Macbeth

Macbeth
MAN AND MYTH

NICK AITCHISON

Foreword by Tony Robinson

SUTTON PUBLISHING

First published in 1999 by
Sutton Publishing Limited · Phoenix Mill
Thrupp · Stroud · Gloucestershire · GL5 2BU

First published in paperback in 1999

This edition first published in 2000

British Library Cataloguing in Publication Data
A catalogue record for this book is available from the British Library

ISBN 0 7509 2640 6

Cover illustration: Macbeth and the Witches, by Henry Fuseli, 1741–1825.
(National Trust, Petworth House, Sussex/Bridgeman Art Library, London)

Typeset in 11½/15 Garamond.
Typesetting and origination by
Sutton Publishing Limited.
Printed in Great Britain by
J.H. Haynes & Co., Sparkford.

For Karen

Contents

Foreword

What a way to go down in posterity! Portrayed as a hen-pecked murderer, and sandwiched between the fictional Othello and the legendary Romeo and Juliet. The poor man doesn't even have the consolation of being thought of as a real person. Macbeth has been ill-served, particularly by that oily-tongued English opportunist William Shakespeare.

So why was Shakespeare so vile about Macbeth? Simply in order to ingratiate himself with King James I. The play bearing Macbeth's name was first performed less than a year after the gunpowder plot, which was designed to blow James to smithereens. It presented its audience with a usurper who is brought low because he kills a king. But not just any old king – Banquo was a direct ancestor of King James! The *Macbeth* which the Royal Shakespeare Company now recreates for our delight isn't a work of art plucked from thin air. It's a piece of royalist propaganda specifically designed to justify the divine right of the Stuart succession and the purge of all those who plot against it.

This might not seem so unfair if Shakespeare had created his fictional king from scratch, or if he had used a real king, but one whose name had already been so blackened that another shovel-full of ordure wouldn't make any difference. But the opposite is the case, as you will see from Nick Aitchison's riveting read. The real Macbeth not only appears to have been a pretty good king, but some might even use the epithet 'great'. He has his own story, which is just as fascinating as Shakespeare's. During his reign Scotland was at a crossroads. Would it turn its back on its heritage, or would it weave its future from its Gaelic past?

Strip away the poetry and drama, and the fictional Macbeth is little more than a Hammer Horror Movie. But the real Macbeth tells us not only what life was like in Scotland a thousand years ago, it also gives us a clue as to why the Scottish nation is once again at crossroads today. Read on.

Tony Robinson
August 2000

Acknowledgements

This book has been a pleasure to research and write. Although the possibility of such a study had already occurred to me, I could not have found the commitment to undertake it without the invitation and support of the publisher. My thanks are due to them, particularly to Jane Crompton, Senior Commissioning Editor, and to Alison Flowers for seeing the book to press so capably.

I am very grateful to Christopher Dingwall and Dr Simon Taylor for their generous advice on Birnam Wood and *Bolgyne* respectively, and to Dr Stephen Driscoll for general points. I would also like to thank the staff of Dundee City Archives, the Map Library of the National Library of Scotland, Perth and Kinross Council Archives and the Scottish Records Office for their (unfortunately unsuccessful) attempts to locate the 1758 Belmont Estate map. The facilities and staff of the British Library at St Pancras have been indispensable throughout. Many organisations (appropriately credited in the relevant figure captions) have given permission to reproduce illustrations. I am indebted to them all, but particularly to the National Monuments Record of the Royal Commission on the Ancient and Historical Monuments of Scotland and its staff.

But my greatest thanks are to Karen for her continuing encouragement, support and patience; to her this book is dedicated.

Introduction

The historical Macbeth is perhaps the most famous of Scottish kings. But he is also one of the least understood because his fame, or rather notoriety, rests on his portrayal as the king immortalised in Shakespeare's compelling study of ambition, temptation, supernatural and evil. The Macbeth of popular perception is invariably Shakespeare's Macbeth. And one can easily see why. Shakespeare's *Macbeth* has an enduring appeal because the tragic hero, brought down by his own ambition, has a startlingly contemporary resonance. The deeds and downfalls of modern Macbeths – whether politicians, businessmen or entertainers – are frequently splashed across newspaper headlines.

Although historians have little problem in distinguishing between Shakespeare's Macbeth and the historical figure, the scarcity of eleventh-century sources has often made them dependent on later material, particularly medieval chronicles. Not surprisingly, the mythological elements present in the chroniclers' accounts of Macbeth and his reign have often been incorporated, consciously or subconsciously, directly into historical analyses. As a result, our knowledge of the historical Macbeth is at best influenced and at worst distorted by later myths and Shakespeare's tragedy. So who was the historical Macbeth, King of Scots, and how much do we know about him and his reign? Leading on from this, how closely was the dramatic Macbeth modelled on his historical counterpart? And how and why did a Scottish king belonging to such a remote period become such a celebrated figure?

Modern perceptions of Macbeth are based on a complex mix of historical, mythological and dramatic sources. This book attempts to unravel the tangled webs that obscure our understanding of Macbeth, the man and his age, and to distinguish the historical Macbeth from his better-known dramatic counterpart. But the intention here is not to discard the myths as being unworthy of historical study. The mythology surrounding Macbeth, its origins, evolution and modern manifestations, is of interest in its own right. While concentrating on the historical Macbeth, the aim here is to provide a wide-ranging survey of Macbeth in all his forms and at the same time demonstrate the manner in which the historical, mythological and dramatic Macbeths are inextricably interlinked.

Chapter 1 outlines the historical background of Macbeth and his reign, beginning with a survey of the complex and challenging evidence on which our understanding of eleventh-century Scotland – and therefore Macbeth – depends. It then looks briefly at cultural and political origins, outlining the various population groups that inhabited early medieval Scotland and how the dominant group – the Scots, migrants from north-eastern Ireland – forged a unified kingdom stretching from northern Scotland to the River Tweed by the early eleventh century. The structures of authority within which power was exercised in eleventh-century Scotland – represented by the offices of king, mormaer and thane – are then discussed. The mid-eleventh century emerges from this as a period of fundamental change in practices of royal succession, probably reflecting or initiating changes within wider society. Chapter 1 continues with a brief discussion of the Church and concludes by looking at Moray, the turbulent northern province and *de facto* kingdom to which Macbeth belonged.

Chapter 2 focuses on Macbeth's early life, before he became king. Discussion ranges from the meaning and significance of his name, through his parentage, boyhood and early career to his physical appearance and his wife, Gruoch. The chapter then examines the historical background to Macbeth's seizure of the Scottish kingship, concentrating on dynastic strife during the final years of the reign of Malcolm II and the military defeats incurred by Macbeth's immediate predecessor, the ill-fated Duncan. The mid-eleventh century was a period of great change and turbulence not only within Scotland but also among adjacent countries. These events are referred to only where they directly concern Macbeth as this book is about Macbeth, not Scotland's relations with its neighbours.

Macbeth's murder of Duncan and the complex combination of factors that drove him to this violent course of action are explored at the start of Chapter 3. Although our knowledge is very limited, Macbeth's experiences during his boyhood and early adulthood were clearly important in shaping his future ambitions on the kingship. Macbeth's aristocratic upbringing, the fate of his father, his relationship with his probable grandfather, Malcolm II, his meeting with King Cnut of England and Denmark and seizure of the Mormaership of Moray all emerge as important factors. These, in conjunction with the influence of Gruoch, who belonged to a dispossessed line of the royal kin group, fuelled Macbeth's desire to acquire the kingship.

The rest of the chapter looks at the few recorded events of Macbeth's reign. Although the scarcity of the sources available inevitably results in a somewhat skeletal biography, these episodes illustrate that Macbeth embodied all the characteristics of a typical early medieval king: war leader, literary patron and benefactor of the Church who went to considerable lengths to demonstrate his royal piety. The events concerned include Macbeth's successful quashing of a rebellion by Duncan's father in 1045 and a possible Northumbrian invasion in 1046, the endowment by Macbeth and his queen of a monastic community, the Culdees of Loch Leven, and, most remarkably of all, his pilgrimage to Rome in 1050. The latter alone sets Macbeth apart; no other Scottish monarch made the pilgrimage to Rome. Chapter 3 continues by looking at the circumstances surrounding Macbeth's defeat in 1054, his withdrawal into his Moray homeland and his ultimate death at the hands of Malcolm III, Duncan's son, in 1057. The chapter concludes by looking at the reign of Lulach, Macbeth's stepson, which lasted only four months.

The evolution of the mythical Macbeth is traced in Chapter 4, from its origins in praise poems composed during Macbeth's reign and presumably recited before Macbeth himself, through the increasingly embellished chronicles of medieval Scotland and then Elizabethan England, before culminating in Shakespeare's *Macbeth*. Modern versions of the Macbeth myth are also considered, from translations of the drama in space and time to the perpetuation of mythical motifs in what are ostensibly historical studies. Shakespeare's tragedy is treated as an integral element within this evolutionary sequence and is not singled out here for detailed study. Instead, discussion concentrates on previously neglected aspects of the mythological Macbeth, such as the praise poem embedded in the *Prophecy of Berchán* and the topographical mythology explored in Chapter 5. Nevertheless, the notes contain detailed references to further reading on Shakespeare's *Macbeth*. Chapter 4 concludes with a wide-ranging discussion examining the nature of the appeal of the Macbeth myth.

The concluding chapter goes in search of Macbeth. It surveys the archaeology, history and mythology of those places that feature so prominently in the Macbeth myth and/or are associated with the historical Macbeth. Travelling in the footsteps of distinguished antiquarians, men of letters and actors of the eighteenth and nineteenth centuries, this chapter begins on the 'blasted heath' where Macbeth and Banquo first encountered the witches. Our itinerary then leads from the castles popularly associated with Macbeth's famous thanages of the Cawdor and Glamis to Macbeth's castle at Inverness, the inauguration place of the early Scottish kings at Scone, the Culdee monastery on an island in Loch Leven and MacDuff's castle. The tour then reaches the famous Birnam Wood and leads inevitably to 'Macbeth's castle' at Dunsinane and the surrounding monuments that, according to tradition, mark the burial places of those who fell in battle there. Chapter 5 concludes, appropriately, by examining the problematic issue of Macbeth's burial place.

Macbeth is a figure of enduring fascination. No Scottish king has captured the artistic and popular imagination as vividly as Macbeth. What emerges forcibly from this study is that the life of the historical Macbeth was every bit as eventful, violent and intriguing – altogether as *dramatic* – as that of the tragic character portrayed by Shakespeare. That this should be the case despite the severe limitations imposed by the sparse contemporary source material is all the more remarkable. But puzzlingly, although there have been many film versions of Shakespeare's *Macbeth* – and despite the recent successes of other films based on episodes from Scottish history, notably Mel Gibson's *Braveheart* – no attempt has ever been made to translate the historical Macbeth to the screen.

As recently as 1990, Professor Gordon Donaldson, the late HM Historiographer Royal for Scotland, described Macbeth as 'something of a man of mystery around whom fantasies have been woven by writers of fiction among whom William Shakespeare was neither the first nor the last'[1] (and one might add 'historians' after 'writers of fiction'). This book dispels much of the mystery surrounding the historical Macbeth and establishes the factual basis behind the better-known Macbeth of myth and drama. It also traces the development of this enduring myth from Macbeth's own lifetime, through the medieval chronicles and Shakespeare's drama, its translation to a range of different media over the past two centuries, to modern manifestations. These myths vividly attest the continued transformation – and therefore relevance – of the myth to the present day.

All dates are AD unless otherwise stated. The end notes give Harvard-style short references, the expanded references for which may be found in the Bibliography. These are intended to provide guidance to both primary sources used and additional reading for readers wishing to pursue the study of Macbeth and his age. They are not essential to the understanding of the text and the casual reader may conveniently ignore them.

CHAPTER 1

Scotland in the Age of Macbeth

The reign of the historical Macbeth (1040–57), King of Scots, straddles the mid-eleventh century. Macbeth's life and kingship are inextricably linked with his wider political and historical context, but what do we know about eleventh-century Scotland? Befitting Macbeth's royal status, whether legitimate or not, the emphasis of this chapter is on socio-political organisation. It sketches the origins and political geography of eleventh-century Scotland, Scotland's turbulent relations with its neighbours, and the nature of those structures of authority that ruled Scotland: kings and kingship, mormaers and provinces and thanes and thanages. The Church, which enjoyed a close relationship with the Scottish kingship, and its organisation are also considered. The chapter concludes with a brief discussion of Moray, the province with which Macbeth was most closely associated.

We may begin by examining the nature of the evidence upon which our knowledge of Macbeth and his age is based.

SOURCES OF EVIDENCE

Macbeth lived a thousand years ago. Before looking at *what* we know about the historical Macbeth, it is worth considering *how* we know about a king who belonged to such a remote period of Scottish history. The evidence is complex and challenging.

Sources are the building blocks of historical research. An understanding of their provenance, nature and, in particular, reliability is essential. This is particularly true in Macbeth's case, where our knowledge of the historical king is potentially distorted by later myths, including Shakespeare's tragedy. Without such an appraisal there is no alternative but to accept sources at face value. But this is likely to cause confusion if a source is erroneous or biased, or if the evidence is fragmentary or contradictory. As a result, the potential to build a cohesive, credible and accurate historical narrative may be lost. Part of the attraction of early medieval history lies in the challenge presented by limited sources which are often terse and obscure. This is particularly true of early medieval Scotland.

Our sources for the historical Macbeth are threefold: contemporary records, contemporary poetry and later chronicles. But these broad categories contain sources that vary widely in form, provenance and veracity. This is not the place for a detailed study of all the sources used here and their reliability, but a brief outline may assist readers unfamiliar with them.

Potentially the most reliable information on eleventh-century Scotland is contained in the annals. Usually compiled within a monastery, the annals comprise a sequence of entries made either annually or at the time of the events they record. Those events are typically battles, *mirabilia* (natural wonders) and the deaths of kings and senior clerics. The annals are therefore contemporary sources, although they usually survive only in much later manuscripts and may have undergone later editing or contain later interpolations. The most useful are the various Irish annals, primarily the *Annals of Ulster*, and the *Anglo-Saxon Chronicle*, which survives in several manuscript versions.[1] Reflecting their context of composition and subsequent manuscript transmission, the Irish annals are usually in Latin, the language of the Church.

Anglo-Saxon Chronicle (MS D). The lower entry, for the year 1054, records Earl Siward of Northumbria's invasion of Scotland and victory over Macbeth (*kyng macbeoðen*) in the Battle of the Seven Sleepers. (By permission of the British Library, MS Cotton Tiberius B. IV, fol. 75v)

But these are external, not Scottish, sources. As a result, they are unlikely to comprise eyewitness accounts, although their compilers may have had access to people with first-hand knowledge of the events recorded. Moreover, the annalists' interpretation of Scottish events is likely to reflect Anglo-Saxon or Irish perspectives. Not surprisingly, these sources sometimes employ terminology that is specific to their own cultural contexts of recording but alien to Scotland. Nevertheless, the Anglo-Saxon and Irish annals demonstrate a keen interest in Scottish affairs, making these valuable sources. In particular, the *Annals of Ulster* contain unique records of events in Moray that are of fundamental importance to the study of Macbeth.

The Scots also had an annalistic tradition. Indeed, the *Annals of Ulster* incorporate records kept in the monastery of Iona during the seventh and eighth centuries.[2]

Continuing that tradition, the *Scottish Chronicle* was compiled in a monastery at Dunkeld during the late tenth century but is preserved in a fourteenth-century manuscript.[3] Based on a combination of oral traditions and earlier documentary sources, it begins during the reign of Kenneth I (Kenneth mac Alpin), *c.* 850, but, unfortunately for our purposes, ends with the reign of Kenneth II (971–95). The *Scottish Chronicle* also contains a regnal list, one of several versions to survive. These simply detail the succession of kings, usually with their reign lengths and supplementary information concerning some kings, often the circumstances and place of their death and burial but occasionally other details.[4] Reflecting this, the Scottish regnal lists are sometimes referred to as the *Chronicle of the Kings of Scotland.* These texts are all descended from an early eleventh-century Irish exemplar, to which entries were added as later kings died. But although the eleventh-century entries are contemporary, the regnal lists survive only in manuscripts dating from the fourteenth century or later and their long histories of textual transmission have resulted in the introduction of scribal errors, particularly in the earlier sections. An eleventh-century verse history of Scottish kings, *Duan Albanach*, is derived from a regnal list.

Another Irish poem provides a unique source of information on Scottish kings and a contemporary insight on Macbeth. Although the *Prophecy of Berchán* is a composite work, dating in its present form to the late eleventh century, its verses on Macbeth comprise a praise poem. Most significantly, this was almost certainly composed by Macbeth's own Court poet and was presumably performed before the king himself. Reflecting their courtly context of composition and performance, these poems are in Middle Irish, not Latin. The eulogistic and prophetic nature of the *Prophecy* means that its contents cannot be accepted at face value. The *Prophecy* is not an objective and factual record of events, although the relevant verses present a fascinating and unique insight into Macbeth's physical appearance, life at his Court and the origins of the mythology surrounding Macbeth.

Other contemporary records are charters recording grants of land and/or income to monastic communities, although again these survive only in much later copies. Of particular interest are those concerning the Culdee community at Loch Leven, which attest Macbeth's close links with the Church and provide the only contemporary record of Macbeth's queen. These endowments are known from later copies of the *Register* of the priory of St Andrews, but they were originally recorded in a Gaelic book kept at Loch Leven and probably took the form of *notitiae*, notes recording legal transactions which were inserted in the

An illuminated page from the *Book of Deer*, a ninth-century gospel book with eleventh- and twelfth-century marginal notes, in Gaelic, recording gifts of land to the monastic church of Old Deer, Aberdeenshire. The illustration is of Abraham. (By permission of the Syndics of University of Cambridge Library, MS Ii.6.32, fol. 4v)

margins of books. Although the original book in which these grants were recorded no longer survives, a ninth-century gospel book, the *Book of Deer*, containing eleventh- and twelfth-century *notitiae* provides a good example of this practice.

But by far the most detailed source of information on Macbeth is the medieval and later chronicles. These range widely in provenance and date. Several English chronicles dating from the twelfth century refer to Scottish affairs but sometimes display a political bias which casts doubt on their historical veracity. The various Scottish chronicles, which exist in Latin and Scots and prose and verse forms, date from the fourteenth to the late sixteenth centuries and attest the increasing mythologisation not only of Macbeth but of Scottish history in general. Although it is simplistic to state that the contents of the earlier chronicles are historically more reliable, these accounts may be relatively free from the accumulated biases, misconceptions and blatant confabulations that colour the later sources. Indeed, the most useful chronicle is the earliest surviving, John of Fordun's *Chronicle of the Scottish People* which dates from about 1370.

The contents of the chronicles can sometimes be corroborated by independent sources, some of which may be contemporary with the events recorded, but other information is often unique. To reject the latter on the grounds that it is neither contemporary nor corroborated would result in a rather minimalist history. There is a valid case for employing such information provided its limitations are recognised and it does not contain later biases. Indeed, it is often the incidental detail, where the chronicler is not attempting to make a particular point, that may be the most reliable. In short, medieval chronicles can flesh out the sometimes rather bare bones of historical analysis, rather than direct the nature of the enquiry itself. But regardless of their historical veracity, the chronicles may be used to trace the evolution of the mythical Macbeth; this is the principal use to which they are put here.

An important external source is the *Orkneyinga Saga* or *Earls' Saga*, the chronicle of the Viking conquest of Scotland's northern isles in the ninth century and the subsequent Viking *Jarls*, or Earls, of Orkney. Committed to writing from oral tradition in about 1190 and incorporating earlier Skaldic verse, the *Orkneyinga Saga* exemplifies the heroic ethos of the Icelandic saga tradition in which the Vikings never lose a battle. But the *Orkneyinga Saga* sometimes demonstrates a poor understanding of Scottish affairs and presents problems of interpretation. It is the only source for events on Scotland's contested northern frontier and is therefore uncorroborated, while its distorted ordering of events – Macbeth appears as a *jarl* (probably meaning a mormaer) in the chapter before his father does – casts doubt on its historical reliability. Although its internal chronology may not be accurate, the *Orkneyinga Saga* nevertheless provides a valuable insight into northern affairs which otherwise would be lost.

Although documentary sources provide the only evidence for the historical Macbeth, placenames[5] and archaeology[6] are also valuable sources of evidence for early medieval Scotland. However, these too are fragmentary and their use presents specific problems.

Placename studies (or onomastics) contribute to the understanding of early medieval Scotland in several ways. Plotting placename types at a national or regional level can illuminate patterns of activity, such as settlement or ecclesiastical organisation, while placename analysis on a regional or local scale can reveal much about the history of an area or assist the identification of archaic or lost placenames mentioned in textual sources. Early medieval Scotland is a particularly fertile field for placename studies because of the range of languages spoken by its various peoples: Gaelic, Pictish, British, Anglo-Saxon and Norse. But successive linguistic changes and the paucity of early documentary sources often hinder the tracing of earlier name forms and interpretation of surviving ones.

Archaeology offers perhaps the greatest, but so far unrealised, potential for adding to our knowledge of eleventh-century Scotland. But it also has limitations. Although some sites belonging to this period may be identified from documentary references, the archaeological evidence is not always preserved or accessible. The continued occupation and sometimes refortification of many royal centres throughout the Middle Ages and beyond means that earlier phases of occupation have often been destroyed or obscured.

Where earlier remains do survive, their dating is problematic. Closely datable artefacts, such as coins, pottery or jewellery, do not occur indigenously in eleventh-century Scotland, although imported examples may be helpful. Scientific dating techniques have made a major contribution to prehistoric archaeology but are of more limited application in historic periods because of the more precise chronologies involved. Despite refinements in carbon-14 dating, the margin of error attached to the results obtained means that it will rarely be possible to date a sample to a specific reign with confidence. However, when employed in combination, artefactual, documentary and scientific techniques may enable a site or a phase of occupation to be dated with reasonable accuracy in specific circumstances. Dendrochronology (or tree-ring dating) is a potential source of accurate calendrical dating, but is dependent on the survival of suitable samples of timber, usually oak, and therefore requires waterlogged conditions.

No archaeological site associated with Macbeth, historically or mythologically, has been excavated since the mid-nineteenth century. A programme of exploratory excavations, conducted to modern standards and employing scientific dating techniques, may not reveal much about Macbeth's reign in particular but could enhance our understanding of the forms and functions of royal centres, their inhabitants and Scotland in general during the eleventh century. Such a project could be modelled on, and perhaps extend, the campaign that Professor Leslie Alcock conducted between 1974 and 1984 on early medieval royal sites in Scotland.[7]

For such a formative period in Scottish history, the eleventh century has received disappointingly little study, perhaps because it has been overshadowed by Macbeth himself. Archaeology, history and placename studies all have a fundamental contribution to make and the sum of their input will be all the greater if those efforts are integrated within a multi-disciplinary framework.

THE ORIGINS OF ELEVENTH-CENTURY SCOTLAND

Macbeth belongs to a transitional period of Scottish history, a twilight zone between the Dark Ages, now usually referred to as the early medieval period, and the High Middle Ages. Early medieval describes the period between the emergence of the historic peoples of what is now Scotland in the mid-first millennium and the forging of the medieval kingdom of the Scots during the eleventh century. During this phase there were fundamental changes in social and political organisation, including the emergence, expansion and sometimes eclipse of kingdoms, the spread of Christianity and the growth of the Church and a remarkable flowering of art, literature and learning.

Another label attached to this period is the Age of Migrations. The centuries after the collapse of the Roman empire saw widespread population movements across Europe. Early medieval Scotland was home to five linguistically and culturally discrete peoples, only two of whom were of indigenous origin.[8] The indigenous peoples were the Picts, who occupied north-eastern Scotland and the northern isles, and the Britons of Strathclyde, Galloway and Cumbria. Lothian and south-east Scotland were occupied from the mid-sixth century by Angles who had pushed north-wards from the Anglian kingdom of Northumbria but originated in what is

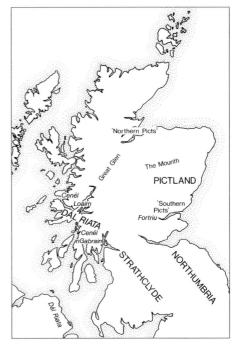

Early medieval Scotland and its neighbours, showing kingdoms, population groups and geographical features mentioned in the text.

now southern Denmark and northern Germany. From about 800, Viking raiders and traders settled in northern and western Scotland, the locations of their farms still attested by placenames. The Scots were also incomers. They are traditionally believed to have been fifth-century migrants from the kingdom of Dál Riata in north-eastern Ireland who founded a kingdom of the same name in western Scotland and gave their name to Argyll, the 'shore of the Gael'. Indeed, the Scots owe their title to the classical and medieval Latin term for the Irish, *Scotti*.

The political geography of early medieval Scotland was fluid. Picts, Scots, Britons, Angles and, later, Vikings competed for power and land, the ebb and flow of their varied fortunes traceable in a succession of battles, sieges and territorial gains and losses. Frequent internal power struggles were another characteristic of the dynamic politics of this period. But although biases in the written record give the impression of near constant warfare, there is evidence that strong social, cultural and economic contacts existed between these peoples in the form of trade, intermarriage, settlement and artistic and linguistic influences. The interplay between some of these peoples is illustrated by the Hunterston brooch.

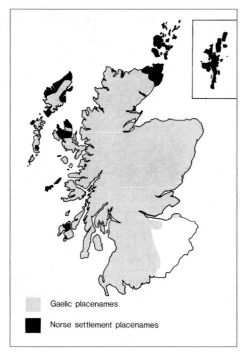

Gaelic placenames

Norse settlement placenames

The distribution of Norse settlement place-names, containing the elements *stathr* ('dwelling place, farm'), *setr* ('dwelling'), *bólstathr* ('farm') and *dalr* ('valley'), and Gaelic placenames in Scotland. This distribution indicates the peripheral nature of Norse settlement in Scotland and that, at its eleventh-century peak, Gaelic was spoken throughout Scotland with the exception of only the south-east.

From its foothold in a peripheral zone of western Scotland, one of these five peoples, the Scots, gradually acquired more territory and extended its influence over its neighbours. In the mid-ninth century, after centuries of both warfare and interdynastic marriage, the Scots under Kenneth mac Alpin (843–58) successfully assimilated the Picts. This must have been a gradual process, but it is portrayed in later mythology as a conquest in which the Pictish nobility was treacherously slain by the Scots at Scone. Kenneth successfully united the Picts and Scots to form the early medieval kingdom of Alba, the embryonic kingdom of the Scots. Alba comprised Scotland north of the Forth– Clyde isthmus, with the exception of the northern isles, which were under Viking control.

The Scots of Dál Riata brought with them their own language, culture and forms of social and ecclesiastical organisation. Reflecting the Scots' origins, these were closely related to those of early medieval Ireland and cultural, ecclesiastical, linguistic and political links between Scotland and Ireland were strong. Absorbed by the Gaelic-speaking Scots, Pictish language, culture and society rapidly disappeared.

The principal royal kin group of Dál Riata, which supplied most of its kings and to which Kenneth belonged, was Cenél nGabráin. During the mid-ninth century, the descendants of Cenél nGabráin migrated eastwards into southern Pictland to occupy the rich agricultural lands of Perthshire, Fife, Angus and the ancient power centres of the Picts, including Scone, with which the Scottish kings were to become so closely associated over the coming centuries. This area, the Pictish province of Fortriu, encompassing Strathearn, Gowrie and Angus, formed the heartland of the newly united kingdom of the Scots. In contrast, the descendants of a less powerful royal kin group of Dál Riata, Cenél Loairn, expanded from Lorn, in northern Argyll, through the Great Glen to settle in Moray, northern Pictland. Moray's fortunes were discrete from those of the Scottish kingship from the outset and strife soon followed. Beyond Ross and Moray, Scotland's northernmost provinces, the Mormaers of Moray contested the Viking *jarls* of Orkney for control of the far north for two centuries, containing Viking settlement on the Scottish mainland north of Strathoykel to Caithness and Sutherland.[9]

With the Grampian mountains, the men of Moray and the Orkney Vikings to the north, the obvious direction for the Scottish kings to expand their territory was south, into the fertile lands of Lothian and Strathclyde. From Kenneth onwards, Scottish kings raided Northumbrian-held Lothian, although Edinburgh was not held

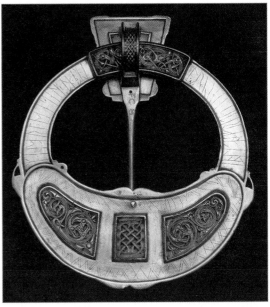

The reverse of the Hunterston brooch, West Kilbride, Ayrshire, attests the contacts between the different peoples of early medieval Scotland. This late seventh- or early eighth-century brooch of Irish type, but perhaps manufactured in Scotland, bears a tenth-century runic inscription, *malbrithaastilk*: 'Mael Brigda owns [this] brooch'. It is a Hiberno-Scottish brooch, bearing a Viking inscription containing a Gaelic name, found within the territory of the Strathclyde Britons. (Photograph © The Trustees of the National Museums of Scotland 1999)

permanently until the mid-tenth century. And, to the south-west, the British kingdom of Strathclyde, which included Clydesdale, Cumbria and Galloway, was a Scottish client state by the late tenth century, its rulers subject to the Scottish kings.

This gradual territorial expansion culminated in the early eleventh century when the Scottish kings extended their authority over the entire region south of the Forth–Clyde isthmus. After gaining territory in Lothian in 1016, the Scots decisively defeated the Northumbrians at Carham in 1018, occupying territory as far south as the River Tweed, which has remained the border between Scotland and England ever since.[10] Reflecting his client status, Owen the Bald, King of the Strathclyde Britons, fought on the Scottish side at Carham. Strathclyde was incorporated into Scotland sometime after 1018, probably after the British kingship died out or was ousted by its Scottish over-

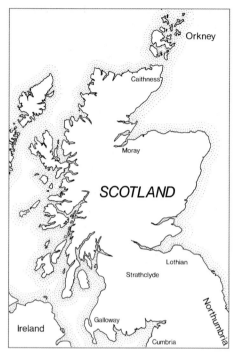

Eleventh-century Scotland and its neighbours, showing kingdoms and provinces mentioned in the text.

kings, while the kingship of Cumbria was retained for the heir apparent to the Scottish throne.

With the southwards expansion of Scottish control, the eleventh century marked the zenith of the Gaelic language. Not only was Gaelic the lingua franca of Scotland north of the Forth, its use also extended into Lothian and the Borders, as place-names attest.11 But from the eleventh century, as Scotland was increasingly subjected to the anglicising influences of its powerful southern neighbour, Gaelic began a long, slow decline.

The opening decades of the eleventh century saw the forging of a unified kingdom of the Scots that stretched from beyond the Moray Firth to the River Tweed and also included Cumbria. This was the kingdom Macbeth acquired only two decades later.

KINGS AND KINGSHIP

The institution of kingship was widespread in western Europe after the collapse of the Roman empire in the fifth century. As Roman imperial authority declined, powerful local war lords, the 'tyrants' of contemporary sources, rapidly emerged to fill the power vacuum. Frequently drawing on actual or fabricated links with the imperial past, the more successful were able to impose their authority over a region and found a ruling dynasty, thus forging kingships and kingdoms. A similar process also occurred beyond the imperial frontiers. Sporadic Roman military campaigns, temporary occupations and then the collapse of Roman rule in adjacent provinces had a destabilising influence on peripheral areas which had never been fully incorporated within the Empire, such as Scotland. All the peoples of early medieval Britain and Ireland (whence insular), native and migrant alike, had their own kingships, and although possessing many common characteristics, they differed in nature. In Ireland, for example, where there had been no direct Roman intervention, a multitude of petty kingships attested a continuity with a prehistoric and perhaps 'tribal' level of kingship.

Although early Scottish kingship was most closely related to that of early medieval Ireland in its theory and practice, there were significant differences. By the mid-ninth century, the kingship of the Scots was a single, powerful national monarchy. Scotland's unitary kingship may be attributed to its origins in a single royal kin group. The ruling kindred of Dál Riata, Cenél nGabráin, gradually extended its power through a combination of military success against, and dynastic intermarriage with, the Picts until it controlled all of mainland Scotland north of the Forth. The nature of the Scottish kingship contrasted with the hierarchical ranks of kingship, surmounted by a notional high-kingship, in Ireland.[12] This confused the Irish annalists, who referred to the King of Scots as they would his perceived Irish equivalent rank, 'high-king of Scotland' (*airdrí Alban*).[13] But, taking account of the absence of junior ranks of kingship in Scotland, Scottish kings were never 'high-kings'. Nor were they 'kings of Scotland' but, reflecting a concept of kingship over people rather than land, were kings of Scots.

Practices of early medieval insular kingship, particularly in Ireland, are often claimed to have perpetuated features of pagan sacral kingship. Indeed, concepts such as the 'prince's truth' (*fír flathemon*), which attributed a kingdom's well-being and the fertility of its people, land and livestock to the just rule of a righteous king, do appear to preserve primitive beliefs.[14] Yet such notions were readily assimilated because they were compatible with the biblical concept of kingship by divine grace, which formed the theoretical basis of kingship throughout medieval Christendom. Practices of medieval kingship, in Scotland as elsewhere, embodied the ideals of Christianity. Indeed, the earliest recorded ordination of a king anywhere in Europe was in Scotland – St Columba's ordination of Aidán mac Gabráin, King of Dál Riata, in 574.[15]

Nevertheless, many features of early Scottish kingship were archaic or even primitive in nature. While the philosophy and rituals of medieval kingship were evolving on the continent and being borrowed from the Merovingians and Franks by the Anglo-Saxons, the Scottish and Irish kingships, on the periphery of Europe, were more conservative. Two of the archaic features displayed there were fundamental to medieval kingship – succession and inauguration.

Scottish kingship was in a state of transition during the mid-eleventh century, as a change in the pattern of royal succession reveals. Before 1040, the kingship passed not from father to son but from brother to brother, uncle to nephew, or cousin to cousin. Over time, as the royal dynasty expanded in size, eligibility to the kingship was shared between collateral branches of the royal kin group, each of which could trace their ancestry to a common royal ancestor, the obscure Alpin, King of Dál Riata and father of Kenneth I. Possession of the kingship alternated between these collateral lines, which offered them a fair share of power and guaranteed that their candidates' turn on the throne would come.

In order to avoid unlimited bids for the kingship, which were a potential cause of instability and violence, eligibility for the kingship was restricted. In Ireland,

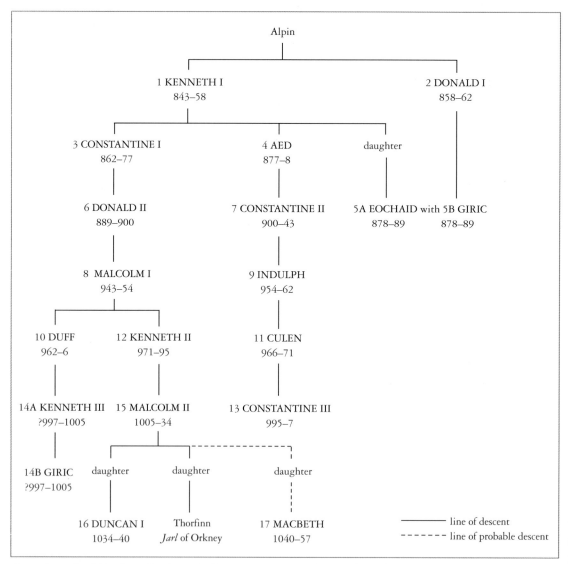

Genealogical table of Scotland's early kings, 843–1057. The numbered sequence reveals the pattern of alternating succession between collateral royal lines, a system that collapsed in the mid-eleventh century with the accession of the ill-fated Duncan.

it rested on membership of the *derbfine* ('certain kin'), comprising the descendants, through four generations, of a common ancestor who had held the kingship. Attesting a stronger desire to minimise the risk of dynastic chaos, eligibility for the Scottish kingship was much tighter, being limited to the sons of kings. Of the twenty-three Scottish kings who reigned between 843 and 1097, nineteen were the offspring of previous kings but did not, under the system of alternating kingship, succeed their fathers in the kingship immediately. Of the four kings who did not fulfil this requirement, one, Eochaid (878–89), was a joint ruler (with Giric). The other three, Duncan I (1034–40), Macbeth and Lulach (1057–8), reigned consecutively, emphasising that the mid-eleventh century was a period of change and instability for the Scottish kingship.

To lessen the risk of aspiring kings attempting to seize the kingship by force or eliminate rival contenders for the kingship, the successor to the kingship was probably designated during the reign of his predecessor. Although not a rigid 'rule' of succession, this was intended to reduce tensions between branches of the royal kin group and aspiring kings by formalising the right of the next in line to the throne. The intended successor was known as the *tanaise* ('appointed one'), from which the system of alternating succession has been known traditionally as 'tanistry'. Although there is no conclusive evidence that the position of *tanaise* existed in early Scotland, it may be inferred from the regularity of the system of alternating succession and by analogy with early Irish kingship, in which the *tanaise* played a prominent role.[16] But despite tanistry, eleven Scottish kings who ruled before 1100 were killed by, or in favour of, their immediate successor. Not surprisingly, the average reign length during this period was only twelve years. Indeed, Irish and Scottish kings died at the hands of their kinsfolk or subjects (the distinction, if indeed it exists, is seldom clear) with such frequency that the Irish annals record their deaths in a chillingly formulaic fashion: *a suis occisus est* ('was killed by his own [people]').[17]

Many tanists probably suffered a similar fate to those kings who were killed in royal succession disputes. Although there is no clear evidence of this in Scotland, it was certainly the case in Ireland, as the Irish annals frequently record. Nevertheless, Boite, whose grandson was killed by Malcolm II (1005–34) in 1033, may have been Malcolm's *tanaise* and seems unlikely to have suffered a better fate than his descendant. Malcolm certainly had a good reason for wanting to eliminate his *tanaise* and his descendants. Rejecting the traditional system of alternating succession, Malcolm sought to retain the kingship for his own direct descendants. In order to do so, he first had to eliminate male members of collateral lines who had a rightful claim to the throne. Malcolm had no sons but he probably had three daughters and three grandsons, one of whom, Duncan, succeeded him in the kingship.

Restricted eligibility to the kingship introduced its own risks, principally that kings would use their influence on their son's behalf and to the detriment of the interests of the collateral branch whose candidate was next in line to the throne. Indeed, confining eligibility to the sons of kings paved the way for the introduction of primogeniture. Malcolm introduced primogeniture to the Scottish royal succession for the first time. Primogeniture limited succession to the kingship to the direct line, under which a reigning king was succeeded by his eldest direct male descendant. This was the system of royal succession most widely practised throughout Europe during and after the Middle Ages. But a strong tendency towards alternating succession survived within the Scottish kingship and resulted in further royal violence after the death of Malcolm III in 1093.

The inherent instability of the system of alternating succession emphasised the importance of strategies of legitimation. In Scotland, as elsewhere in medieval Europe, kings sought to demonstrate the legitimacy of their kingship in an attempt to project themselves as unchallengeable and deter potential pretenders to the throne. This was achieved by invoking notions of divine kingship and appealing to the past, both of which feature prominently in royal inauguration rites. Inauguration according to traditional practice was essential for the legitimacy of a kingship. It was an explicit acknowledgement of a king's hereditary right to the throne and established his status as a just and lawful ruler.

Scottish kings were ritually inaugurated at the royal centre of Scone, Perthshire. An archaic and distinctive feature was that Scottish kings were not crowned but enthroned according to an apparently ancient ritual. Little is known of the form this took before the mid-thirteenth century, although the inherently conservative nature of kingship and ritual, as well as the emphasis on the past, might suggest that earlier inaugurations were similar in character.

The strategies of legitimation employed in these royal rituals are illustrated by the inauguration at Scone in 1249 of Alexander III, who was then only eight years old. This is the earliest-known description of an inauguration of a Scottish king. According to Fordun, the earls, barons and lords of Scotland assembled at Scone in the presence of the Bishops of St Andrews and Dunkeld and the Abbot of Scone.[18] The event began with arguments about whether it was an auspicious day for making a king and whether Alexander should first be knighted. The assembled throng gave its approval that Alexander should be installed in the kingship that day without the prerequisite of knighthood, perhaps indicating that the new king was publicly proclaimed. Some nobles, principally the Earls of Fife and Strathearn, then led Alexander to a cross in the graveyard at the east end of the church. There they sat him on the royal throne, which was draped in rich cloths. The throne held the famous Stone of Destiny, on which the Scottish kings were traditionally inaugurated.[19] This was in front of a large earthen mound, Moot Hill, on the flat top of which inaugurations originally may have been conducted. The Bishop of St Andrews then consecrated the King, after which the nobles spread their garments under the King's feet. The ritual culminated in a poet reciting, in Gaelic and from memory, the King's royal pedigree, back through fifty-six generations to Fergus the first King of Scots and from him back to the earliest Scots, the mythological Gaidheal Glas, son of Neoilus, King of Athens, and the eponymous Scota, daughter of the Egyptian Pharaoh Chenthres.[20]

The Scottish royal inauguration ritual contains rich layers of symbolism.

Moot Hill, Scone, Perthshire. This large, flat-topped mound was, for several centuries, the ritual focus of the Scottish kingship. Until 1296, Scottish kings were inaugurated by being installed on the Stone of Destiny either on top or in front of Moot Hill. Although his inauguration is unrecorded, this is where Macbeth would have been made King of Scots in 1040. The neo-Gothic mausoleum is a much later feature and probably incorporates the fabric of the old parish church, first recorded in 1624. (The Author)

The ceremony was conducted before, and with the approval of, the assembled nobility, representing the entire nation of the Scots. The King was installed by the most senior bishops and earls of Scotland. The participation of the bishops symbolised divine sanction and attests the close links that existed between the kingship and the Church. The Earls of Fife and Strathearn belonged to collateral branches of the royal kin group that had been excluded from the kingship during the early eleventh century but whose loyalty was retained partly through according them a prominent political role as king-makers. The inauguration was performed on or before a mound, raising the King above his subjects. The mound may have been modelled on a prehistoric funerary monument or perhaps was even a real one, symbolising the inauguree's ancient and presumably royal ancestry. This link with the past is expressed more explicitly through the recital of the royal pedigree, tracing the inauguree's direct descent from a long line of kings.

The inauguration of Alexander III on or in front of the Moot Hill at Scone, Perthshire, as depicted in a fifteenth-century illustration in Walter Bower's *Scotichronicon*. The bard is seen reciting the king's pedigree. (CCC MS 171, f. 206r. The Master and Fellows of Corpus Christi College, Cambridge)

Turning to the practice of kingship, early Scottish kings were, first and foremost, war leaders. Kings thrived on prestige, a principal source of which was military success. Newly installed kings often sought to establish their initial reputation on the battlefield, sometimes with disastrous results. In 1006, the year after his accession, Malcolm II misguidedly tried to besiege Durham and the Scots were heavily defeated. His successor, Duncan, tried to make his mark by attempting unsuccessfully to assert his authority over Caithness, then held by the Orkney Vikings.

Early Scottish kings effectively embodied the state. They possessed an extensive range of powers: legislative, judicial and fiscal as well as military. This authority was not exercised from a single location, a static royal 'capital', but from several royal centres, both fortresses and palaces. Little is known about the eleventh-century royal centres and few are referred to in contemporary sources, although their identities may be inferred from earlier and later references. Several royal centres, most notably Scone and the palace complex of Forteviot,[21] were clustered in southern Perthshire, the political heartland of the Scottish kingdom, and of the Picts before them. Their recorded status as royal centres in both earlier and later centuries strongly suggests that they performed a similar function in the eleventh century including, presumably, during Macbeth's reign.

The Scottish kingship was peripatetic: the king, accompanied by his entourage, travelled around his kingdom dispensing justice, collecting and consuming taxes in the form of food renders and asserting royal authority, as Duncan did:

For he observed the praiseworthy custom of traversing all the provinces of his kingdom once a year to comfort graciously with his presence his own peaceful people. . . . When . . . Duncan was making his annual progress through the kingdom in this way, it was his practice to correct abuses unlawfully inflicted on the lower classes by the more powerful, to prevent unjust and irregular imposts on the part of his officials, to crush the wickedness of brigands and other criminals, who raged violently among the people, with a kind of judicious severity, and to calm down the internal disputes of his subjects.[22]

But it required more than an annual tour to administer and exert royal power throughout Scotland. The size and geography of the kingdom required the representation of royal authority at both regional and local levels. This was carried out by two tiers of royal officials.

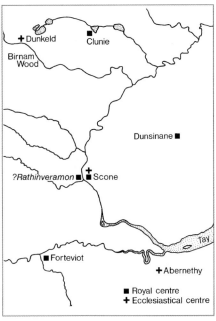

Southern Perthshire, the political heartland of the early Scottish kingdom, showing royal and ecclesiastical centres mentioned in the text.

MORMAERS

Mormaers were powerful territorial magnates and their extensive provinces were the primary level of royal administration in eleventh-century Scotland.[23] *Mór maer* means 'great steward' and this Gaelic title is first recorded in 918, although its origins are unclear. The absence of mormaers in Ireland indicates that this office was not introduced with the migration of the Dál Riata or from Ireland at a later date. Instead, the predominantly north-eastern distribution of the Scottish provinces recorded as having mormaers suggests that this office had Pictish origins. It may have originated in the provincial kingships that lost their royal status as the kingship of the Picts became increasingly centralised. However, the disappearance of the earlier Pictish provinces[24] and their names suggests a degree of political and administrative reorganisation after the eclipse of Pictish power in the mid-ninth century. Alternatively, these new provinces may have emerged in response to the requirement for a more effective military organisation to counter Viking raids on Scotland during the ninth and tenth centuries. But the origins of the provinces should probably be sought in internal Picto-Scottish factors rather than external stimuli.

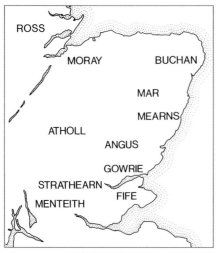

The provinces of eleventh-century Scotland.

As their name suggests, mormaers were, at least originally, royally appointed officials, administering their province on behalf of the king. They probably combined a range of fiscal, judicial and military functions: collecting dues and tribute and, when required, raising and leading into battle a provincial army. Reflecting the annalists' interests, the most visible role of the mormaer is that of war leader. The Irish annals record the presence of Scottish mormaers fighting alongside their king, Constantine II (900–43), against a Viking army at the Battle of Corbridge in Northumbria in 918, the participation of three named Scottish mormaers in an expedition led by two Irish kings in 976 and the death of the Mormaer of Mar in the battle of Clontarf, near Dublin, in 1014.[25] Some mormaers may have held other offices simultaneously. For example, Crinán, (lay) Abbot of Dunkeld, also appears to have had a role similar to that of Mormaer of Atholl and led an army against Macbeth in 1045.

Although it is often claimed that mormaers were descended from autonomous tribal kingships, this is unlikely. 'Tribal' kingship implies a more primitive and much earlier level of socio-political organisation. Instead, mormaers were probably scions of the royal kin group who were no longer eligible for the kingship and had declined in status, becoming nobles. For example, a rival branch of the royal kindred, the descendants of Duff (962–6), was excluded from the kingship by Malcolm II, and was probably relegated to the Mormaership of Fife. The descendants of the son of Duff held the medieval earldom of Fife, the origin of Shakespeare's MacDuff.[26]

Yet mormaers' extensive powers meant that they were provincial kings in all but name; in effect, regional sub-kings. Before the ninth or tenth centuries, a mormaer's functions would have been performed by a provincial king. For example, Atholl was ruled by a Pictish king in 739, but the status of its ruler had shrunk to that of 'governor' (satrapas, probably a Latin translation of mormaer) by 966.[27] This shift, from provincial kings to nobles, attests a growing centralisation of power under the Scottish kingship during the late first millennium. However, this trend was not universal, particularly among those provinces most distant from the political heartland of the Scottish kingship. In particular, a powerful hereditary Mormaership of Moray existed by the eleventh century and it was from this regional power base that Macbeth successfully challenged the Scottish kingship in 1040.

Mormaers were the equivalent of the Anglo-Saxon *eorl* and Viking *jarl*. Although there was no direct equivalent in Ireland, a similar role was performed there by one of the ranks of over-king or provincial king. Unfamiliar with the rank of mormaer, the Irish annalists were particularly confused by the more autonomous Mormaers of Moray, whom they described as 'King of Scots' (*rí Alban*), probably meaning '*a*' rather than '*the*' King of Scots, or 'king of Moray' (*rí Muireb*).[28] A similar confusion probably also accounts for the *Anglo-Saxon Chronicle*'s reference to the young Macbeth as an 'other king'. Regardless of the reliability of these sources, they reflect external, not Scottish perceptions; the Mormaers of Moray were not kings, even though they possessed many of the characteristics and powers of regional kings.

The title of mormaer disappeared during the late eleventh or early twelfth centuries, probably as a result of increasing external influences, firstly Anglo-Saxon and then Norman, on the Scottish kingship. But the functions and provinces of the mormaers survived under earls, which are first recorded in Scotland by the mid-twelfth century. The title *comes* ('earl') was used earlier as the Latin equivalent of mormaer; a *Comitis* of Angus is recorded in 995.[29] Indicating a strong degree of continuity, the medieval earldoms retained the forms and names of the earlier provinces, while some earls, though referred to as *comes* in Latin, were still described as mormaers in vernacular sources.[30] There is no evidence to support the chroniclers' claim that Malcolm III created the first Scottish earls or the episode in Shakespeare's *Macbeth* where Malcolm elevates to earldoms those thanes who had supported him against Macbeth.[31]

THANES AND THANAGES

The secondary tier of royal administration in eleventh-century Scotland was the thanage.[32] The principal distinction between the two levels is that mormaers, as scions of the royal kin group, probably held their provinces by right from the king, while thanes were not members of the royal kin group but officials, each administering a smaller royal estate or demesne for the king. The two types of administration were therefore complementary. Provinces were not divided into thanages; although thanages could be located within provinces, the thane held his land directly from the king, not the mormaer.

Thane is a late title in Scotland and is derived from Anglo-Saxon *þegn*, 'one who serves'.[33] Thanes and thanages are not recorded in Scotland before the twelfth century, so that references to them in an eleventh-century context are, strictly speaking, anachronistic. The sole exception is a reference to 'Crinán the thane' in an early eleventh-century context. This, however, occurs in an English source, and its author may have applied what he perceived to be the closest equivalent Anglo-Saxon rank to the office he identified Crinán as holding.[34] In reality, Crinán held a position more consistent with that of Mormaer rather than Thane of Atholl, although he was actually Abbot of Dunkeld.

But regardless of the terminology used, the office of thane and the form of administration to which it related were considerably older than the twelfth century. The names of, and obligations attached to, thanages give the impression of antiquity. As early as about 1370, Fordun noted that thanages had existed 'from ancient times indeed'.[35] Moreover, like the provinces, the seventy-one thanages recorded are concentrated in north-eastern Scotland, indicating that they originally formed a level of Pictish socio-political organisation. The equivalent Gaelic term for a thane was either *tighearn* ('lord') or *toísech* ('leader/chief'); *toísech* is the only noble rank other than mormaer recorded in the *Book of Deer*.[36] Yet a mormaer could also be a *toísech*, as a note in the *Book of Deer* records, because he was also the head of his own kin-group.[37] Perhaps significantly, *tighearn* is used in the *Annals of the Four Masters* to describe the lowest grade of Irish king, which was earlier known as a *rí tuaithe*, 'king of a people/tribe/kingdom'.

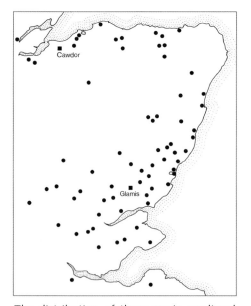

The distribution of thanages in medieval Scotland, showing their concentration in what was formerly the kingdom of the Picts, north-eastern Scotland. Two of these thanages, Cawdor and Glamis, have become intimately associated with Macbeth, although there is no evidence of any historic link.

The thane was the basic and most common rank of noble in eleventh-century Scotland. This is indicated by the Laws of the Brets and the Scots, an eleventh-century law of status that records the compensation payable for killing people of different social ranks. It defines the blood payment for killing a thane as 100 cows, while that of every other rank is a multiple or fraction of this.[38] Like mormaerships, thanages tended to become hereditary. However, their status as royally appointed officials and smaller power bases presumably made it more difficult for thanes to pose a credible threat to the kingship and easier for a king to remove thanes from office. During the late twelfth century the (non-hereditary) Thanage of Arbuthnott in Kincardineshire appears to have had a new thane on average every five or six years, although it is unclear if this was typical or can be applied to earlier periods.

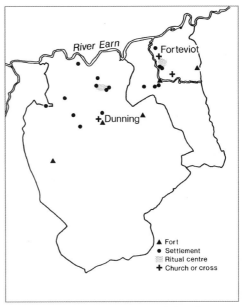

A conjectural reconstruction of the thanages of Dunning and Forteviot, Perthshire, based on old parish boundaries. (After Dr Stephen T. Driscoll)

Thanes had a range of administrative, fiscal, judicial and military responsibilities. A thane's primary function was to manage his thanage, a royal estate or demesne, and collect royal revenues. The latter comprised 'cain', or regular tribute, and 'conveth', the obligation of hospitality, scotticised terms derived from Gaelic *cáin* and *coinnmed/coinmheadh* respectively. Conveth was originally levied as food and accommodation for the King and his retinue for a specified number of nights as they progressed around the kingdom but later comprised food renders in lieu, from which the thane deducted his own share. The importance of conveth as the defining basis of thanages is attested by two thanages called Conveth, in Banffshire and Kincardineshire.[39]

The thanage was the standard unit of royal demesne in Scotland north of the Forth. Thanages were an important element of a complex but ordered pattern of social organisation, territorial administration and agricultural exploitation. Each one had three principal components: a *caput* or main royal residence, a ritual centre and several farms, from which conjectural maps of thanages may be constructed.[40] The *caput* (Latin, 'head') was the administrative and symbolic centre of the thanage. This was where royal power, represented by the thane or – while visiting during a progress – the King in person, resided. Many of these centres would have been fortified, reflecting the requirements of the King and his thane for both defence and to give architectural expression to their status. Attesting their close identification, the thanage often derived its name from its *caput*, not from a district.

Emphasising its significance, the ritual centre was often located at or near the *caput*. This was where inauguration ceremonies, assemblies and popular courts were held. The ritual centre was sometimes focused on a prehistoric monument, often a burial mound, or a complex of such sites, thus conferring the legitimacy of the past on the activities performed there and the socio-political élites conducting them.[41] Alternatively, a mound of later construction or of natural origin was sometimes used. The best-known example of this is Moot Hill at Scone, which acquired a much wider significance by virtue of its role as the inauguration place of the Scottish kings. The former locations of these court or moot hills are sometimes identifiable only by placename evidence, usually a variant of Cuthill, from Gaelic *comhdháil*, 'assembly, meeting'.[42] The frequent collocation of ritual centres and early churches attests the close relationship that existed between secular and ecclesiastical élites.

The main farms within a thanage comprised the dependent estate associated with the *caput*. The thanage therefore conformed to the model of the 'multiple estate', a form of managing royal and noble demesnes which is found throughout early medieval Britain.[43] The conveth raised from these farms was delivered to, and ultimately consumed at, the *caput*. The farms were worked by free farmers, ordinary commoners of free legal status. Below them would have been various grades of peasants and bonded workers, semi-free or unfree agricultural workers who owed a lengthy or permanent duty of obligation to their lord and were therefore tied to the land. These lower social ranks are scarcely represented in historical sources.

The thanage has been of enduring interest to historians from Fordun's time, probably because several survived throughout the Middle Ages but were obviously archaic and of obscure origin. Boece claimed that many thanes were made earls by Malcolm III in return for supporting him in his defeat of Macbeth, implying that this resulted in the disappearance of the rank of thane.[44] In reality, thanes and thanages survived, although mormaers are absent from medieval chronicles, possibly because the greater antiquity of mormaerships and their early transformation into earldoms ensured obscurity. As a result, Macbeth is consistently but inaccurately portrayed as a thane, not a mormaer, in medieval chronicles and, of course, Shakespeare's *Macbeth*.

The thanage declined in importance as a result of the feudalisation of Scotland north of the Forth during the late twelfth and thirteenth centuries. In its place, the sheriffdom became the primary unit of royal administration throughout Scotland during the thirteenth century. Some thanages became the centres of sheriffdoms, the offices of sheriff and thane perhaps merging, while other thanages were alienated by the Crown to lay landlords or occasionally the Church. Nevertheless, more than half the thanages recorded survived after 1300, co-existing with the new feudal tenancies. Most thanages appear to have remained under royal control, with incoming Norman settlers being granted lands previously forfeited by the Crown from mormaers or earls who had fallen out of royal favour. Although the fourteenth century saw a more extensive alienation of thanages, some survived within earldoms while the lands of others were held as baronies. Indeed, so established was the concept of the thanage within the innately conservative pattern of landholding in medieval Scotland, that eleven were still in existence during the seventeenth century. Two of these surviving thanages, Cawdor and Glamis, had long since acquired a special significance within the Macbeth myth.

THE CHURCH

There was no single, organised 'Church' in eleventh-century Scotland, while vague concepts of a 'Celtic' Church are even less helpful. Instead, Christianity exhibited a regional character, reflecting the different churches of the various peoples who became the medieval Scots. Angles, Britons, Picts and Scots each had their own distinctive forms of ecclesiastical organisation, liturgy, saints and architecture.[45] This was a result of the different routes by which Christianity first reached these peoples during the mid-first millennium and the varied influences subsequently exerted on their churches. In addition to these regional variations, there was also great ecclesiastical diversity even within the same regions of Scotland, chiefly between churches that were monastic in character and others that served secular communities. Not until the ecclesiastical reorganisations of the twelfth century, which saw the introduction of a full diocesan structure and the systematic establishment of parishes, was uniformity imposed.

North of the Forth, strong Irish influences on ecclesiastical organisation, liturgy and architecture prevailed. However, this was not due to St Columba's mission, which introduced Christianity to this region in the sixth century, or the subsequent influence of Columba's foundation of Iona, but the result of those close cultural connections the Scots maintained with their ancestral homeland after the forging of the kingdom of the Scots in the mid-ninth century. This Irish legacy is particularly evident in Scottish placenames, many of which refer to ecclesiastical offices, customs and institutions of Irish origin.[46] These placename elements include Appin (*apdaine*), the territory under the jurisdiction of an abbot; Annat (*annaid*), a patron saint's church or church

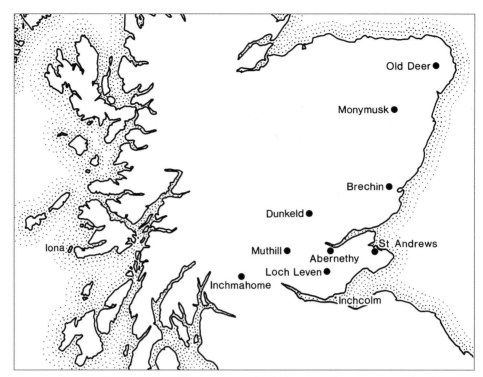

Major ecclesiastical sites in eleventh-century Scotland, showing places mentioned in the text.

containing the relics of its founder; Dysert (*dìsert*), a solitary place of contemplation and, most commonly of all, Kil- (*cill*), a church or chapel. Placenames also attest the presence in Scotland of the cults of many Irish saints. For example, Inchmahome (*Innis mo-Cholmáig*) in the Lake of Menteith attests its dedication to, and perhaps even its foundation by, Colmán, an Ulster saint, while Inchcolm in the Firth of Forth commemorates Colum Cille, St Columba. The 'Kil'- placename element in particular was usually prefixed to the name of the saint to whom the church was dedicated.

Our knowledge of ecclesiastical organisation in Scotland between the ninth and eleventh centuries is limited. The Scots probably adopted or adapted a pre-existing, Pictish episcopal structure. Pictish foundations, such as those at Abernethy, Brechin, St Andrews and possibly Dunkeld, continued as important ecclesiastical centres under the Scots, although they may have become monastic churches of Irish type, each headed by an abbot. These churches owned extensive but often widely distributed lands, the result of piecemeal endowments made by kings and nobles. The legacy of this may be traced in the fragmented geography of the medieval dioceses of Brechin, Dunkeld and St Andrews. Fossilising an

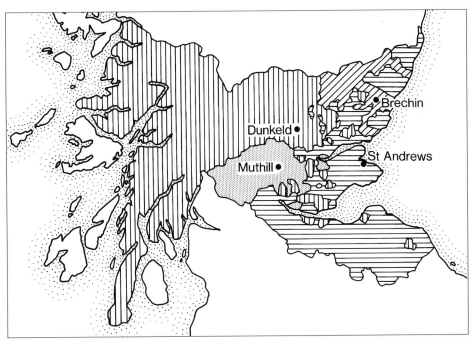

Dioceses and cathedrals in central Scotland before *c.* 1180, showing the fragmented geography of the dioceses. The widely distributed detached portions were the result of piecemeal endowments of land and churches made to monastic churches by kings and nobles. These monastic churches later became cathedrals and, when new diocesan boundaries were created during the episcopal reorganisation of the twelfth century, several parishes became enclaves surrounded by the territory of a neighbouring diocese. (After Dr Alan Macquarrie)

earlier pattern of landholding, these dioceses possessed a multiplicity of enclaves scattered throughout eastern Scotland. This occurred during the episcopal reorganisation of the twelfth century, when remote churches within the *parochiae*, or monastic confederations, of Brechin, Dunkeld and St Andrews were transformed into parishes within the newly created dioceses but became physically detached from their mother church when the new diocesan boundaries were created.

Although there was probably a combination of episcopal and monastic churches, the details of their organisation, interrelationships and functions are unclear. The existence of a hierarchy of churches, comprising chief churches with subsidiary or dependent churches, is apparent from notes in the *Book of Deer*.[47] Under an episcopal organisation, a bishop ministered to the people within a defined territory or see, while under a monastic organisation an abbot ruled his monastery and ministering to the people was not conducted on a territorial basis. However, the distinction was probably blurred and no uniform ecclesiastical organisation may have existed in Scotland north of the Forth before the twelfth century. Indeed, as in Ireland, both abbatial and episcopal offices could be held simultaneously; Tuathal, who died in 865, was Chief Bishop (*prímescop*) of Fortriu (and therefore possibly of all Scotland) as well as Abbot of Dunkeld.[48] The title *prímescop* implies the existence of other, lesser bishops. A similar office, implying a comparable episcopal organisation, was still in existence during the reign of Malcolm III (1057–93), when the pre-eminent status of the Bishop of St Andrews was distinguished by his Gaelic and Latin titles *árd escop* and *summus episcopus*, 'chief bishop'.[49]

By the eleventh century, most clerics were probably not celibate and many ecclesiastical posts had become hereditary. In addition, some churches had undergone a gradual secularisation, so that the abbot was often the lay administrator of a church's temporalities, its properties and revenues. Some of these offices may have been in the gift of the King; Crinán, Abbot of Dunkeld, was the son-in-law of Malcolm II and, underlining his influence, the father of Duncan. These abbots acted like secular lords; an earlier Abbot of Dunkeld was killed in a battle between two contenders for the Scottish kingship in 965.[50] Crinán may also have been Mormaer of Atholl and was himself killed in battle against Macbeth in 1045.

The *Céli Dé* ('Clients of God'), or Culdees as they are usually scotticised, belonged to an ascetic revival movement which originated in eighth-century Ireland,[51] possibly in reaction to the increasing secularisation of the Church. Its members were originally committed to lives of austerity, contemplation and devotion, although some Culdee communities also underwent a gradual secularisation. Two types of Culdee community appear to have existed in Scotland between the tenth and thirteenth centuries. The first comprised communities of secularised clergy who ministrated in the bishops' churches of Abernethy, Brechin, Monymusk, Muthill, St Andrews and probably Dunkeld. The second, which included the island communities of Iona and Loch Leven, was eremitical in character. The dedications and insular locations of some medieval abbeys and priories, such as Inchcolm and Inchmahome, also point to their origins as early monasteries and, possibly, eremitic Culdee communities. These, presumably, were the types of community to which Turgot, Bishop of St Andrews (1108–15), was referring to in his *Life of St Margaret* when he portrayed eleventh-century Scotland as a land of hermits: 'At that time in the kingdom of the Scots there were many living, shut up in cells in places set apart, by a life of great strictness, in the flesh but not according to the flesh; communing, indeed, with angels upon earth.'[52]

Royal and ecclesiastical élites enjoyed a close relationship in early medieval Scotland.[53] During the eleventh century this is particularly evident from grants of royal lands and incomes to the Church. For example, Malcolm II endowed the monastery of Old Deer, Aberdeenshire, with royal revenues from his nearby lands at Biffie in Buchan, as a note in the *Book of Deer* records,[54] while Macbeth and his queen gave lands to the Culdees of Loch Leven. This mutually supportive relationship between royal and ritual structures of authority began with kings granting land to saints for the establishment of ecclesiastical communities, as various foundation legends, including those of Iona and Loch Leven, record. While royal gifts were often made, at least overtly, in return for prayers for the souls of their donors, they also ensured the Church's continuing support for the kingship. The legitimation of royal authority by Christianity is most apparent in later royal inauguration ceremonies. A similar relationship existed at a local level between the nobility and the Church; notes in the *Book of Deer* record a mormaer and his wife and a *toísech* freeing the community from secular obligations due on their lands.[55]

Although few surviving structures can be dated confidently to the eleventh century, Irish influence is clearly detectable in early ecclesiastical architecture north of the Forth.[56] Churches were usually small, unicameral (single-cell) buildings, mostly of timber, which explains why so few have survived. Only the more important churches were of stone, although these are likely to have mirrored their wooden counterparts in size and form. The tiny St Columba's Shrine on Iona,[57] with its high gables and steeply pitched roof, is probably typical of both masonry and timber churches of the ninth to eleventh centuries. Originally free-standing, St Columba's Shrine was later incorporated into the thirteenth-century Benedictine abbey.

St Columba's Shrine, Iona. Once free-standing, this simple, unicameral (single-cell) chapel of probably eleventh-century date is now joined to the Benedictine abbey. The abbey, constructed between about 1200 and 1638, was restored in the late nineteenth and twentieth centuries and St Columba's Shrine was extensively reconstructed in 1962. (Crown copyright: Historic Scotland)

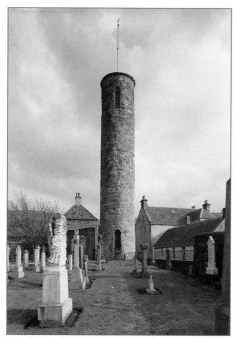 

Abernethy round tower, Perthshire. Different phases of construction are detectable in its masonry, adding to uncertainty about its date. Although the Romanesque belfry windows (one of which is visible near the top of the tower) are of twelfth-century date, these belong to a later phase of rebuilding. The original construction of the free-standing tower, and its surviving lower courses, probably dates to the eleventh century and possibly to Macbeth's reign. (Crown copyright: Royal Commission on the Ancient and Historical Monuments of Scotland).

The round tower, Brechin Cathedral, Angus. Originally free-standing, the tower is now joined to the nave of the thirteenth-century cathedral by a modern aisle. A church contemporary with the round tower would have stood on the site now occupied by the cathedral. Although the tower is probably eleventh century in date, the conical roof was added in the fourteenth century. (Crown copyright: Royal Commission on the Ancient and Historical Monuments of Scotland)

Irish influence is particularly evident in the round towers at Abernethy and Brechin.[58] Essentially bell towers and originally free-standing, these are the only known Scottish examples of a distinctively Irish form of ecclesiastical architecture; about ninety examples are recorded in Ireland. Dates ranging from the late tenth to early twelfth centuries have been proposed for the towers, although the later dates probably relate to secondary phases of construction or reconstruction. These towers, or at least their earliest phases, probably predate the Anglo-Saxon tastes introduced by Malcolm III and Queen Margaret and may belong to Macbeth's reign.

Religious sites reflect the diversity of ecclesiastical organisation in Scotland during this period. They range from simple places of worship, comprising a single-cell church, to large ecclesiastical centres. The latter, approaching the size and status of towns, would probably have contained a larger principal church, several smaller churches, associated ancillary domestic and industrial buildings, a cemetery and religious sculpture such as high crosses. Such specialised and impressive architectural works as the round towers and their late eleventh- and twelfth-century square counterparts,[59] would have been the preserve of only the most powerful and opulent ecclesiastical centres. All these structures would usually have stood within an enclosure, often defined by an earthwork and sub-circular or sometimes rectilinear in plan. A characteristic feature of early medieval monastic sites, this marked the boundary of the abbot's rule and symbolically demarcated the sacred and secular worlds. Some eremitic communities placed an added emphasis on the spiritual salvation that physical isolation from the material world brought and sought the solitude of

St Rule's or St Regulus' Church, St Andrews, Fife. This church, and particularly its tower, exhibits strong similarities with late Anglo-Saxon and early Anglo-Norman ecclesiastical architecture, indicating a late eleventh-century date for its construction. The ruins of the twelfth-century cathedral stand in the background. (Crown copyright: Royal Commission on the Ancient and Historical Monuments of Scotland)

island sites. One such community, that of St Serf at Loch Leven, appears to have been of special significance to Macbeth and his queen.

THE PROVINCE OF MORAY

The province of Moray is central to any study of Macbeth. Macbeth belonged to the hereditary aristocracy of Moray; his father was a Mormaer of Moray and this was presumably where Macbeth was born and brought up. Moray's unique character must have exerted an enduring influence on the young Macbeth, with profound consequences; he murdered Duncan in this province and it was from this powerbase that he seized the Scottish kingship.

The medieval province of Moray was much larger than the modern local authority district of the same name. At its maximum extent it stretched from the North Sea to the Atlantic and from the River Dee to Ross; the Mormaers of Moray ruled over a great swathe of northern Scotland. The Dee was a significant boundary; Macbeth withdrew north of the Dee after his defeat by Malcolm III and Earl Siward in 1054, retaining his northern province as a residual kingdom for a further three years before his defeat and death. But it was the Grampian mountains, known traditionally – and still referred to by historians – as the Mounth (from Gaelic *monadh*, 'mountain'), that separated Moray physically from the rest of Scotland to the south. Moray lay beyond the Mounth, distant from the principal power centres and historic heartland of the kingdom of the Scots.

Moray's peripheral and partially isolated location resulted in it developing a discrete identity from the rest of early medieval Scotland. The existence of Moray as a separate political entity is apparent from as early as the eighth century. Bede described in 731 how 'the provinces of the northern Picts . . . are separated from those of the southern Picts by a range of steep and rugged mountains',[60] implying that the Picts comprised two groups on either side of the Mounth. More specifically, the existence of a 'king of the Picts on this side of the Mounth' (*rex Pictorum citra Monoth*)[61] in 782 indicates that the Mounth marked a political division between the northern and southern Picts, both of whom presumably had their own kings.

Moray retained a separate political identity after the assimilation of the Picts by the Scots in the mid-ninth century. This may have been the result of several influences, including the appropriation by the Scots of an existing power structure within Moray, possibly the kingship of the northern Picts, the intermarriage of incoming Scots with members of the native Pictish royal dynasty and Moray's distance from the political core of the Scottish kingdom. Another factor lay in the internal politics of Dál Riata. While the descendants of Cenél nGabráin migrated eastwards to the historic heartland of the former Pictish kingdom and dominated the Scottish kingship, the descendants of a lesser royal kindred, Cenél Loairn, moved from northern Argyll up the Great Glen to settle in Moray, where they held the hereditary mormaership. The descendants of these two kindreds formed different branches of the Scottish royal kin group, one drawing its power from the south, the other from the north. These two branches are usually and conveniently, but anachronistically and somewhat inaccurately, referred to as the House of Atholl or Dunkeld and the House of Moray respectively. Although probably involving several complex

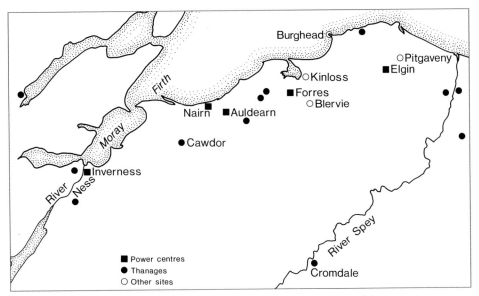

Moray, showing royal centres, thanages and other locations mentioned in the text.

processes, the origins of tensions between the Mormaers of Moray and the Scottish kings may be traced to dynastic rivalries between the descendants of two royal kin groups of Dál Riata.

Moray's political and economic heartland, the power base of its mormaers, occupied an area delineated by the River Spey in the south-east, the Grampian mountains to the south, the River Ness in the west and the Moray Firth to the north. Moray's appeal to settlers from the earliest times is apparent from its geography and its archaeological remains. It has a long coastline, with natural harbours and easily defended promontories, and a rich agricultural hinterland, the Laigh (or Laich) of Moray. Most prehistoric and medieval settlement was inland, beyond the coastal sand dunes and heavy estuarine silts, which were unsuitable for early cultivation.[62]

Although several promontory forts along the Moray coast, including the massive one at Burghead, were built by the Picts, there is no evidence that their occupation continued into or beyond the late first millennium. Instead, the power centres of Moray were situated further inland by at least the mid-tenth century, as the recorded deaths of kings at and near Forres indicate. Like kings, mormaers were probably peripatetic, progressing around their province, carrying out administration, collecting and consuming food renders and dispensing justice. This business was probably conducted from fortified power centres, of which the Mormaers of Moray may have had several.

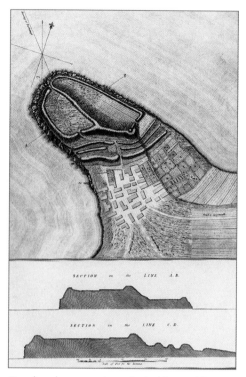

Burghead promontory fort, Morayshire, as depicted in General William Roy's *The Military Antiquities of the Romans in North Britain* (1793) but based on his military survey of 1747–55. Defended on three sides by the waters of the Moray Firth, the landward side was fortified with four timber-reinforced ramparts, up to 6 m high, across the neck of the promontory. Most of these defences were destroyed when the present village was built in 1805–9. The fort is probably a Pictish stronghold of the mid-first millennium AD. (Crown copyright: Royal Commission on the Ancient and Historical Monuments of Scotland)

There were several thanages in Moray and their distribution suggests an attempt by the Scottish kingship to limit the powers of the Mormaers of Moray. Most of these thanages form a ring surrounding the rich agricultural lands around Elgin and Inverness, important power centres of the Mormaers of Moray, and may indicate the presence of royal estates within Moray considerably earlier than the province's forfeiture by the Crown in 1130. In later attempts to strengthen royal authority, Moray power centres were appropriated by the Crown for royal burghs, each with its own royal castle; Elgin and Forres by 1153, Inverness, Nairn and Auldearn by 1214. That such strongly fortified symbols of royal authority were required in Moray attests the province's turbulent state. These castles probably occupied the sites of the mormaers' earlier fortresses, but Moray's violent later history has ensured that there are few surviving remains of even these medieval castles.

Although owing at least nominal allegiance to the King of Scots, the Mormaers of Moray were regional kings in all but name. Indeed, they are described in Irish sources as kings. Although this reflects external perceptions of their status, in terms of the multiplicity of ranks of Irish kingship, it is revealing that no other Scottish mormaers are described as kings. Irish sources indicate that Moray was perceived as a sub-kingdom within the kingdom of the Scots, implying that its mormaers wielded substantial powers and enjoyed a (perhaps varying) degree of autonomy from the Scottish kingship. Moray's *de facto* status was a kingdom within a kingdom.

Whatever the extent of Moray's autonomy, it was evidently insufficient for its mormaers and yet too great for the Scottish kings. For over three centuries, relations between Moray's rulers and the Scottish kingship were characterised by sporadic strife, as the *Scottish Chronicle* and regnal lists record. In response to intermittent rebellions, the Scottish kings regularly led their army north to reassert royal authority over Moray, at least in theory if not always in practice. Donald I died at Forres in 900 on the earliest recorded royal expedition into Moray.[63] This is supported by later events. Donald's son, Malcolm I (943–54), later 'went with his army into Moray and slew Cellach'.[64] Cellach, probably the Mormaer of Moray or a member of its ruling kin group, may have been killed in revenge for Donald's death. But Malcolm failed to subdue Moray. In 954, perhaps during the same campaign on which Cellach was slain, Malcolm was 'treacherously killed by the men of Moray', probably at Blervie, 3.5 km south-east of Forres.[65] The *Verse Chronicle* inserted in the *Chronicle of Melrose* expresses its contempt for the men of Moray with the comment that Malcolm 'fell by the deceit and guile of an apostate people'.[66]

Another King of Scots, Duff, was killed at Forres in 966 and his body hidden under a bridge at Kinloss.[67] And, of course, Duncan I was killed by Macbeth in Moray in 1040, the fourth Scottish king to have been killed in Moray in 140 years. Yet of the rebellious Mormaers of Moray, only Macbeth went on to seize the Scottish kingship, effectively uniting the province of Moray with Scotland south of the Mounth.

But there were also periods when the authority of the Scottish kings extended over Moray. Malcolm II is styled 'King of the Mounth' in *Duan Albanach*,[68] indicating that he ruled on both sides of the Grampians. Rather than imposing this by force, it seems more likely that peace was effected by political means through the marriage of a close female relative of Malcolm's, probably a daughter or possibly a sister, to Findlaech, Mormaer of Moray. As these were Macbeth's parents, this provides a plausible explanation for Macbeth's close links with the Scottish kingship and his own claim to the throne.

Another factor that may have brought the Mormaers of Moray into a closer relationship with the Scottish kingship during the early eleventh century was the threat posed by the Vikings of Orkney and Caithness. Moray lay on a frontier; across the Moray Firth were Ross and Sutherland, control of which alternated between the Scots and Orkney Vikings. And beyond Sutherland lay Caithness and Orkney, which had been settled by the Vikings in the ninth century.

The *Orkneyinga Saga* conveys an impression of frequent warfare between the Viking *jarls* of Orkney and the Mormaers of Moray. Macbeth, his father and uncle

Sueno's Stone, Forres, Morayshire. This massive cross-slab (the cross, on the west face, is not seen here), standing over 6.5 m high, probably dates to the ninth or tenth centuries. Its east face is covered by an extensive and unique battle scene, in four panels, and probably records a historical confrontation between the armies of a King of Scots and a Mormaer of Moray. (Crown copyright: Historic Scotland)

are all described as separately leading armies into battle against the Orkney Vikings. To the *Orkneyinga Saga*, which made no distinction between Moray and Scotland 'proper', these were Scottish *jarls* and armies, but according to the saga only one campaign was led by the King of Scots himself. Moray not only occupied a peripheral location within Scotland but effectively acted as a buffer zone between the kingdom of the Scots and the Orkney Vikings.

The violence of Moray's early history is graphically attested in the extensive battle scene on the reverse face of the remarkable monument known as Sueno's Stone, on the outskirts of Forres. Although not closely datable, this cross slab may belong to the ninth or tenth centuries. Traditionally believed to mark a Scottish victory over a Scandinavian army led by Sueno during the reign of Malcolm II, this unique scene is now thought to commemorate the killing of Duff in 966 or the Scots' defeat of the northern Picts in the mid-ninth century.[69]

Moray's independence and violent history did not end with Macbeth's death. Lulach, Macbeth's stepson, continued the struggle against Malcolm III for a few months after Macbeth's death until he, too, was killed in battle by Malcolm. Lulach's son, Máel Snechtai, was the next to take up the fight against Malcolm. On invading Moray in 1078, 'Malcolm captured Mæl-slæhta's mother [*sic*, i.e. Lulach's widow] . . . and all his best men, and all his treasures and his cattle, and he himself escaped with difficulty'.[70] The death of Máel Snechtai, 'King of Moray', is recorded in 1085.[71] Although the circumstances are not noted, Máel Snechtai's death notice appears in a list of Irish clerics who 'ended their lives happily'. The implication is that Máel Snechtai was forced into exile in 1078 and died, possibly in Ireland, after entering a monastery.

Moray was the scene of sporadic strife over the next 150 years, indicating that the Scottish kingship was still incapable of consistently imposing its rule over the recalcitrant province. These rebellions were led by descendants of Lulach and later leaders of Moray. Sometimes the evidence is very meagre, as in 1116: 'Ladhmann son of Domnall, grandson of the King of Scotland, was killed by the men of Moray'.[72] The rebellion of Lulach's grandson, Angus, Earl of Moray, in 1130 is better documented. Angus invaded Scotland and reached Stracathro in Angus before being defeated and killed by an army led by Edward, the Constable of David I: 'A battle between the men of Scotland and the men of Moray in which four thousand of the men of Moray fell with their king, Angus son of the daughter of Lulach; a thousand, or a hundred, which[ever] is more accurate, of the men of Scotland [fell] in a counter-attack.'[73] Another source records that 'Angus was killed by the raiding-army of the Scots, and there was a great slaughter with him'.[74] Following this, the earldom was forfeited by the crown and the lands were granted to Flemish settlers in an attempt to weaken the position of Moray's native landowners.

An ally of Angus, the obscure Malcolm mac Heth, then rebelled, but was captured and imprisoned in 1134. The next rebellion was led by Wimund, Bishop of the Isles, who claimed to be a son of the Earl of Moray, presumably either Angus or Malcolm. Sometime after 1142, Wimund was captured, blinded and forced to spend the rest of his life in Byland Abbey, Yorkshire. Malcolm IV ('the Maiden') (1153–65) led an army against a subsequent rebellion by the men of Moray and in 1163 either transplanted the defeated rebels or expanded the introduction of Flemish settlers into Moray.[75]

William ('the Lion') (1165–1214) faced a more serious uprising. Donald mac William, a descendant of both Duncan II (1094) and the Earls of Moray, claimed the Scottish kingship during the 1160s and rebelled in 1179. Although only one royal castle, Auldearn, fell, Donald's uprising was not crushed until 1187. A challenge by the sons of mac Heth and mac William resulted in their heads being presented to Alexander II in 1215. The mac Williams again revolted in 1230 and, once defeated, the mac William line was wiped out when its youngest member had her brains dashed out against the mercat cross at Forfar. This was the last occasion on which the men of Moray rebelled; the subjection of Moray by the Scottish kings had been a protracted and costly affair.

Against this background, Macbeth may be viewed as a typical Mormaer of Moray: warlike, ambitious and fiercely independent. Macbeth was by no means the only ruler of Moray to defeat and kill a Scottish king. Yet, of all the rebellious mormaers and Earls of Moray only Macbeth usurped the Scottish kingship. What drove him to this course of action, enabled him to succeed and then maintained him on the throne for the next seventeen years?

CHAPTER 2

The Path to the Throne

The historical Macbeth is an enigmatic figure. This is a result of the limited amount of surviving contemporary sources and the extent to which our perceptions of Macbeth have been influenced by later myths and, of course, Shakespeare's play. However, as these are the only sources available, this fragmentary, complex and often contradictory evidence must form the basis of any study of the historical Macbeth and his reign. Although it is not possible to write a historical biography in the recognised sense, the available texts present us with a series of 'snapshots' of Macbeth the man. When pieced together, placed in chronological sequence and examined within the broader geographical and historical context of eleventh-century insular kingship, these seemingly isolated incidents provide genuine insights into the principal events in Macbeth's life and reign, enabling us to construct a skeletal narrative history. Moreover, the evidence also offers a tantalising glimpse of the factors that may have shaped Macbeth's personality and led him to seize the Scottish kingship.

MACBETH'S NAME

Befitting such an enigmatic figure, the uncertainties surrounding Macbeth extend to his name. These doubts concern not only the form, meaning and significance of the name, but even its relationship with the king. Contemporary sources preserve Macbeth's name in its original form. The *Chronicle* of Marianus Scotus, although in Latin, records Macbeth's full name in its Gaelic form, 'Macbethad mac Finnloech', while the Irish annals confirm it as 'Mac Bethadh mac Findlaich'.[1] Macbeth's name appears in *Duan Albanach*, written within a generation of his death, as 'MacBeathadh' (pronounced *mok b'a-ha*).[2] The St Andrews *Register* renders his name in Latin as '*Machbet filius Finlach*' and '*Macbet filio Finlac*'.[3]

But non-Gaelic sources spell Macbeth's name in forms that were more familiar to their scribes. Macbeth appears in the *Anglo-Saxon Chronicle* as 'Macbeoðen', 'Mealbæaðe' and 'Mælbæthe' and in the *Orkneyinga Saga* as

'Magbjóthr'. This sometimes makes it difficult to identify references to Macbeth in external sources. Macbeth's name also underwent a transformation in the Latinised form used in later Scottish chronicles. His name is rendered 'Machabeus' by Fordun and 'Maccabaeus' by Boece, a name shared with Judas Maccabaeus, who led the Jews against their Hellenisation by the Seleucid kings.[4] Scottish chroniclers simply may have sought a recognised name from which to standardise the Latin spelling of 'Macbeth' and settled on 'Maccabaeus' as the most authoritative. But Judas Maccabaeus had a special significance for the medieval Scots; Robert I ('the Bruce') (1306–29) is described in the Declaration of Arbroath as 'another Maccabeus' because of his role as a warrior king and defender of his kingdom and people.

Vernacular Scots spellings of Macbeth also vary considerably. 'Makbeth', used by Wyntoun and Bellenden, is simply a scotticisation of the Gaelic original, displaying a contraction of the final syllable. But the translation of Latin chronicles into Scots during the sixteenth century resulted in further variant spellings: 'MakCobey', in Stewart's translation of Boece's chronicle, and 'Machabie' in Leslie's *Historie*. This indicates continued confusion about the correct form of Macbeth's name. Against this background it is perhaps unsurprising that some Scottish historians formerly claimed that 'Macbeth . . . is commonly supposed [to be] no name at all'.[5]

The earliest recorded appearance of Macbeth as a personal name is in 891, when three Irish pilgrims arrived at the Court of Alfred the Great; the name of one was recorded in the different manuscripts of the *Anglo-Saxon Chronicle* as 'Macbeathadh', 'Maccnethath', 'Machbethu' and 'Maccbetu'. The name is not recorded in Irish sources until the eleventh century, when it appears in both royal and ecclesiastical contexts. Two Ua Conchobair (O'Connor) Kings of Ciarraige (Kerry), both called Mac Bethad, died in 1014 and 1086. In addition, Mac Beathadh, Abbot of Cork, and Mac Bethad, a principal member of the learned order of Armagh, died in 1041 and 1106 respectively.[6] The name appears to have been fashionable in south-west Ireland during the eleventh century. Yet, with the exception of Macbeth, King of Scots, recorded examples of the name are rare in Scotland before the twelfth century, when various forms appeared, and it disappeared as a first name in about 1300.[7]

Gaelic *mac* means 'son' and was used with the father's first name to denote filiation, descent being all-important in a kin-based society. These patronymics have evolved into many of today's Scottish surnames. The two elements are now usually run together, for example, as MacDonald, while the contraction of *mac* and the disappearance of the initial capital of the father's name results in Mcdonald.

Macbeth survives as various Scottish surnames, not only MacBeth. Scotticised forms derived phonetically from the Gaelic name form Mac Bheatha (pronounced *mok v'a-ha*) have resulted in a range of names such as MacBey, MacVeagh and MacVey.

Although Macbeth conforms to the structure of a Gaelic patronymic, the name carries no notion of filiation but expresses a more obscure concept: Macbeth means 'son of life, a righteous man'.[8] Other proposed etymologies, deriving Macbeth from 'a corrupt form of *macc-bethad*, "one of the elect"' or *beath*, a birch tree,[9] are not widely accepted. 'Macbeth' denotes one who is saved spiritually, a Christian. The concept is illustrated by the twelfth-century *Life of St Colmán*, which describes how an Irish saint heard the voice of a 'son of life' (*filii vite*) amidst the howls of a group of murderous robbers and resolved to save the youth from the 'death-in-life' of outlawry.[10] '*Filii vite*' is a literal translation of 'Macbeth' and represents the expression in Latin, the language of the Church, of an Irish concept. Colmán evidently believed that the 'Son of Life', alone among the brigands, was worth saving, perhaps because his voice revealed his ecclesiastical education.

This episode *may* suggest that Macbeth was a religious name, assumed by someone entering the Church. This interpretation has prompted claims that Macbeth was not his original name but his 'name in religion' and that only the latter is now known, it being the form favoured by monastic scribes and a result of the monopoly of the Church in keeping written records during this period.[11] This theory suggests that Macbeth may be referred to in some sources under another name and deserves closer examination.

Devotional names were common in early medieval Scotland and Ireland. They typically comprise a devotional prefix, usually *Céle* ('client, vassal'), *Gilla* ('servant') or *Máel* ('tonsured, devotee'), compounded with a saint's name. But devotional names were not restricted to clerics and acquired a much wider currency during the early medieval period. Three of Macbeth's close relatives had devotional names: his uncle, Máel Brigte ('Devotee of St Brigit') and cousins, Gilla Comgán ('Servant of St Kevin') and Máel Coluim ('Devotee of St Columba'). Although Macbeth may have originated as a devotional name, it had lost this significance by the eleventh century, as the Kings of Ciarraige and Macbeth, King of Scots, demonstrate. Consequently, there is no evidence that Macbeth's was an adopted name of religious significance or that he was previously known by another name.

The familiar form, Macbeth, is as old as the name's earliest recorded appearance. Shakespeare made Macbeth the universally popular form and, not surprisingly, this is the name by which Macbeth is most commonly known today in all his manifestations, historical, mythological and dramatic. But even here there are variations. The capital 'B' is sometimes restored to give 'MacBeth', 'to prevent confusion' or in deference to the name's original form.[12] However, if authenticity is the objective, it is unclear why those advocating 'MacBeth' as the correct form do not use the original Gaelic spelling, Mac Bethad. Indeed, it is increasingly fashionable to employ the original spelling of historic names and references to 'Mac bethad' (*sic*) now appear frequently.[13] However, this spelling is not followed here. As the name's most widely used and recognised form, 'Macbeth' is used throughout this book, except where quoting sources which employ an alternative spelling.

MACBETH'S ORIGINS AND BOYHOOD

Macbeth's year of birth is unknown. Although he is widely claimed to have been born in 1005, this is uncorroborated. Births were rarely recorded in early medieval sources and frequently have to be inferred from other dates, where available, including those of marriage, accession to the throne, death and the birth and/or death of parents, siblings or children. In Macbeth's case, the chronological points of reference are his father's death (1020), description as a 'sub-king' (1031), Mormaership of Moray and marriage (probably 1032), kingship (1040) and death (1057). As these leave considerable uncertainty about Macbeth's year of birth, 1005 can only represent an estimate. Macbeth's place of birth is also uncertain but was probably in Moray. The absence of references to any siblings suggests that, if there were any, they died in childhood.

Macbeth's genealogical origin is better documented. He belonged to the hereditary aristocracy of Moray. His full name, Macbeth mac Findlaech, enables his father to be identified as Findlaech mac Ruadri (Finlay son of Rory), Mormaer of Moray. The eleventh-century Mormaers of Moray claimed descent from the Cenél Loairn Kings of Dál Riata. This is recorded in their genealogy, which is preserved in an Irish source,[14] although its veracity is unclear. It may have been fabricated in order to bolster Macbeth's claims of an impeccable royal pedigree, a practice which is well attested in early medieval Ireland.

Little is known about Findlaech, although the *Orkneyinga Saga* relates how Sigurd the Stout, *Jarl* of Orkney, overcame Findlaech ('Finnleik') in battle in Caithness with the aid of his magic banner, sometime between 995 and 1014:

a Scottish earl called Finnleik challenged Sigurd to fight him on a particular day at Skitten . . .

> Earl Sigurd . . . got the support of the Orkney farmers by giving them back
> their land-rights, then set out for Skitten to confront Earl Finnleik. The two sides
> formed up, but the moment they clashed Sigurd's standard-bearer was struck
> dead. The Earl told another man to pick up the banner but before long he'd
> been killed too. The Earl lost three standard-bearers, but he won the battle.[15]

Findlaech survived to fight another day.

The identity of Macbeth's mother is less clear, although she was almost
certainly a close relative of Malcolm II. She does not appear in contemporary
sources and the medieval chronicles are inconsistent, describing Macbeth as a
nephew of either Malcolm or Duncan, specifically the son of Duncan's sister.[16]
Historians sometimes identify Macbeth's mother as Malcolm's sister, but this
would place Macbeth a generation too early. Both Duncan, whom Macbeth
killed for the kingship, and Gruoch, Macbeth's wife and who already had a son
by a previous marriage, belonged to the next generation.

A more plausible identification appears in one of the later and otherwise less
reliable chronicles and is given added weight by the inclusion of Macbeth's
mother's otherwise unrecorded name. According to Boece, Macbeth's mother
was Doada, a second daughter of Malcolm II; he describes Macbeth and Duncan
as 'sisters' sons'.[17] Although Fordun claims that 'Beatrice' (Bethoc), Duncan's
mother, was Malcolm's only daughter, he may have been referring only to
Malcolm's legitimate offspring.[18] Another daughter married Sigurd, leaving
open the possibility that Malcolm had a third daughter. Her marriage to a
Mormaer of Moray certainly fits the pattern of diplomatic unions with
powerful local rulers that Malcolm followed for his other daughters. But one
thing is clear – Macbeth's mother belonged to the principal branch of the royal
kin group. Her marriage to Findlaech, therefore, may have been a diplomatic
one, intended to draw together the houses of Atholl and Moray.

Macbeth's presence at the meeting between Malcolm II and Cnut in 1031
confirms that Malcolm and Macbeth had a close relationship. That their
relationship was perceived to be one of king and sub-king need not preclude
their status as grandfather and grandson. The young Macbeth is described in a
later chronicle as living in the King's house. Although Wyntoun,[19] who has a
habit of conflating characters, identifies the King as Duncan, only Malcolm fits
the context. Macbeth may have been fostered by Malcolm, or at least joined the
royal Court. Fosterage was important in Gaelic society, where it originated out
of the necessity for establishing political alliances beyond one's immediate kin.
Macbeth's fosterage would have been particularly appropriate after his father's

death in 1020. One does not need to look far to find a parallel. The *Orkneyinga Saga* relates how: 'Thorfinn was only five years old when his father [Sigurd] was killed [in 1014], living with his grandfather, King Malcolm [II] of Scotland. The King of Scots gave Thorfinn Caithness and Sutherland, granted him the title of earl [*jarl*, presumably meaning mormaer, the equivalent Scottish rank], and appointed counsellors to govern with him.'[20] Malcolm may have held Macbeth in similarly high affection and Macbeth, like Thorfinn, may have been brought up at Malcolm's Court.

Little is known about Macbeth's childhood, but it was probably spent following the typical pursuits of a boy of royal or noble birth, including practising martial skills. Macbeth is also described as going hunting with two greyhounds.[21] Several factors, including his probable grandfather's position as King of Scots, may have exerted a powerful influence on the young Macbeth. His father's position as Mormaer of Moray may have been even more influential. Apart from any time at Malcolm's Court, most of Macbeth's childhood was presumably spent in Moray, where his father's status and power would have determined his lifestyle, company and developing expectations. As the apparently only son of a powerful local ruler, Macbeth would have possessed status and power from an early age. Mormaers, like kings, most likely led a peripatetic existence and the young Macbeth may have accompanied his father on business around Moray.

Moray must have exerted a strong influence on the young Macbeth. Scotland's most northerly province, Moray's peripheral location, between the Scottish heartland and the Orkney Vikings, gave it an identity of its own and a degree of autonomy. This situation probably resulted in the emergence of a 'marcher' society similar to those found on other medieval frontiers, notably the Anglo-Scottish border.[22] In addition to their independence and resilience, a defining characteristic of these societies was their organisation for war on a permanent basis. As the son of a Mormaer of Moray, these qualities were likely to have been instilled in Macbeth from an early age. Violence or its threat must never have been far from the young Macbeth. He would have been exposed to it through his father's status as a war leader and from seeing preparations for war and hearing tales of heroic deeds on the battlefield. We can be confident that Macbeth became inured to violence during his boyhood.

Violence was not confined to the Viking wars. Disputed successions were usually determined by violence, albeit probably on a small scale, the killing of the incumbent king or mormaer providing both a symbolic and a practical, if only temporary, conclusion to the conflict. The military forces involved in such internal strife were war bands rather than armies. During the eleventh century Moray appears to have suffered from similar intra-dynastic power struggles to those which periodically afflicted the Scottish kingship. Although this violence may be attributed to contested successions, the disputes themselves are obscure.

The violence of early eleventh-century Moray directly affected the young Macbeth. As one of the most significant events of Macbeth's youth, his father's death in 1020 may be expected to have influenced Macbeth's development profoundly. This can only have been exacerbated by the manner of his father's demise. Mistakenly describing him as '[a?] king of Scotland', one Irish annal uses the standard formula to record that Findlaech 'was killed by his own [people]', although another identifies his killers as 'the sons of his brother Máel Brigte'.[23] Macbeth's murderous cousins may be identified as Malcolm (Máel Coluim) and Gillacomgain (Gilla Comgán). Macbeth must have been about fifteen years old at the time.

The exact circumstances of Findlaech's death are not recorded but the motive seems clear: he died in a dynastic dispute. As in the system of royal succession, the Mormaership of Moray did not pass directly from father to son but alternated between collateral branches of the noble kin group. Findlaech's brother, Máel Brigte, was probably mormaer before him; Máel Brigte, '[a?] *jarl* of Scotland', died in Moray in battle against the Orkney Vikings, according to the *Orkneyinga Saga*.[24] This battle appears to have been fought sometime between 985 and 995. If Findlaech had been mormaer since Máel Brigte's death, by 1020 his nephews may have seen their opportunity to succeed him slipping away and sought to create a vacancy by killing their uncle.

MACBETH'S EARLY CAREER

One of Macbeth's cousins presumably became mormaer after killing Findlaech. Under the traditional system of alternating succession, the mormaership should have passed to Macbeth on the death of whichever cousin had seized the office. The risk for Macbeth was that the other cousin would then want his slice of the cake and succeed as mormaer and that on his death the title would pass to one of the cousins' sons. There was a genuine possibility for Macbeth that he and his descendants would be excluded permanently from eligibility for the mormaership. Macbeth, therefore, may have been perceived as a potential threat to his cousins' interests.

Macbeth's response to the killing of his father is unknown, although he probably fled Moray for his own safety, unless he was already present at the Court of Malcolm II. Time spent, probably in the heartland of Scotland, would also have enabled Macbeth to take stock until he was in a stronger position to avenge his father's death and recover the mormaership by force. Macbeth's exile was probably spent at Malcolm's court, particularly if Malcolm was Macbeth's grandfather. This is supported by the earliest historical reference to Macbeth, in which he appears alongside Malcolm.

Cnut, the powerful ruler of England and Denmark, invaded Scotland in 1031, perhaps provoked by an alliance between Malcolm and Cnut's Scandinavian opponents or a Scottish offer of support to them: 'Cnut . . . went to Scotland, and Malcolm, the King of Scots, submitted to him – and two other kings, Mælbeth and Iehmarc'.[25] But Cnut's victory was short-lived: 'the King of Scots surrendered to him and became his man, but he only held to that for a little while'.[26] The significance of Cnut's incursion and the veracity of Malcolm's submission are debatable. The location of the meeting is not recorded, although Cnut's invasion is thought to have reached the River Tay. A fragment of Skaldic verse referring to the submission of 'the princes in the north from the midst of Fife' may support this.[27] Of perhaps more relevance is the parallel offered by the invasion of William I ('the Conqueror'), who received the submission of Malcolm III in 1072 at Abernethy, an important religious centre in south-east Perthshire, near the Firth of Tay. In selecting this venue, was William emulating his predecessor?

The identification of 'Mælbeth' as Macbeth has been challenged, partly because the names are dissimilar, but also because Macbeth's name is recognisable, as Macbeoðen in the *Chronicle*'s D text.[28] However, a spelling in one text is irrelevant to a spelling in another and Mælbeth is an acceptable Anglo-Saxon rendering of Macbeth.[29] This mis-spelling presumably resulted from a scribe confusing the *mac* patronymic with the *Máel* devotional prefix, for which parallels exist in twelfth-century Scottish charters. The range of spellings recorded indicates that many non-Gaelic scribes found Macbeth a difficult name; that it posed particular problems for Anglo-Saxon scribes is apparent from a reference to Macbeth as 'the King of Scots with an outlandish name' (*rex Scottorum nomine barbarus*).[30]

Macbeth's presence at the meeting between Malcolm and Cnut supports the suggestion that Macbeth may have joined Malcolm's court after his father's murder. It reveals that he was a prominent political figure by his mid-twenties, involved directly in one of the major diplomatic events of Malcolm's reign. The source emphasises Macbeth's status by referring to him as a king, paralleling the description of the Mormaers of Moray in Irish sources. 'Iehmarc' is probably Echmarcach Rognvaldsson, who may have succeeded his father as King of the Isles in 1005 and later became King of the Dublin Vikings. In 1031 he probably ruled the Western Isles, the Isle of Man and the Rhinns of Galloway.[31]

The presence of Echmarcach and Macbeth and their description as 'other kings' suggests that they were both powerful local rulers, the former possibly allied with Malcolm against Cnut and the latter nominally subject to the Scottish king. By linking them in this manner, the *Anglo-Saxon Chronicle* implies that Echmarcach and Macbeth were of similar status, perhaps because they ruled peripheral, semi-autonomous regions of Scotland, the Western Isles and Moray respectively. But this requires Macbeth to have become Mormaer of Moray by 1031, when this does not appear to have occurred until 1032. However, this small discrepancy may be attributed to either the relevant entry in the *Annals of Ulster* being erroneously inserted under the following year, or the entry in the *Anglo-Saxon Chronicle* being recorded *after* 1031, by which time Macbeth had become mormaer. Alternatively, Macbeth may have been described as a 'king' because he was, or was perceived to be, a powerful noble by birth, *before* becoming Mormaer of Moray.

After killing Findlaech in 1020, Macbeth's cousins became Mormaer of Moray in turn. Little is known of their rule of Moray. The only record is a note in the *Book of Deer*, recording that Malcolm son of Máel Brigte granted the lands of Elrick to the monastery at Old Deer.[32] Malcolm died in 1029.[33] Although his death notices imply that he died from natural causes, too much significance should not be attached to this. The circumstances of his death may not have been known in Ireland and a violent death seems more probable, although no details are recorded. Under the traditional system of alternating succession between collateral branches, the mormaership should then have passed to Macbeth. But his surviving cousin, Gillacomgain, excluded Macbeth and retained the office, albeit briefly, for himself.

Gillacomgain died violently in 1032: 'Gillacomgain son of Máel Brigte, Mormaer of Moray, was burned together with fifty of his men'.[34] Although no further information is recorded about Gillacomgain's death, the fire in which he died was probably deliberate. The men killed with Gillacomgain probably comprised his war band or *comitatus*,[35] while their deaths in a fire, rather than in open battle, indicates either the outcome of a siege, probably of a fortress or a feasting hall, or perhaps that they had sought refuge in a church. The firing of buildings, complete with their occupants, was an established practice in early medieval warfare and features frequently in the Irish annals[36] and Icelandic sagas. The most likely context of such violence in Moray towards the end of the reign of Malcolm II was a power struggle between the various factions of Moray's ruling aristocracy.

This section of the Bayeux Tapestry illustrates the use of fire in early medieval warfare. Here a building is being fired by Norman soldiers during the invasion of Anglo-Saxon England in 1066. (The Bayeux Tapestry – eleventh century. By special permission of the City of Bayeux)

There can be little doubt that Macbeth was responsible for Gillacomgain's death. He certainly had sufficient motive: to avenge his father's murder twelve years earlier and assert what he must have perceived to be his birthright to the Mormaership of Moray. Macbeth was certainly Mormaer of Moray by 1040 and the most obvious context for acquiring the office was on Gillacomgain's death. Macbeth probably seized the mormaership after burning Gillacomgain and his warband to death. Moreover, Macbeth's involvement in his cousin's death is supported by the fate of Gillacomgain's widow, whom Macbeth then took as his wife. Given their close relationship, Malcolm II may have assisted Macbeth's bid to become Mormaer of Moray. Indeed, the challenges Malcolm faced towards the end of his reign suggest that he may have sought to replace a troublesome mormaer with a more loyal candidate, his grandson Macbeth.

These episodic outbreaks of internecine strife reveal the existence of great tensions within, and perhaps suggest the disintegration of, the ruling kindred of Moray. This was possibly as a result of sustained external pressures, posed either by the Orkney Vikings or the Scottish kingship, or perhaps rapidly changing socio-political circumstances. Whatever the cause, these events underline Moray's turbulent character during the eleventh century.

No further details are known about Macbeth's early career. Yet it seems reasonable to presume that he served Malcolm II in a military capacity, while at the same time developing the martial skills required of a mormaer, enabling him to avenge his father's killing and become Mormaer of Moray. Fighting for his king, perhaps against Cnut, would have been an obvious way of combining both activities, while Macbeth's subsequent performance as a capable war leader implies that he had previous military experience.

The other arena in which Macbeth was probably active militarily was, like his father before him, against the Orkney Vikings. Indeed, the *Orkneyinga Saga* relates how Macbeth and an unnamed Scottish king provided an army for Skuli, an Orkney Viking who was attempting to seize the jarldom from his brother, Ljot.[37] After Skuli and his Scottish army were defeated in Caithness, Macbeth led an army against Ljot, but was routed at Skitten. Here, however, the saga's chronology is confused: Macbeth appears as a *jarl* (i.e. Mormaer of Moray) before his father does. Alternatively, the saga may confuse Macbeth and his father, as Findlaech is also claimed to have fought a battle at Skitten. Macbeth's appearance in this context is either mistaken, perhaps reflecting his later fame, or indicates his involvement in the long-running struggles between the Scots and the Orkney Vikings.

MACBETH'S APPEARANCE

Any attempt to determine Macbeth's appearance presents particular difficulties because no contemporary likenesses of him survive in any medium. The earliest contemporary portrait of a Scottish king, Malcolm IV, is over a century later. Where evidence is lacking, imagination has filled the void, leading to the visual interpretation of Macbeth according to later tastes and fashions. Macbeth has been played and portrayed in various anachronistic guises – frequently crowned, sometimes in full armour belonging to a style some centuries later, as a tartan-bedecked Highland chief, or even a combination of both. Drawing directly on Shakespeare's portrayal, Macbeth is stereotypically depicted as a dark and brooding or disturbed character. Despite their enduring influence, all these portraits are mythical, the artistic equivalents of the literary and topographical mythology surrounding Macbeth.

Although no contemporary images of Macbeth are available, a contemporary description survives. The *Prophecy of Berchán* incorporates three stanzas on

sita est sup ripam fluminis Tvede. in loco q

David I and his eldest grandson Malcolm IV, sitting in state with their regalia. This is an initial capital from the charter of Kelso Abbey, 1159. (National Library of Scotland/by courtesy of the Duke of Roxburghe)

Macbeth which originally belonged to a praise poem composed during his own lifetime.[38] These describe Macbeth as 'the red king', 'the red, tall, golden-haired one' and 'the furious red one'. Reflecting modern stereotypes of 'Celtic' appearance, the recurring references to 'red' are often thought to refer to describe Macbeth's hair. Yet Macbeth is specifically described as 'yellow haired', suggesting that he had a ruddy complexion instead. His face may simply have had a weather-beaten appearance or he may have suffered from a medical condition which produces a reddening of the facial skin. Alternatively, 'furious red one' may describe Macbeth's battle frenzy, an oblique reference to his martial prowess.

Despite their terseness, these brief descriptive phrases present a unique insight into Macbeth's physical appearance and characteristics. Not only do they date from Macbeth's reign, but, belonging to a eulogy, Macbeth must have heard himself described in these very terms. This should sound a note of caution

– that these phrases were intended to flatter Macbeth suggests that they may describe idealised rather than actual handsomeness. That the poet was attributing stereotyped royal good looks to Macbeth is apparent from a reference to 'stately yellow-haired company' and similar descriptions of other early Scottish kings: Constantine I (862–77) is 'the tall fair[-haired?] one'; Donald I (858–62) is 'ruddy-faced', Constantine II (900–43) is 'red-limbed', while Malcolm I (943–54) is 'the red scald-crow'.[39] This provides an insight into early medieval Irish and Scottish concepts of male and/or royal handsomeness, which were consistently associated with a vividly pigmented appearance. This range of meanings is conveyed by Old Irish *dath*: 'complexion', 'hue', especially 'beautiful complexion' of the face or skin.[40] This is how the *Prophecy of Berchán* describes Indulf (954–62) and *Duan Albanach* portrays Aed (877–8) and Duncan (1034–40); 'handsome', 'high-coloured' and/or with a 'severe complexion'.[41]

So was Macbeth really tall, blonde-haired and red-faced? That the eulogist appears to have been observing a poetic convention indicates that even these brief descriptive details cannot be accepted at face value. But is it conceivable that Macbeth would have been described inaccurately in a praise poem that was presumably written for and performed before him? Macbeth may not have been flattered if he was described in terms which he visibly failed to live up to. Alternatively, the praising of imaginary qualities, which is well known in other royal contexts, may have had an established role in boosting the royal ego. Without corroboration from independent sources it is impossible to be confident about Macbeth's appearance, although he *may* have lived up to his description as tall, flaxen-haired and ruddy-faced.

GRUOCH: MACBETH'S QUEEN

Alongside St Margaret (1070–93), queen of Malcolm III, Macbeth's queen is one of medieval Scotland's most famous women. Yet, unlike Margaret, her fame arises not from anything she did during her own lifetime, but from her portrayal at the hands of later chroniclers and, of course, Shakespeare. But paradoxically, what little is known of her suggests that the historical 'Lady Macbeth' is even more interesting than her dramatic counterpart.

The name and lineage of Macbeth's queen are recorded in a contemporary source. A note copied in the later St Andrews *Register* records an endowment of land to the Culdee community of Loch Leven made jointly by Macbeth and 'Gruoch, daughter of Bodhe . . . queen of Scots' (*Gruoch filia Bodhe . . . regina Scottorum*).[42] Bodhe may be identified as the Boite son of Kenneth (Boete mac

Cineadha) whose grandson was killed in 1033.[43] Although it is unclear if Boite's father was Kenneth II (971–95) or Kenneth III (997–1005), Gruoch not only belonged to the royal kin group but was also directly descended from a previous King of Scots. Gruoch's status as a member of the royal kin group in her own right is emphasised by her description as a queen rather than a consort. Her royal status would have been particularly prominent if her grandfather was Kenneth II, which would have made her a niece of Malcolm II, but subsequent events suggest that Gruoch was a grand-daughter of Kenneth III.

Macbeth was not Gruoch's first husband. Intriguingly, she had previously been married to Macbeth's cousin, Gillacomgain, who, with his brother, had murdered Macbeth's father, Findlaech, in 1020. This lends weight to the interpretation that Macbeth killed Gillacomgain, and that he married Gruoch sometime, probably soon, after Gillacomgain was burned to death in 1032. Although confused, Wyntoun's account is revealing.[44]

Lady Macbeth as a pre-Raphaelite vision. Dame Alice Ellen Terry playing Lady Macbeth in Sir Henry Irving's 1888 production, as portrayed by John Singer Sargeant. (Tate Gallery, London 1999)

Conflating Macbeth's murders of Gillacomgain and Duncan, Wyntoun mistakenly claims that, after murdering Duncan, Macbeth married his widow, but this clearly refers to Gillacomgain's murder and Macbeth's marriage to Gruoch. In taking Gruoch as his bride, Macbeth may have been emphasising the completeness of his victory by marrying the widow of his dead opponent. Yet Gruoch was no chattel, but a woman of status. Marriage to her clearly had political implications and may have been intended to heal the intra-dynastic strife that had destabilised Moray for over a decade. This desire to effect a reconciliation may suggest that, on first becoming mormaer, Macbeth's position was not a strong one. Moreover, Gruoch's royal descent brought wider political dividends; Macbeth's actions were borne of political expediency and ambition.

Little else is known about Gruoch. She had a son, Lulach, by her first husband, whom Macbeth adopted out of loyalty to his new wife or from an obligation to foster his victim's offspring. But Macbeth also made Lulach his heir, indicating that he and Gruoch had no children of their own, or at least any who survived childhood. Macbeth's acceptance of Lulach, the son of his father's killer and whose father Macbeth himself had killed, also indicates a degree of magnanimity, perhaps even compassion, on Macbeth's part. Macbeth may have been influenced by the loss of his own father while still a boy. Lulach's adoption supports the interpretation that Macbeth was attempting to reconcile previously opposed branches of Moray's aristocratic kindred.

Gruoch's endowment of land to the Culdees of Loch Leven has been interpreted as evidence that she or her family had a local association, perhaps in the form of estates in Fife. Gruoch's probable status as a great granddaughter of Duff supports this. The collateral royal line that traced its descent from Duff was probably compensated for its exclusion from the kingship by being given the Mormaership of Fife. The medieval Earls of Fife belonged to the kindred of mac Duff, the son of Duff, and the origin of Shakespeare's mythical MacDuff, Thane of Fife. Gruoch, or at least her kin, may therefore have owned extensive lands in Fife. But as the endowment was made jointly with Macbeth it may not reflect exclusively on Gruoch's background. Moreover, Gruoch may have made gifts to other communities, either jointly with Macbeth or by herself, of which no record now survives. Nevertheless, the endowment probably reflects a special association with, or affection for, Loch Leven and its Culdee community, suggesting that Gruoch may have been a regular visitor.

With the notable exception of Margaret, Gruoch's saintly antithesis, the role of queens in early medieval Scotland is almost completely unrecorded. Indeed, even their existence is largely invisible. What little is known about Gruoch points to her status and influence, perhaps even genuine power. As a granddaughter of Kenneth III or niece of Malcolm II, and daughter of Boite, sometime *tanaise* of Malcolm, Gruoch was at the centre of Scotland's royal kindred. Her powerful position is attested by her marriage to two successive Mormaers of Moray and her subsequent position as Queen of Scots. Furthermore, the hostility between the descendants of Kenneth II and Kenneth III and the exclusion of her lineage from the kingship suggests that Gruoch was opposed to Malcolm II and, by implication, his successor. Another event probably hardened her opposition.

THE END OF MALCOLM II'S REIGN

The killing of Boite's unnamed grandson, Gruoch's nephew, by Malcolm II in 1033 is recorded in the *Annals of Ulster* in characteristically terse manner: 'The grandson of Boite son of Kenneth was killed by Malcolm son of Kenneth [Malcolm II]'.[45] Royal succession disputes were the cause of most violence within the royal kin group and the death of Boite's grandson appears to have been no exception. By 1033, Malcolm had already reigned for twenty-eight years. Not only was this long by early medieval Scottish standards, but it would have seemed all the longer by coming immediately after a series of short reigns; between 943 and Malcolm's accession in 1005, Scotland had eight kings (although two, Kenneth III and Giric, may have reigned jointly). Malcolm's long reign must have put additional pressures on the traditional system of royal succession, under which the kingship alternated between two branches of the royal kin group. Members of the other segment may have become increasingly restless at the delay before their candidate could be installed in the kingship. Of even greater concern to them, the longer Malcolm spent in the kingship, the more opportunity he had to consolidate his power and exclude their lineage from the kingship altogether. Malcolm certainly had an established track record of political violence, having killed his predecessors, Constantine III (995–7) and Giric (?997–1005), in battle to acquire the kingship.[46]

This political context suggests that Boite was a son of Kenneth III, whose lineage was excluded from the kingship by Malcolm II, Kenneth's successor. Presumably conscious that he was the third generation of his lineage who had not held the kingship since Kenneth III, Boite's grandson may have attempted to seize the throne but was defeated and killed by Malcolm. However, as Kenneth III was killed in 1005, his great-grandson is unlikely to have been able to mount a challenge for the throne as early as 1033. Boite's grandson may have been referred to in error for Boite's son, a simple error caused by the accidental duplication of *meic* ('son of') during the copying of the annals. If the unsuccessful challenger was Boite's son, not grandson, he would have been Gruoch's brother, bringing Gruoch even closer to the disputed succession. Alternatively, Boite may have been a son of Kenneth II, and therefore a brother of Malcolm II.

The challenge mounted by Boite's grandson suggests that Boite himself was perceived to have had a special claim to the kingship. This is supported by the description of Lulach, Macbeth's stepson, as 'the nephew of son of Boite'.[47] This defines Lulach's relationship to Boite through the male line and not, as 'grandson of Boite', through the female line. This was presumably because royal succession was, with only rare exceptions, restricted to the male line. Thus, Lulach's claim to the kingship rested on his position as 'the nephew of Boite's son'.

The significance attached to Boite by his descendants indicates that he probably had been named as the *tanaise*, or appointed heir, of Malcolm II. But after Boite's death, Malcolm appears to have excluded Boite's descendants from the succession in a successful bid to secure the kingship for his own direct descendants. By challenging Malcolm, Boite's grandson was attempting to reassert the right of Boite's descendants to the kingship. And by defeating Boite's grandson, Malcolm was ensuring that he would be succeeded by his own grandson, Duncan.

The killing of Boite's grandson attests the eruption into violence of intra-dynastic tensions over the succession to the kingship only seven years before Macbeth seized the throne from Duncan. As Boite's daughter, Gruoch's loyalties may be expected to have lain with her kin group, thereby placing her in opposition to Malcolm II and, presumably, his successor, Duncan. However, as Gruoch was probably married to Macbeth by 1033, her opportunities for supporting any opposition to Malcolm were probably severely restricted, particularly if Macbeth was Malcolm's grandson. But Malcolm's death was soon to change this situation dramatically.

Malcolm II died at Glamis in 1034.[48] His presumably advanced years, after a twenty-nine-year reign, might imply that he died from natural causes but early Scottish kings were more likely to have died at the hands of their kin in competition for the kingship. Malcolm had already killed Boite's grandson the year before; where there was one unsuccessful challenger for the throne there might also be others who were more fortunate. Suspicions that Malcolm met a violent death are supported by a stanza in the *Verse Chronicle* inserted in the *Chronicle of Melrose*: 'A free [death] carried off the king, in the village of Glamis: he perished underfoot, after laying low the enemy'.[49] Moreover, he died in battle against his own kin according to the *Prophecy of Berchán*:

> He will conquer ten battles – angels who have prophecy –
> thirty-five years and his time over Scotland in high-kingship.
> Until the day he goes to battle in meeting with the kin-slayers;
> to a swift leap in the morning at the mountain,
> woe to Scotland facing them.[50]

It is unclear if Malcolm died in an intra-dynastic succession dispute or in revenge as a result of one. Nevertheless, the descendants of his victims,

Constantine and Giric, conspired against Malcolm and ambushed him near Glamis. Malcolm was mortally wounded and died three days later 'at the age of eighty and upwards'.[51]

DUNCAN AND HIS REIGN

Despite his murder, the succession of Malcolm II was secure, at least initially. Presumably inspired by his earlier manipulation of the royal succession through violence and emboldened by his long reign, Malcolm's ambition was to abandon the traditional system of alternating succession. In its place, he sought to establish a unitary royal lineage within which succession to the kingship was passed through the direct line. But Malcolm had no sons. At least, insular sources do not record any and the *Verse Chronicle* inserted in the *Chronicle of Melrose* states specifically that 'Malcolm had no son'.[52] In contrast, the eleventh-century Burgundian chronicler Rudulfus Glaber claims that Cnut received Malcolm's son straight from the baptismal font.[53] Although this may represent the giving of a hostage to ensure Malcolm's good behaviour, perhaps after the meeting in 1031, Glaber's account is uncorroborated.

On Malcolm's death the kingship passed to Duncan I. Duncan was the son of Malcolm's eldest or only legitimate daughter, Bethoc, and Crinán, Abbot of Dunkeld. Crinán probably combined his hereditary lay abbacy with a powerful secular office and may have been Mormaer of Atholl. This fits with his association with Dunkeld, which was probably the power centre of the province of Atholl. Fordun describes Crinán as 'a man of great vigour and power' but displays some confusion about his titles.[54] Unable to comprehend or accept the existence of lay ecclesiastical offices, Fordun describes Crinán as 'Abthane of Dul', claiming that 'abthane' was the 'chief of the thanes', and 'Steward of the Isles', whose duties were 'to keep the account of the king's rents, and monies in his treasury, performing . . . the duties of housekeeper or chamberlain' to Malcolm II. Yet 'Abthane of Dul' is mistakenly derived from the district known as Appin of Dull (*abthania de Dul*) in Perthshire, while the functions described are those of the later High Stewards of Scotland. Nevertheless, Fordun's account may reflect Crinán's power and influence during Malcolm's reign.

Duncan was Malcolm's appointed heir. Malcolm II gave Cumbria to Duncan and Duncan's kingship of Cumbria is reflected in the description of Malcolm III as 'son of the King of the Cumbrians' in several medieval chronicles.[55] According to Fordun, Duncan did not do homage to Cnut for Cumbria because, as Malcolm inventively claimed, this was due only to kings of English descent and Cnut was a Dane.[56] Duncan, in turn, reserved the kingship of Cumbria for his own son and *tanaise*: 'immediately after his coronation [Duncan] gave Malcolm the province of Cumbria'; Malcolm still held the title 'King of the Cumbrians' when he became King of Scots.[57]

Against this background it is difficult to explain why Duncan did not attend Malcolm's meeting with Cnut in 1031. Malcolm may still have been hoping for a male heir late into his reign, with the result that, contradicting Fordun, Duncan did not become *tanaise* until after 1031. This provides an obvious context and motive for the unsuccessful challenge mounted by Boite's grandson in 1033, who may have been spurred into action by Duncan's appointment as *tanaise*, reinforcing the exclusion of Boite's descendants from the kingship. It also suggests that Duncan may have had little time to consolidate his power base before Malcolm's death in 1034. Alternatively, Duncan may have been present at the meeting with Cnut but the Anglo-Saxon chroniclers, unaware of the significance of his position as *tanaise*, omitted him from their record of the event.

The significance of Duncan's accession is that he was the first King of Scots to have succeeded in the direct line, a radical departure from the traditional system. Duncan's status as appointed heir was probably attributable to his being the eldest son of Malcolm's eldest or only legitimate child, Bethoc. Although complicated in this instance by Duncan's descent through the female line, this marks the adoption of primogeniture, the right of succession of the first born, by the Scottish kingship. However, rather than resolving those intra-dynastic rivalries that periodically erupted into violent succession disputes, this had the immediate effect of exacerbating these tensions. Under the new system, collateral royal lineages were permanently excluded from eligibility to the kingship, possession of which was now restricted to Malcolm's direct descendants. Malcolm had initiated a fundamental change which was destined to rebound on his chosen successor with tragic consequences.

In addition to his position as Malcolm's *tanaise*, Duncan's accession to the kingship may have been assisted by geography. Gordon Donaldson suggested that 'Duncan became king, possibly because he was the eldest or ablest, but just as likely because, on Malcolm's death, he managed to beat his rivals to the scene of royal inaugurations at Scone, much as in England Henry I beat his brother Robert to Winchester'.[58] This is supported by the *Prophecy of Berchán*,[59] which states that Duncan 'takes sovereignty after him without delay', and corroborated by Marianus Scotus, who records that Malcolm II was killed on the seventh day before the Kalends of December (25 November 1034), and that Duncan 'reigned . . . from the Mass of St Andrew' (30 November).[60] Duncan probably exploited the geographical advantage presented by the location of his power centre at or near Dunkeld, his father's abbatial seat, only 18 km from Scone. In contrast, Macbeth's Moray power base lay much further north, beyond the Mounth, with the effect that he was less well placed to hurry to Scone on Malcolm's death.

Duncan's accession cannot have been welcomed by the hereditary aristocracy of Moray. However it is viewed, the change in the system of succession consolidated the House of Atholl's hold over the Scottish kingship and further marginalised the position of the House of Moray. Paradoxically, these changes created problems for Malcolm's successor not by excluding collateral royal lineages from the kingship, though this can hardly have helped, but by alienating Malcolm's other direct descendants, Duncan's cousins. The marriage of an otherwise unidentified daughter of Malcolm to Sigurd, *Jarl* of Orkney, produced a son, Thorfinn. The other (probable) cousin was Macbeth. Family ties, however, were evidently no impediment to the latter's ambitions for the kingship.

Duncan owed his kingship to his grandfather, Malcolm II, rather than to any personal qualities. By abandoning the traditional system of royal succession, Malcolm created future problems for his grandson. According to the traditionally accepted system of alternating succession, Duncan was not the rightful successor to the kingship and therefore was likely to attract challenges from those who believed they had a stronger claim and those ambitious enough to try their hand at seizing the throne. Moreover, Duncan was not suitable kingly material. The early Scottish kingship was frequently seized by force and then had to be defended against future challengers, while kings also had to protect Scotland from external enemies. Kings were essentially war leaders first and foremost; their survival and the well-being of their kingdom depended on it. Crucially, Duncan displayed little military ability.

Contemporary and later sources say little about Duncan's reign. Even Fordun is uncharacteristically terse, enigmatically stating only that 'Nothing worthy of mention happened in the kingdom during this short time of Duncan's reign'.[61] His choice of words is interesting. Was Fordun unable to discover anything about Duncan's reign, or did he prefer not to record events which he found unpalatable for some reason? The impression that Fordun may have sanitised his account is reinforced by both external and later sources, which paint a rather different picture of Duncan's reign.

Again, the *Orkneyinga Saga* provides the only commentary on events on Scotland's northern frontier, where the Scots appear to have suffered a series of defeats against the Orkney Vikings.[62] On becoming King of Scots, 'Karl Hundason', attempted to reassert Scottish control over Viking-held Caithness and appointed his nephew Muddan or Mutatan as *Jarl* (probably Mormaer) of Caithness. But Thorfinn the Mighty, *Jarl* of Orkney, who had been granted Caithness by his grandfather, Malcolm II, refused to pay any tribute for it. To enforce the collection of tribute, Muddan raised an army and advanced into Caithness, but withdrew when opposed by a superior Viking force. In the aftermath, Thorfinn subdued Ross and Sutherland and plundered throughout Scotland. Karl himself then led eleven warships in a surprise assault on Thorfinn's fleet off Deerness, Orkney, only to be defeated. Scottish losses included Karl's own flagship, although Karl escaped with a soaking.

Karl then raised an army from across Scotland, 'both in the east and the west as far south as Kintyre', which also included Irish forces. At the same time, Thorfinn mustered 'all the troops from Caithness, Sutherland and Ross' and advanced southwards, while Thorkel the Fosterer, Thorfinn's foster-father, killed the Mormaer of Caithness in Thurso before rendezvousing with Thorfinn and his army. The Viking and Scottish armies joined battle at *Torfnes*, which is usually identified as Tarbat Ness, between the Dornoch and Moray Firths.

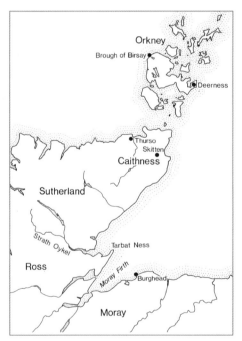

Duncan's wars against the Orkney Vikings, northern Scotland, showing locations mentioned in the text.

This location may be consistent with the description of the battle in the earlier Skaldic verse incorporated in the *Orkneyinga Saga*: 'Slim blades sang there/south on Oykel's bank'. However, the saga explicitly (but perhaps mistakenly) locates *Torfnes* on the southern shore of the Moray Firth. Another proposed identification is Burghead, a large Pictish promontory fort on the south side of the Moray Firth, although there is nothing to corroborate this.

Despite its numerical strength, Karl's army was defeated, the Skaldic verse proclaiming 'Well the red weapons/fed wolves at *Torfnes*'. Karl fled the field although, in the confusion of battle, some of the saga-tellers' sources claimed that he was killed. Thorfinn's victory subsequently left Scotland exposed to Viking raids, although the saga's claim that Thorfinn conquered Scotland as far south as Fife is exaggerated.

The identity of 'Karl Hundason' has stimulated much debate, with opinion evenly split between Macbeth and Duncan, although those advocating Macbeth are currently in the ascendant. Other identifications, including claims that 'Karl' was an otherwise unrecorded Mormaer of Ross and/or Sutherland,[63] are inconsistent with his description as King of Scots and have received little support. Despite the controversy, there are strong grounds for equating 'Karl' with Duncan. The *Orkneyinga Saga* explicitly states that, after Malcolm's death, 'the next man to take over power in Scotland was Karl Hundason'.[64] This can only refer to Duncan, Malcolm's successor. Furthermore, Duncan is not mentioned by name within the saga, in contrast to Macbeth, who makes a single but readily recognisable appearance as 'Magbjóthr'. Internal evidence within the *Orkneyinga Saga* firmly identifies 'Karl Hundason' as Duncan.

The historical context lends weight to Karl's identification as Duncan. The Scots and the Orkney Vikings were competing for territory and influence in northern Scotland decades before Duncan's reign. Sigurd had defeated Findlaech, Macbeth's father, at Skitten. Furthermore, the marriage of one of Malcolm's daughters to Sigurd was presumably a political match, intended to effect or seal a truce or treaty between the Scots and the Orkney Vikings. Malcolm's desire to foster healthy relations is apparent; he made Thorfinn, his grandson, *Jarl* or Mormaer of Caithness. Although effectively granting Caithness to the Orkney Vikings, this may only have formalised the status of an area which had already seen extensive Viking settlement. These actions indicate that containing the power of the Orkney Vikings posed a problem to the Scottish kingship.

The identification of Karl with Duncan is supported by other sources. The *Prophecy of Berchán* describes how Macbeth assumed the Scottish kingship 'after slaughter of Gaels, after slaughter of Vikings',[65] an unambiguous reference to warfare between Scotland and the, presumably Orkney, Vikings during Duncan's reign. Although a much later source, 'the wars of King Duncan against the Danes', that is, the Vikings, feature prominently in Boece's *History*.[66] Another indication of warfare between Duncan and Thorfinn is that, after he had acquired the kingship from Macbeth, Duncan's son, Malcolm III, married Ingibjorg, Thorfinn's widow or daughter. This has the appearance of a political marriage, an attempt to effect a reconciliation between the Orkney Vikings and Duncan's descendants.

The accommodation reached between Malcolm II and firstly Sigurd, then Thorfinn, did not survive Malcolm's death and Thorfinn may not have felt bound by it after Duncan's accession. But although it is claimed that Thorfinn himself had ambitions on the Scottish kingship, this rests on a single verse in the *Orkneyinga Saga*:

> The Man of the Sword,
> Seeking Scotland's throne,
> Ever won victory.
> Fire flamed fiercely,
> Fast fell the Irish host,
> And flower of Welsh manhood.[67]

And this translation is not supported by the original text, which is more accurately rendered:

> The warrior laid waste
> now the Welsh, now the Irish,
> now feasted the Scots
> with fire and flame.[68]

Although the *Orkneyinga Saga* claims that the Orkney Vikings plundered throughout Scotland after their victories over 'Karl Hundason', there is no evidence that Thorfinn ever attempted to assert, or even genuinely held, any ambitions on the Scottish kingship. Instead, his concerns were more localised. The saga relates how Duncan's accession posed a threat to Viking control of Caithness, leaving them no alternative but to defend their interests. This is credible. Medieval kings often sought to prove their military prowess by leading a hosting soon after their accession, and such expeditions frequently ended in defeat, as Malcolm's siege of Durham did in 1006. Duncan appears to have marked his coming to throne by over-ambitiously attempting to impose his kingship over Caithness. Duncan's motives may have been borne of jealousy and personal animosity towards Thorfinn, perhaps provoked by his grandfather's gift of Caithness and his cousin's control of a province on the Scottish mainland.

Macbeth's apparent absence from the war between Duncan/'Karl' and the Orkney Vikings is intriguing. As the mormaer of one of Scotland's northernmost and most powerful provinces, he may be expected to have played a central role in the battles against the Norsemen. Did the saga-tellers, with their limited knowledge of Scottish personalities and understandably emphasising the personal involvement and defeat of the Scottish King, simply ignore

Macbeth's role in these battles? Or did Macbeth, predicting the outcome in advance, choose not to participate in the conflict? And if the latter, was this simply for reasons of self preservation, or did he have an ulterior motive? Macbeth may have deliberately chosen not to become involved so that Duncan bore the brunt of the Viking onslaught, thus weakening Duncan's kingship and presenting Macbeth with a potential opportunity to gain the throne. But it is easy to speculate in the absence of any concrete information concerning Macbeth during Duncan's reign.

The Brough of Birsay, Orkney, viewed from the air. This tidal island off the north-west coast of Orkney's mainland was a Viking power centre between the ninth and twelfth centuries. The remains of the seat of the Viking *Jarls* of Orkney and their later church, overlying an earlier Pictish settlement, may be seen. (Cambridge University Collection of Air Photographs: copyright reserved)

Duncan's problems were not confined to Scotland's northern frontier. To the south, Scotland and Anglo-Danish Northumbria were vying for control of Cumbria during the eleventh century. Duncan had close links with the Earls of Northumbria through marriage. Before becoming king, Duncan had married Suthen, an unspecified but close relative, probably a sister or cousin, of Siward.[69] Siward, a Dane, had been made Earl of York by Cnut in 1033 and conquered Northumbria, one of the three great Anglo-Danish earldoms in 1041. A combination of royal appointee and client ruler of a powerful regional kingdom, Siward secured his position by marrying into the Northumbrian aristocracy, namely Aelfleda, daughter of Ealdred, Earl of Northumbria. Duncan's younger brother, Maldred, married Ealdgyth, daughter of Earl Uhtred of Northumbria (1006–16), granddaughter of King Aethelred II of England, and sister of Eadulf, future Earl of Northumbria (1039–41). Further cementing these links, Siward married Ealdgyth's niece. Both Duncan and Maldred held lands in Cumbria, suggesting a division of their possessions, with Duncan owing allegiance to the King of Scots and Maldred owing allegiance to the Earl of Northumbria.

On becoming Earl of Northumbria in 1039, Eadulf, 'being exalted with pride, ravaged the Britons with sufficient ferocity',[70] probably in an attempt to assert

Durham, the target of unsuccessful Scottish attacks in 1006 and 1039 or 1040, from the air. The medieval city, with its cathedral dedicated to St Cuthbert (centre) and its castle (behind the cathedral), occupied a naturally-defended promontory high above the meandering River Wear. (Cambridge University Collection of Air Photographs: copyright reserved)

Northumbrian control over Cumbria. Possibly in reprisal, Duncan led a Scottish raid on Durham. Duncan may also have been attempting to redeem his military reputation after his defeats against the Orkney Vikings, distract attention from the inadequacies of his kingship and emulate Malcolm II's great victory over the Northumbrians at Carham in 1018. Although the raid on Durham is undated, it is most likely to have occurred in 1039 or early 1040. This adventurism was without an obvious strategic objective; Durham lay too far south for its possession to have helped secure Scotland's southern border, while Lothian had remained in Scottish hands since 1018.

Duncan's target was presumably the treasures that this major ecclesiastical site, the cult centre of St Cuthbert, held.

Regardless of Duncan's motives, Durham was a difficult prize, occupying a naturally defended promontory high above the River Wear. Moreover, the precedents were ominous; the army of Malcolm II had been comprehensively defeated by Uhtred while besieging Durham in 1006. History was to repeat itself: 'Duncan, King of the Scots, advanced with a countless multitude of troops, and laid siege to Durham, and made strenuous but ineffective efforts to carry it. For a large proportion of his cavalry was slain by the besieged, and he was put to a disorderly flight, in which he lost all his foot-soldiers whose heads were collected in the market-place and hung up upon posts.'[71] Duncan again survived, but his days were numbered.

CHAPTER 3

Macbeth, King of Scots

SEIZING THE KINGSHIP

Duncan's defeat at Durham may have sealed his fate; his next was to cost him his life. This time the enemy was not Northumbria but Macbeth.

There is no record of Macbeth's involvement in the battles against Thorfinn or the attack on Durham. Nevertheless, as Mormaer of Moray, Macbeth may have played an important role in the intermittent struggle against the Orkney Vikings, just as his father had. But although Macbeth's role as a war leader is compatible with his position as a mormaer, no contemporary source ascribes this role to him. Instead, Macbeth's traditional portrayal as Duncan's commander is derived directly from later chronicles and/or a misinterpretation of a contemporary reference, in the *Chronicle* of Marianus Scotus, to Macbeth as Duncan's *dux*. *Dux* (literally 'duke') was a late Roman title for high-ranking military officers and its use survived into the post-Roman period. In sixth-century Gaul, a *dux* was a royally appointed official with administrative and military responsibility for a region, while in Britain the legendary Arthur is famously referred to as *dux bellorum* ('duke/leader of battles') in the *Historia Brittonum* attributed to Nennius. Although this corresponds with one of the functions of a mormaer, the significance of the title of *dux* changed over time. Hiberno-Latin sources from the mid-ninth century onwards refer to the lowest grade of Irish king as *dux*, reflecting an erosion of their status and power. Marianus was simply expressing in his own idiom that Macbeth was a petty king, the Irish equivalent of a mormaer. Consequently, there is no basis for assuming that Macbeth led any of Duncan's ill-fated military expeditions.

Regardless of his involvement, Duncan's disastrous attack on Durham may have spurred Macbeth into action and provided the opportunity required. While Duncan licked his wounds in the south, Macbeth may have rebelled in the north. Fordun comments that Duncan was too trusting, even naïve, neither taking action against nor protecting himself from 'certain members of an ancient family of conspirators' who were said to have 'conspired to kill the king

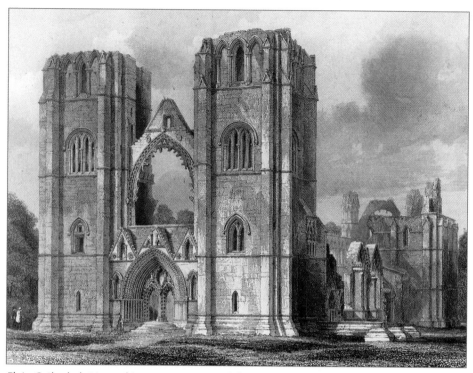

Elgin Cathedral, Morayshire: an engraving of the west towers by R.W. Billings, c. 1852. The cathedral was founded in 1224, when the seat of the bishopric of Moray was transferred from Spynie. (Crown copyright: Royal Commission on the Ancient and Historical Monuments of Scotland)

just as they had conspired to kill his grandfather, his predecessor'.[1] The head of this family was Macbeth, although Fordun mistakenly identifies Macbeth's kin as the killers of Duncan's grandfather and great-grandfather. In the face of increasing evidence of a conspiracy, or even open revolt, Duncan may eventually have been compelled to act against Macbeth, with fatal consequences.

Duncan's murderer is unambiguously identified in the *Chronicle* of Marianus Scotus: 'Duncan, King of Scots, was killed . . . by his *dux*, Macbeth (*a duce suo Macbethad*) son of Findlaech'.[2] The regnal lists record that Duncan was murdered by Macbeth at *Bothirgouane* or *Bothgouanan*, 'Hut of the Blacksmith'.[3] Fordun states that Duncan was fatally wounded by Macbeth at *Bothgofnane* and carried to Elgin, where he died.[4] The place concerned is usually identified as Pitgaveny, 3 km north-east of Elgin.[5] Duncan certainly died in or near Elgin; in 1235, Alexander II endowed a chaplaincy in Elgin Cathedral to celebrate mass in perpetuity for the soul of his ancestor.[6] Elgin was an important administrative and ecclesiastical centre in Moray and almost certainly one of Macbeth's power centres.

The location of Duncan's death perhaps supports the interpretation that he had advanced against Macbeth, possibly to put down a revolt. Alternatively, Duncan may have been surprised by Macbeth while on progress around his kingdom.

Duncan was killed 'in the autumn (on the nineteenth day before the Kalends of September)'.[7] This date, 14 August, is generally accepted, although a marginal note in the same source adds that 'Duncan reigned for five years: that is, from the Mass of St Andrew [30 November 1034] . . . to the Nativity of St Mary'. Although the latter is on 15 August in the Roman calendar, it was celebrated by the Scots on 16 August. This was 'not long after' Duncan's return from his unsuccessful siege of Durham.[8] Duncan's reign, of five years and nine

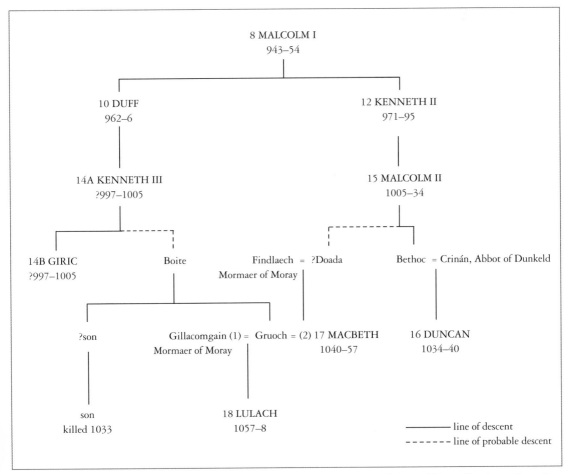

The genealogy of Macbeth. This shows how Macbeth's marriage to Gruoch brought together two alternative claims to the Scottish kingship: the dispossessed descendants of Boite, represented by Gruoch, and Macbeth, a probable grandson of Malcolm II.

months, may seem short, particularly in comparison to the three long eleventh-century reigns of Malcolm II, Macbeth and Malcolm III, but it was not unusual. Although Duncan had three sons, he 'was killed by his own [people] at an immature age'.[9] This may not mean that he was young but simply that he met a premature death. Duncan's genealogy suggests that he was middle-aged; as his birth is usually dated to about 1001, he would have been about thirty-nine years old when he died.

The sequence of events that led to Duncan's murder and Macbeth seizing the kingship began several years earlier. Malcolm II became king by killing his predecessors and then rejected the traditional system of alternating royal succession in favour of his own direct descendants. Malcolm's actions initiated a cycle of violence that led not only to his own death, but also that of the grandson who succeeded him. The continuity of the system of lineal succession introduced by Malcolm was assured by Duncan's sons. Immediately after his accession, Duncan 'gave Malcolm the province of Cumbria',[10] indicating the appointment of the eldest as *tanaise*. Macbeth's motive for killing Duncan is clear; with Duncan's succession established, Macbeth's only chance of becoming king was through violence.

Having examined the events leading up to Duncan's death, Macbeth's motives and the basis of his claim to the throne may now be established. The three principal elements were:

- *Descent*: Macbeth was of royal blood, a member of the aristocratic ruling dynasty of Moray and probably a grandson of Malcolm II. Macbeth may have viewed his claim to the kingship as being at least as strong as Duncan's, especially as Duncan became king only as a result of changes Malcolm made to the system of royal succession. Macbeth's royal descent was the basis of his claim and, according to established practice, he was entitled to use force in asserting his claim.
- *Marriage*: Macbeth's wife, Gruoch, was also of royal blood, a daughter of Boite, the sometime *tanaise* of Malcolm II and a direct descendant of Kenneth II or Kenneth III. Gruoch's lineage possessed its own claims to the kingship, the strength of which may be reflected in her title of queen rather than consort. Through her marriage to Macbeth, Gruoch brought these claims with her into the hereditary aristocracy of Moray. Although their marriage did not, strictly speaking, strengthen Macbeth's own claim, it enabled Macbeth to combine discrete claims to the kingship. Crucially, it also appears to have brought two like-minded people together in a

common purpose. Macbeth's marriage to Gruoch was fundamental in stimulating his ambitions for the kingship.

- *Royal and martial qualities*: Early Scottish kings were, first and foremost, war leaders. Duncan's defeats at Durham and against the Orkney Vikings revealed that he was not a capable war leader, and possibly that he was not fit to hold the kingship. This was in addition to existing doubts about the legitimacy of Duncan's kingship. Macbeth may have believed that he embodied the required regal and martial qualities more fully than Duncan; not only that he would make a more capable ruler, but that this gave him a stronger claim to the kingship.

Individually, none of these claims are very convincing. But in conjunction they make a persuasive case, particularly in contrast to Duncan's ineffectual kingship. Although traditionally portrayed as an usurper, Macbeth had a valid claim to the kingship, though not necessarily the strongest one.

In addition to the various strands of his claim, several psychological factors probably contributed to Macbeth taking the kingship by force. Although it is clearly impossible to produce a psychological assessment of Macbeth from the very limited evidence available, it is possible to identify tentatively some personality traits from Macbeth's background, upbringing and early career. These characteristics are likely to have had a profound affect on him, stimulating his hunger for power and ultimately driving him to seize the throne by force:

- *Jealousy/sense of injustice*: Macbeth may have resented Duncan's succession, particularly as both were equally close and direct descendants of Malcolm II. These feelings may have been exacerbated by the change to the system of succession that brought Duncan the kingship. Left unchecked, these feelings may have led Macbeth to conclude that, as the kingship was rightfully his, any means were justified in achieving the end of acquiring the kingship. Gruoch, too, probably harboured a sense of injustice and may have been politicised by the dynastic violence of Malcolm's reign; Malcolm had killed her probable grandfather, Kenneth III, to seize the kingship, then excluded her descendants from eligibility to the kingship and murdered her nephew in 1033.
- *Predisposition to violence*: Macbeth's upbringing in the marcher society of Moray would have exposed him to much violence, both internecine and against the Orkney Vikings, from an early age. This, combined with his father's murder by his cousins, may have had profound psychological

consequences, drawing him into a cycle of violence. Macbeth's desire for revenge and readiness to resort to violence is indicated by the burning to death of one of his cousins and fifty men twelve years later. Macbeth probably found it easy to justify the use of violence.

- *Ambition*: Macbeth's ambition probably had several sources. From an early age, Macbeth more than likely expected to succeed his father as Mormaer of Moray. Macbeth's probable presence at Malcolm's Court and his meeting with Cnut in 1031 may have kindled his ambitions to acquire the kingship. Perhaps significantly, Wyntoun describes Macbeth's first prophetic vision of his future kingship occurring in a dream while he was still a boy living in the king's household.[11] Seizing the Mormaership of Moray in 1032 may have fuelled Macbeth's ambition, impelling him to attain even higher office and greater power, as well as demonstrating that violence pays. Lastly, the influence of his wife cannot be dismissed. Had her father not been excluded from the kingship, Gruoch would have been a princess. Gruoch may have regarded Macbeth as an opportunity to achieve not only the status denied her by Malcolm, but to become queen.

These characteristics provide an insight into the motives that spurred Macbeth into taking his violent course of action. No single element led Macbeth to seek the kingship and there appears to have been no defining moment that prompted his ambitions. Instead, Macbeth possessed a complex and powerful combination of motivating factors; a genuine, though not very strong, claim to the kingship, together with a range of personality traits that may have origins in experiences he had during his childhood and early adulthood. These experiences included Macbeth's exposure to his father's status, responsibilities and fate as Mormaer of Moray, particularly in Findlaech's battles against the Orkney Vikings and murder by his nephews, as well as growing up in a marcher society that was permanently organised for war, whether against the Orkney Vikings or the Scottish kingship. Macbeth probably believed that his marriage to Gruoch strengthened his claim to the kingship, but it may also have reinforced his sense of injustice and encouraged his ambition.

One final factor may be identified in Macbeth's bid for the kingship, self-defence. Duncan's place of death suggests that he may have been advancing on Macbeth, possibly to suppress a conspiracy or revolt. Threatened in this manner, Macbeth may have felt that he had no alternative but to attack Duncan. Although this might suggest that Macbeth's murder of Duncan was not premeditated and that his seizing the kingship was simply opportunistic, this

A woodcut illustration from Holinshed's *Chronicles* (1577) that shows Macbeth receiving the crown and sceptre of the Scottish kingship: 'Then having a companie about him of such as he had mad privie to his enterprise, he caused himselfe to be proclaymed king, and forthwith went to Scone, where by common consent, he receyved the investure of the kingdome according to the accustomed maner'.

seems unlikely. Although Duncan's presence in Moray may have forced Macbeth to act sooner than he had intended, it also presented Macbeth with the advantage of being on his own territory. Macbeth exploited the opportunity fully.

Murdering Duncan did not, in itself, make Macbeth king. Scotland's medieval kings were installed ritually in accordance with ancient tradition at Scone in Perthshire. Royal inauguration ceremonies were of great political significance, formally establishing the inauguree's possession of the kingship by hereditary right and, at least in theory, deterring rivals from mounting future challenges. After killing Duncan, Macbeth would have needed to legitimise his position by being inaugurated in the traditional manner and at the appointed place. As a result, he probably hurried south from Moray before a rival candidate could reach Scone.

Although no records of Macbeth's inauguration exist, the ritual probably incorporated many of the same elements exhibited by that of Alexander III in 1249. Macbeth was likely to have been installed in the kingship by ritually sitting on the Stone of Destiny, which was perhaps housed in a throne, on or before the Moot Hill at Scone. Scotland's most senior nobles and clerics probably played an important role in the ceremony. The legitimacy conferred by the past may have been invoked by the recital of Macbeth's genealogy, tracing his royal pedigree

The Stone of Destiny, on which Scottish kings were inaugurated at Scone. Seized by Edward I of England in 1296, the Stone was removed to Westminster Abbey, where it became an integral element of firstly English and later British royal coronation rituals. The Stone was returned to Scotland in 1996 and is now on display in Edinburgh Castle. (Crown copyright: Historic Scotland)

back through his probable grandfather, Malcolm II, and the long lineage of early Scottish kings to the mythological progenitors of the Scots.

The measure of Macbeth's achievement was not simply Duncan's elimination but his ability to replace Duncan as King of Scots. For the mormaer of a peripheral province, this represented a considerable feat. Macbeth's success in acquiring the kingship from a narrow power base, geographically distant from the southern Perthshire power centre of the Scottish kingship, requires explanation. Several factors were probably involved. Macbeth may have been assisted by Duncan's unpopularity. Although we should be wary of his later mythologisation, even some later chroniclers, despite being hostile to Macbeth, are unsympathetic to Duncan, characterising him as a weak, oppressive or unrighteous king. Duncan's poor performance as a war leader, a central role of early medieval kings, may have lost him support among his nobles, leaving him vulnerable to challenge from the more disaffected nobles who wished to further their own ambitions.

Unlike Duncan, Macbeth had not held the kingship and was not tainted by failure. Moreover, Macbeth may have been perceived as a more effective leader. Certainly, his actions in seizing firstly the Mormaership of Moray, then the Kingship of Scots reveal him as bold and decisive, while his abilities as a war leader are attested by later events. Macbeth probably received support from important elements of the nobility; tacit support from nobles who primarily sought an end to Duncan's kingship and active support from Macbeth's own followers. The latter presumably included contacts Macbeth made at the Court of Malcolm II. It is worth recalling that Macbeth, not Duncan, is known to have accompanied Malcolm at the meeting with Cnut in 1031, a possible reflection of their relative status, and perhaps influence, at Malcolm's Court.

These factors reveal that it is simplistic to portray Macbeth's seizure of the kingship as a Moray take-over of the rest of Scotland, the peripheral northern province conquering the kingdom to which it belonged. Just as Macbeth probably had 'southern' support when he took the Mormaership of Moray in 1032, he could probably count on the assistance – active or passive – of a wide range of Scottish nobles. Indeed, Macbeth's success, not only in seizing the kingship, but also in securing it for the next seventeen years, indicates that he enjoyed a wide degree of support. This would have come from Macbeth's kinsfolk, allies and those disaffected by Malcolm's changes to the system of royal succession and/or by Duncan's rule.

Members of royal lineages that had been excluded from the kingship were another likely source of support for Macbeth. Boite's lineage, including Gruoch, Macbeth's queen, is the obvious example, but Malcolm's elimination of his predecessors and collateral candidates suggests that there were others. After Malcolm's death, Duncan would have been the natural focus of their opposition. These may be the 'swarms of malcontents' who supported Macbeth against Duncan.[12] Although more anti-Duncan than pro-Macbeth, their role was probably decisive. Opposition to Duncan from various sources may have coalesced around Macbeth to form the 'very powerful resources' with which Macbeth seized the kingship.[13] Although this may only have been a temporary alliance, held together by the objective of removing Duncan, it was of sufficient strength and duration to enable Macbeth to secure the kingship after Duncan's murder.

The area of greatest uncertainty concerning not only Macbeth's acquisition of the kingship but his entire reign is what role, if any, the Orkney Vikings played in these events. The sources are silent, although the Vikings' presence looms large. Duncan had suffered a series of defeats against Thorfinn the previous decade; is it realistic to expect the men of Orkney to have played no part in the events of 1040? It is often claimed that Macbeth and Thorfinn allied themselves to overthrow Duncan and that they then divided Scotland between them. This rests on Thorfinn's obituary in the *Orkneyinga Saga*, which claims that Thorfinn 'won for himself nine Scottish earldoms, along with the whole of the Hebrides and a considerable part of Ireland'.[14] This, however, is heroic hyperbole; there is no evidence of such an alliance or the division of Scotland.

Taking the alliance theory a step further, Macbeth's murder of Duncan is sometimes linked with Thorfinn's victory over 'Karl Hundason' at *Torfnes*. The commonest interpretation rests on the identification of *Torfnes* with Burghead, 12 km north-west of Elgin; after his defeat by Thorfinn, Duncan/'Karl' fled the battlefield but was intercepted and fatally wounded by Macbeth near Elgin.

Intriguing though this is, there is no evidence to support it. Contemporary sources are consistent; Duncan was fatally wounded at *Bothgouanan*, Macbeth was the perpetrator and there is no reference to Thorfinn or a battle against the Orkney Vikings. This interpretation conflates two separate events, Duncan's defeat by Thorfinn at *Torfnes* with his murder by Macbeth. These occurred several years apart and there is no evidence that they were linked.

Other interpretations of events on Scotland's northern frontier are more plausible. Thorfinn's neutrality may have been sought or offered in return for Macbeth confirming Viking possession of Caithness and possibly Ross and/or Sutherland. This would have left Macbeth free to challenge Duncan without having to worry about his rear. Alternatively, Duncan's death may have provided Thorfinn with the opportunity to consolidate his hold over Caithness, without the need for an alliance with Macbeth. Their objectives may have been confined to mutually compatible spheres of interest; Macbeth winning the Scottish kingship while Thorfinn was preoccupied with domestic affairs.

The *Orkneyinga Saga* reveals that Thorfinn had to cede two-thirds of Orkney to his nephew, Rognvald Brusason, in return for assistance in suppressing a revolt in his lands in the Western Isles and Ireland.[15] This led inevitably to conflict between the two *jarls*, culminating in Rognvald's death, while Thorfinn's summer raiding expeditions targeted Scotland's Western Isles and coast and the Irish Sea littoral, areas that were peripheral to Macbeth's interests. Rather than a formal alliance between them, Macbeth and Thorfinn may have realised that it was in their mutual interests not to interfere in each other's affairs. Similarly, there is no evidence to support claims that Malcolm III's ultimate success over Macbeth may be linked to Thorfinn's death, the year of which is unclear but may not have been until about 1065 and several years after Macbeth's death.

But the impression of peaceful relations between Scotland and the Orkney Vikings during Macbeth's reign may simply reflect the poorly documented history of northern Scotland during the eleventh century. One must be wary of inferring too much from negative evidence; in reality, the situation could have been very different.

SUPPRESSING THE OPPOSITION

There is no evidence that Macbeth encountered any opposition in seizing the kingship or immediately afterwards. If any occurred, Macbeth must have emerged victorious to consolidate his hold on the throne. The most obvious source of opposition was from Duncan's relatives and supporters, while the most likely direction of a future challenge was from Duncan's legitimate sons, Malcolm Canmore ('Big Head') and Donald. Their ages are unclear, but they were born while Duncan's grandfather, Malcolm II, was still alive,[16] making them at least six or seven years old in 1040. But Malcolm's appointment as *tanaise* on Duncan's accession in 1034 suggests that he was somewhat older.

Macbeth was aware of the potential threat Duncan's sons posed and attempted to eliminate them: 'Macbeth hunted down with all his might Duncan's sons, Malcolm Canmore (who should have succeeded Duncan) and his brother Donald, striving to kill them; but they resisted as best they could and remained in the kingdom for almost two years hoping for victory, while few of the people gave assistance openly either to Macbeth or to them.'[17] Fordun infers that Malcolm and Donald spent these two years in hiding and/or on the run. Their youthfulness suggests that they were incapable of mounting any effective opposition to Macbeth's rule during this period, although their successful survival and escape indicates that they received some assistance. Despite Macbeth's efforts, Malcolm and Donald evaded him: 'When . . . they did not dare to continue the struggle any longer, Donald went to the Western Isles and Malcolm to Cumbria, since it was abundantly clear that death rather than life awaited them, if they had remained.'[18]

In the absence of Duncan's sons, his father was the most likely source of opposition, although this did not materialise immediately. Instead, opposition appears to have simmered quietly beneath the surface before erupting into open revolt. In 1045, 'A battle [was fought] between the Scots, on one road; and Crinán, Abbot of Dunkeld, was killed in it; and many along with him, namely nine score fighting men'.[19] Although the circumstances and location of the battle are not recorded and there is no reference to Macbeth, it clearly represents the outcome of a rebellion against Macbeth's kingship. 'On one road' may be translated as 'upon a united expedition' or 'in a mass levy', implying 'an army . . . composed of different elements, which divided into hostile parties'.[20] This implies a large-scale mobilisation, perhaps reflecting the extent of the revolt Macbeth faced. The body count, if reliable, indicates a sizeable encounter. This battle is the first indication of internal unrest during Macbeth's reign.

Crinán evidently retained his abbacy for five years after Macbeth's accession. After seizing the kingship, Macbeth did not eradicate even the closest of Duncan's supporters or, at least in this case, replace them with his own appointees. It is uncertain whether this reflects Macbeth's magnanimity, his limited influence over the Church, or his belief that they posed no serious threat. Regardless of this, Crinán's position suggests that Dunkeld, the power centre of the Mormaers of Atholl, was a centre of opposition to Macbeth during the early years of his reign. But it is unclear why this should not have broken into open revolt until 1045. Crinán possibly lacked sufficient support within Scotland to mount an effective challenge to Macbeth and had to bide his time, perhaps waiting for foreign assistance.

The *Annals of Durham* record just such an external intervention in 1046: 'Earl Siward came to Scotland with a great army and expelled King Macbeth and appointed another, but after his departure Macbeth recovered the kingdom'.[21] Duncan's murder and Macbeth's accession presented Siward with a unique opportunity, that of securing his northern frontier, or even extending his territory into southern Scotland, in return for assistance in restoring Duncan's relatives to the kingship.

But the entry from 1046 is problematical and uncorroborated. It is most unlikely that Macbeth was expelled from Scotland; a region of Scotland, presumably Lothian, was probably intended. It may mean that, after making some initial gains, perhaps including the conquest of Lothian, a Northumbrian invasion was repulsed. But it is unclear if this was a separate attempt to oust Macbeth from that mounted by Crinán in 1045; either the Irish or Northumbrian annalists may have misplaced one of these events by one year. Crinán's and Siward's actions may have been concerted; having to fight on two fronts simultaneously might explain why Macbeth temporarily lost his kingdom or part of it. Alternatively, Siward may have made a belated attempt to exploit Macbeth's internal difficulties the year after Crinán's unsuccessful rebellion. A third, but less likely, possibility is that the entry represents a confused, duplicated and misplaced account of Siward's invasion of 1054.

This entry, if reliable, is significant. It attests Northumbrian intervention in Scotland eight or possibly nine years before Siward's offensive with a combined Northumbrian and Scottish force in 1054 and suggests that Duncan's relatives and supporters in Scotland and Northumbria were already cooperating to oust Macbeth. The identity of Siward's appointee to the Scottish kingship is unclear. Malcolm would have been too young to have been a credible contender for the kingship, suggesting that Siward's intention may have been to install Duncan's brother, Maldred, who was related to Siward by marriage, on the throne. It is presumably significant that the next Northumbrian offensive did not occur until eight years later, probably reflecting the strength of Macbeth's grip on power and the scale of the defeat(s) suffered by both the internal opposition and Northumbrian forces in 1045/46.

In the face of Macbeth's strong rule, opposition to his kingship may have taken the form of clandestine conspiracies rather than open rebellion. Fordun relates how some magnates plotted to persuade Malcolm, whom they regarded as the rightful heir to throne, to return and take the kingship.[22] But they were betrayed and Macbeth had the conspirators killed or imprisoned, or their property confiscated. The ringleader, MacDuff, 'Thane of Fife', escaped, whereupon Macbeth besieged his castles, confiscated all his lands and property, and banished him permanently. But such was MacDuff's popularity that this produced a 'great murmuring throughout the whole kingdom, and especially among the nobles'.

Fordun's account is unsubstantiated; the characterisation of Macbeth as a tyrant indicates its mythological nature and MacDuff is not recorded in contemporary sources. But it may have a historical basis, reflecting the political intrigue of Macbeth's reign, the destabilising effect of Malcolm's continued presence in Northumbria and Macbeth's heavy handed attempts to suppress any opposition to his rule. Moreover, the MacDuff medieval Earls of Fife took their name from the son of Duff and Duff's descendants may have held the Mormaership of Fife during the eleventh century. That the lands of the Mormaers of Fife were forfeited by the Crown during the eleventh century is suggested by the limited possessions of the Earls of Fife by the early twelfth century. Fordun's account of MacDuff may have a basis in historical fact.

MACBETH'S REIGN

Little is known about Macbeth's reign. Medieval chroniclers describe it as a period of tyranny or prosperity (or both), their contradictory and stereotyped portrayals attesting the later mythologising of Macbeth. Indeed, the paucity of contemporary textual sources means that only seven events may be identified during Macbeth's reign: Crinán's defeat in 1045, the repulsing of the Northumbrian invasion in 1046, Macbeth's (undated) gifts of land to the Culdees of Loch Leven, his pilgrimage to Rome in 1050, reception of Norman exiles in 1052, the Northumbrian invasion and ensuing battle in 1054, and his ultimate defeat and death in 1057. The limited nature of the evidence is all the more apparent when one considers that it is from a seventeen-year reign.

Nevertheless, these incidents not only enable a skeletal historical narrative to be constructed but also provide revealing insights into Macbeth's kingship. In particular, his patronage of the Church, pilgrimage and role as a war leader indicate that he was typical of eleventh-century insular monarchs, conscious of and responsive to changing practices and fashions of kingship. This suggests that Macbeth, like his insular counterparts, was a patron of the arts and literature. However, our inability to date precisely Scottish architecture, sculpture and metalwork of this period means that no specific works of art can be assigned to Macbeth's reign, let alone attributed to Macbeth's patronage.

In contrast, a poem in *Lebor Bretnach*, a Middle Irish translation of the *Historia Brittonum*, may have been composed during Macbeth's reign. The poem beginning *What Assembled the Picts in Britain* (*Cruithnig cid dosfarclann*), a mythological tract on Pictish origins, is possibly by the Irish poet Flann Mainistrech, who died in 1056.[23] The version preserved in the fourteenth- or fifteenth-century *Book of Ballymote* records that 'mac Bretach' was then reigning and the king concerned is widely identified as Macbeth (Mac Bethad). This reference implies that the poem was intended for recital at Macbeth's court and was perhaps even composed under his patronage. Set in the mid-ninth century, it tells how the Scots invited the Pictish nobility to a feast at Scone, waited until their guests were drunk, then murdered them. This widely found myth, which survives in several medieval versions, is better known as *The Treachery of Scone* (*Braflang Scoine*), from the recorded title of a lost tenth-century Irish tale.[24] Its appeal to Macbeth is evident. The myth not only relates how Macbeth's ancestors conquered the Picts and founded the Scottish kingdom, but also concerns the use of violence in the pursuit of power. Is the Scots' betrayal of the Picts' trust an oblique reference to Macbeth's murder of Duncan through an act of treachery? Although uncorroborated, it is an intriguing possibility.

MACBETH AND THE CULDEES OF LOCH LEVEN

In common with established patterns of Christian kingship throughout western Europe, a close relationship between kingship and the Church is evident in early medieval Scotland, although there was no unified ecclesiastical organisation during this period. In Macbeth's case, this relationship was probably complex. In particular, the position of Duncan's father as Abbot of Dunkeld until 1045 is likely to have strained Macbeth's relationship with at least this important ecclesiastical centre. Macbeth may have enjoyed a close relationship with other ecclesiastical communities. These may have included the possible Culdee community at Scone, where Macbeth was presumably inaugurated, and St Andrews, an important royal and ecclesiastical centre from the eighth century.[25] However, there is evidence of Macbeth's association with only one ecclesiastical foundation, the monastery on St Serf's Island in Loch Leven, Kinross-shire. This relationship provides a unique insight into Macbeth's kingship and, perhaps, character.

Land was an important source of income, in the form of rents and agricultural produce, for medieval monasteries. Most monastic lands were granted by the Crown and many monastic communities kept a cartulary or donations book, in which such endowments were recorded. The Culdee community on Loch Leven maintained its cartulary in Gaelic. Although it no longer survives, it may have comprised marginal notes inserted in a gospel book, like the *Book of Deer*. After the monastery and its library were acquired by the Priory of St Andrews in the mid-twelfth century, this cartulary

An aerial view of the remains of the medieval monastic foundation on St Serf's Island, Loch Leven, Kinross-shire. The ruined Romanesque chapel (centre) probably occupies the site of an earlier church belonging to the Culdee community endowed and perhaps visited by Macbeth and his queen. Faint traces of other buildings belonging to the medieval monastery lie beyond the chapel. (Cambridge University Collection of Air Photographs: copyright reserved)

was summarised in Latin in the St Andrews *Register* and, although this too has disappeared, copies and summaries of some of its contents survive.

Many of the gifts of land recorded in the Loch Leven cartulary were made by kings and other members of the royal kin group. Three notes are of particular interest.[26] One records a grant of land, the *villa de Bolgyne*, made by Macbeth to the 'hermits' of Loch Leven 'with the utmost veneration and devotion'. The other two record the gift of the *villa de Kyrkenes* to the Culdees by Macbeth and Gruoch. Both placenames still survive.[27] *Bolgyne* is Bogie, near Kirkcaldy in Fife, an important royal estate, income from which was also granted to Dunfermline Priory by Malcolm III and Margaret.[28] *Kyrkenes* (Church of/on the Promontory) survives as Kirkness, near the south-east end of Loch Leven. Its name, which is distinctively Scandinavian in form, indicates the presence of an ecclesiastical site there. *Kyrkenes* was given by Macbeth and his queen 'from motives of piety and for the benefit of their prayers'. The rent from this land was probably used to finance a chantry priest who celebrated mass and prayed for the benefactors' souls at a specially dedicated altar in either the church at Kirkness or St Serf's Monastery.

These grants of land have strongly influenced modern interpretations of Macbeth's kingship and character. But although it is often claimed that Macbeth gave these lands to the Culdees of Loch Leven in absolution for murdering Duncan, the endowment of altars was practised widely by monarchs and nobles throughout the Middle Ages. These gifts of land are also cited widely as evidence that Macbeth was a devout and generous benefactor of the Church, implying that he was a 'good' king, in contrast to his later portrayal. But Macbeth's motives remain unclear. As the relevant entries were originally recorded by the Culdees themselves, their expressions of devotion may comprise an ecclesiastical interpretation of the gifts, rather than reflect Macbeth's exact sentiments. As recipients of the endowments, the Culdees' impressions of Macbeth were, not surprisingly, favourable.

The evidence – two endowments of land made to the same community within seventeen years – is insufficient to determine whether Macbeth was generous even to the Culdees of Loch Leven, let alone the Church in general. The areas of land concerned are unclear but are unlikely to have been large, given the other grants of land in these areas made to the community. Furthermore, one of the gifts was made jointly by Macbeth and Gruoch, perhaps reflecting the influence of his queen. Nothing here proves that Macbeth was a generous benefactor. Yet the fragmentary nature of the evidence leaves open the possibility that Macbeth may also have endowed other ecclesiastical centres, but that no records of this survive.

Was Macbeth a generous and pious king? The best indication is provided by analogy; comparable gifts made by other kings are not difficult to find. The St Andrews *Register* also records several other endowments of land made to the Culdees of Loch Leven during the eleventh century. The donors included Malcolm II, Malcolm III and his queen, Margaret, and Edgar (1097–1107), but were not confined to monarchs; Ethelred, a son of Malcolm and Margaret who was probably Abbot of Dunkeld and Earl of Fife, also gave land to the community.[29] This was clearly a well-established practice in eleventh-century Scotland and began before Macbeth's reign.

Macbeth's gifts prove neither that he was generous to the Church nor that he was a pious king. There is no evidence of acts of significant generosity, such as the foundation of new religious houses, only minor endowments of land to an existing community. Not until the next century, and the reign of David I (1124–53) in particular, did such royal foundations appear, but by that time the character of Scottish kingship had changed considerably as a result of Norman influences. Instead, Macbeth's gifts to the Culdee community on Loch Leven reveal that he was a Christian king who conformed to the established practices of kingship in eleventh-century Scotland.

But why did Macbeth endow this particular community? It may reflect the importance of St Serf's Monastery and the influence of its abbots. Or perhaps Macbeth was a regular visitor. Loch Leven lies on the route between the southern Perthshire power base of the Scottish kingship and Dunfermline, a prominent royal centre during the reign of Malcolm III. If Dunfermline was already important during Macbeth's reign, the community of St Serf may have featured on Macbeth's progresses around his kingdom. Alternatively, the grants to Loch Leven may reflect the power of Gruoch, as the joint nature of one endowment supports. If Gruoch and/or her kin had estates in Fife, they may have had a close relationship with the Culdees of Loch Leven and Gruoch's influence may be detected behind the gifts.

MACBETH'S PILGRIMAGE TO ROME

One of the most intriguing episodes in Macbeth's reign is his pilgrimage to Rome. For the king of a small nation on the northern fringes of Europe to take the long (about 2,000 km) and hazardous road to the Eternal City was a committed act of piety and devotion, second only to undertaking a pilgrimage to Jerusalem itself.[30] The contrast with the evil and tyrannical Macbeth of the later chroniclers and Shakespeare seems complete. Indeed, so remarkable does this episode appear that some Scottish historians even denied that Macbeth ever visited Rome.[31]

Our knowledge of Macbeth's presence in Rome comes from a single source, but one that is nearly contemporary and is known to be reliable in its reporting of other events. Marianus Scotus was an Irish monk, his epithet being derived from the Latin name for the Irish, *Scoti* or *Scotti*. Known in Irish as Maél Brigte, Marianus was expelled from Moville, Co. Down, an important centre of monastic learning, in 1056. He then followed in the footsteps of the *peregrini*, wandering Irish monks who preached and studied on the continent, and went to what is now Germany.[32] Marianus entered the Monastery of St Martin at Mainz in 1069, where he completed his *Chronicle of World History (Chronicon)* in 1073, and remained there until his death in 1082 or 1083. Scottish monks were also active on the continent. In 1072, Marianus' unnamed amanuensis made a marginal note in Latin and Gaelic in Marianus' *Chronicle* recording that he was from Scotland and that he, too, had travelled to the continent after being expelled from his monastery, evidently an occupational hazard.[33]

Marianus records that, in 1050, 'The King of Scots, Macbeth, scattered silver like seed to the poor in Rome'.[34] Marianus was writing only a few years later and, despite his eremitic lifestyle, clearly had access to a wide range of sources. Indeed, the contents of his *Chronicle* attest Marianus' extensive connections across the continent and the existence of a monastic information network stretching from Rome all the way to Ireland, Scotland and Germany. The entry concerning Macbeth appears to have been based on an eye-witness account and probably reached Marianus from one of three sources: his Scottish amanuensis, who would have had an obvious interest in recording Macbeth's presence in Rome; a (possibly Irish or Scottish) pilgrim whose visit to Rome coincided with that of Macbeth and who later sought hospitality on his homeward journey in a monastery in Germany, perhaps Mainz itself; or a cleric in the Irish monastery in Rome, *Sanctae Trinitatis Scottorum* (*Holy Trinity of the Irish*).[35]

This brief account provides a remarkable insight into Macbeth and his reign. Marianus does not state that Macbeth was in Rome on pilgrimage, but there was no other reason for an insular king to visit Rome during the eleventh century. In addition, Macbeth's charity to the poor parallels that of other royal pilgrims and his visit was probably recorded by Marianus because of its religious significance.

What drew Macbeth to Rome and how should his pilgrimage be interpreted? Pilgrimage is an act of public penance for sins committed and a quest for absolution from those sins. Does this reveal aspects of Macbeth's character? Was Macbeth seeking papal absolution for murdering Duncan, as is frequently claimed? Our knowledge about early medieval insular pilgrimage is drawn from Anglo-Saxon and Irish sources, and these provide a valuable historical context against which Macbeth's pilgrimage may be studied.

Rome, the Holy See and cult centre of saints Peter and Paul, was one of the three great pilgrimage centres of medieval Christendom. Encouraged by the new millennium and the thousandth anniversary of Christ's death, Christians placed an increased emphasis on the spiritual benefits of pilgrimage, particularly to Rome, during the eleventh century. Nevertheless, the motives of individual pilgrims probably varied enormously. Even if some of these were genuinely spiritual, other factors featured prominently. For example, Irish saints' lives reveal that the social status of pilgrims was enhanced with the 'consideration and honour' they received from the Pope.

For kings, the rewards of making the pilgrimage to Rome were potentially greater still. The adoption of Christian concepts of kingship throughout western Europe during the early Middle Ages led kings to seek divine sanction for their office, authority and succession. Charlemagne's two sons were consecrated by anointing in Rome in 781 and the practice, based on Old Testament models, spread rapidly throughout western Christendom. Although there is no evidence that Macbeth was anointed, his pilgrimage would certainly have had a political significance.

The political dimension of royal pilgrimage is apparent from Cnut's travels. Although there are some doubts about the number of pilgrimages he made to Rome and their dates, he appears to have made the journey twice, in 1026–7 and 1031. Cnut's motive was to create a pious image for himself as part of a strategy of aligning himself with, and seeking support and legitimation from, a Church that was growing rapidly in power and wealth.[36] Although displaying some hyperbole, medieval chroniclers give a flavour of the magnificent spectacle of Cnut's presence in Rome and the impression his actions created. Symeon of Durham describes how:

A public display of royal piety. King Cnut and Queen Emma (known as Aelfgyfu to the Anglo-Saxons) present an altar cross to New Minster, Winchester, witnessed by Christ in His majesty, c. 1031. (From the *Liber Vitae* of the New Minster, by permission of the British Library, MS Stowe 944, fol. 6r)

Cnut . . . went with great pomp to Rome, and bestowed upon [the church of] St Peter, the chief of the apostles, large gifts in gold and silver, and other precious articles; and obtained from Pope John [XIX] that the school of the Angles [in Rome] should be freed from all tribute and custom; and in going and returning he laid out large alms on the poor, and abolished (by paying a great price) many gates on the road where a toll was exacted from strangers; and before the tomb of the apostles he vowed to God that he would amend his life and conversation.[37]

The opulence displayed by Cnut on his pilgrimage was unparalleled, according to the *Chronicle of Huntingdon*: 'No king of the western parts displayed so much magnificence in his pilgrimage to Rome. Who can reckon the alms, and the offerings, and the costly banquets which the great king gave during his pilgrimage?'[38] Cnut's conspicuous largesse indicates that his pilgrimages were motivated by more than just piety. Insular kings were not only seeking spiritual gains, but an international stage on which to enhance their prestige through opulent displays of royal wealth and power. Making the pilgrimage to Rome conferred legitimacy and status on royal pilgrims.

Cnut was the most powerful and influential insular king of his time and his pilgrimage to Rome rapidly established a vogue for the practice amongst other insular rulers. Although no Scottish kings other than Macbeth are known to have made the journey, several Irish kings soon followed in Cnut's footsteps. In 1028, Sitric, King of the Dublin Vikings, and Flannacán, King of Brega, also made the pilgrimage to Rome, followed by Flaithbertach ua Néill, High-King of Cenél nEógain, in 1030–1.[39]

Cnut may even have been responsible for inspiring Macbeth's pilgrimage to Rome. In 1031, 'as soon as he came home' from his (second?) religious expedition to Rome, Cnut went to Scotland, where he met Malcolm II and Macbeth.[40] Fresh from his pilgrimage, did Cnut's tales of Rome and its holy splendours inspire Macbeth to follow the same path nineteen years later? Was Macbeth, by scattering his silver to the poor, trying to emulate Cnut's earlier display of generosity?

Like Cnut, Macbeth's pilgrimage to Rome must also have had a political dimension. Although Macbeth's silver was directed at the poor, his act of public charity was for the consumption of a wider and more influential audience. By making a conspicuous entrance to the city, Macbeth was attempting to impress other high-ranking pilgrims, the ecclesiastical authorities in Rome and perhaps the Pope himself. But there is nothing to support claims by some English historians that Macbeth was attempting to bribe either the papal court or even the Pope.[41] Instead, Macbeth may have been trying to dispel those preconceptions that would have been attached to him as the king of what was perceived to be a remote, poor and backward nation. This was public relations, medieval style. Most pilgrims arrived in Rome for the great festivals of the Christian calendar, when the Eternal City was thronged with pilgrims and worshippers. By timing his arrival to coincide with this, Macbeth could have ensured maximum publicity for his opulent entrance. Although the time of year Macbeth arrived in Rome is unrecorded, it seems most likely to have been Easter 1050.

If Macbeth intended to impress he evidently succeeded; reports of his charity not only reached Germany but also touched Marianus sufficiently for him to record the event. Marianus' agricultural metaphor was probably chosen carefully to imply that Macbeth intended to harvest the future dividends of his generosity: 'sow and you shall reap'. The poor may not have been the only recipients of Macbeth's generosity. Macbeth may have made donations to the recently founded Irish monastery in Rome, perhaps influencing the favourable account of his pilgrimage that reached Marianus.

The route Macbeth took to Rome was probably already well established by previous pilgrims and ecclesiastics; as early as 721, two bishops from what later became Scotland, a Pict and a Strathclyde Briton, attended a council in Rome. Nevertheless, the journey carried considerable risks and several kings did not either reach their destination or return from it. Travelling through England could be hazardous for foreign dignitaries, even on pilgrimage; Indrechtach ua Fínechta, Abbot of Iona, and Amlaíb son of Sitric, King of the Dublin Vikings, were killed by the Saxons on their way to Rome in 854 and 1034 respectively.[42] England was not only unfamiliar but potentially hostile territory for Macbeth; Northumbria's rulers were related to Duncan, while Duncan's eldest son, Malcolm, was in exile there and had been received by Edward the Confessor. The absence in contemporary Anglo-Saxon sources of references to Macbeth's presence in England may indicate that he either followed a different itinerary or, less probably, travelled incognito. From Scotland, Macbeth is more likely to have sailed down the eastern coast of England, avoiding the overland route altogether.

Macbeth probably crossed the English Channel at its narrowest point, the Strait of Dover. From there, he would have followed the route taken by Irish and presumably other insular pilgrims: through northern France or the Low Countries, then up the Rhine to Switzerland and through the Alpine passes into northern Italy. A network of hostels existed on the continent for the relief of Irish pilgrims on their way to Rome and Macbeth may have used these facilities. Alternatively, as befitted someone of his status, he may have been hosted more lavishly by local kings or bishops. Important ecclesiastical centres along the route provided convenient stopping places for pilgrims on their way to Rome: Cnut visited St Omer;[43] Irish pilgrims rested in Liège in the ninth century;[44] while the son of Aelfgar, Earl of East Anglia and Mercia, died in Rheims in the mid-eleventh century. As the journey to Rome took several months, Macbeth may have left Scotland in 1049, in which case Rheims may have provided an attractive stopping point on his journey. Rheims Cathedral was consecrated on 2 October 1049, in the presence of Pope Leo IX and the Holy Roman Emperor, Henry III, and Leo then

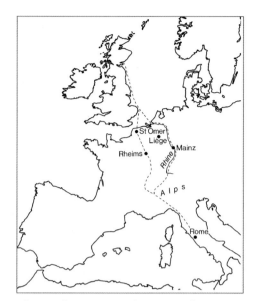

The road to Rome. This map of western Europe shows possible routes taken and some of the ecclesiastical centres that might have been visited by Macbeth on his pilgrimage from Scotland to Rome in 1050. Also shown is Mainz, where Marianus Scotus, a monk in the monastery of St Martin, recorded Macbeth's pilgrimage.

presided over an important ecclesiastical synod.[45] This would have given Macbeth sufficient time to reach Rome by Easter the following year.

Macbeth probably travelled with a retinue, which would have both served him and protected him from the robbers who, according to Irish saints' lives, posed the greatest danger to pilgrims on their way to Rome. It is not known if Gruoch went with Macbeth. Although it was unusual for kings to take their queens on pilgrimage, it was not unheard of. Laidcnén, King of Gailenga, who died in Rome in 1051, was on pilgrimage with his wife,[46] while the large entourage that accompanied Tostig, Earl of Northumbria, to Rome in 1061 included his wife. Emphasising the rigours involved, even for high-status pilgrims, Tostig and Aldred, Archbishop of York, were attacked and robbed on the return journey.[47]

We can only speculate about Macbeth's activities in Rome, in addition to distributing alms, but eminent pilgrims were sometimes received by the Pope. Cnut met John XIX in 1031,[48] while Thorfinn, *Jarl* of Orkney, 'had an audience with the Pope and received absolution from him for all his sins'.[49] If the Pope could grant an audience to Thorfinn, Macbeth's royal status and Scotland's established and distinguished Christian tradition would presumably have guaranteed him a meeting. Leo IX (1049–54) was an outstanding eleventh-century pontiff and an ardent reformer who laids the foundations of the papal monarchy.[50] It is an intriguing, but uncorroborated, possibility that Macbeth may have been drawn to Rome by Leo's impressive reputation and that this may reflect Macbeth's own interests in ecclesiastical reform.

This meeting, if it occurred, would probably have been the highlight of Macbeth's pilgrimage, symbolising his social, political and religious acceptance by the holy see and, in the process, enhancing his status, honour and prestige in the eyes of both his subjects and foreign kings. Yet there is no record that Macbeth and

Leo ever met and the fact that Leo spent only six months of his five-year papacy in Rome suggests that, if they did, it was not in Rome.

Although Macbeth's pilgrimage to Rome provides a remarkable insight into his reign and character, it does not prove that Macbeth was a king of exceptional piety. Indeed, his pilgrimage cannot be interpreted simply as a religious act. Going on pilgrimage to Rome was an important and fashionable feature of eleventh-century insular kingship, involving kings of widely different status, from Irish petty kings to the mighty Cnut. Macbeth was a monarch of his age and his pilgrimage was in keeping with evolving practices of kingship. Only when viewed within this wider context does the political dimension become apparent. Against this background, it is most unlikely that Macbeth, while on his pilgrimage, sought absolution for murdering Duncan.

Pope Leo IX (left) blessing a monastery offered by Warinus, Abbot of St Arnulf. This is a miniature from a manuscript produced in Metz during the second half of the eleventh century. (Burgerbibliothek, Bern)

DOWNFALL AND DEATH

Macbeth's pilgrimage to Rome marks approximately the mid-point in his reign, when his power may have been at its height. Certainly, Macbeth's absence from Scotland for at least several months attests the strength of his grip on the kingship and his confidence at retaining power on his return. The defeat(s) inflicted by Macbeth on Crinán and the Northumbrian invasion four or five years previously may have successfully quashed any potential opposition for several years, enabling Macbeth to travel to Rome without concern.

Macbeth appears to have learned from his predecessors' mistakes and not indulged in any misguided attacks against either the Orkney Vikings or Northumbria. But Scotland could not be insulated from events in neighbouring kingdoms. The strong links between Duncan's family and Northumbria ensured a continued, if only occasionally active, Northumbrian interest in Scottish affairs, as Siward's intervention in 1046 demonstrates. Events further south were also felt in Scotland. When Godwine, Earl of Wessex, returned from exile in Bruges in 1052 he expelled the Normans introduced to England by Edward the

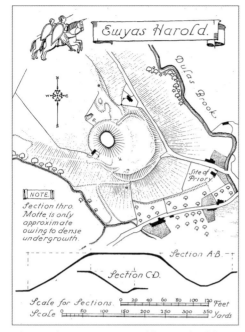

The castle at Ewyas Harold, Herefordshire. A castle was first built on this naturally defended promontory by Osbern Pentecost in the mid-eleventh century. The surviving motte and stone walls probably belong to later phases of refortification. (English Heritage, © Crown copyright)

Confessor.[51] Although most went to Normandy, some Normans fled west to the castle of Osbern Pentecost.[52] Subsequently, 'Osbern . . . and his ally Hugo, surrendered their castles . . . and went to Scotland, and were there kindly received by Macbeth, King of Scots'.[53] This marks the earliest recorded Norman presence in Scotland.

Osbern's castle is identified with a naturally defended promontory, occupied by a slightly later motte and bailey castle, at Ewyas Harold, Herefordshire.[54] Its location, right on the Anglo-Welsh border, suggests that Osbern had received a small lordship in return for building a castle and protecting this part of the frontier from Welsh raids. Osbern, therefore, was familiar with Norman fortification techniques. Macbeth's reception of these Norman castellans cannot be attributed to Scottish hospitality alone. Instead, Macbeth probably valued their expertise and, although it is not known if he used their knowledge of fortifications, he did employ their military skills.

The origins of Macbeth's downfall may be traced to the first two years of his reign, when he failed to eliminate all potential sources of opposition. Although any challenge was most likely to come from Duncan's close relatives, Macbeth was unable to prevent Duncan's sons from escaping into exile in 1042 and did not act against Duncan's father until he rebelled in 1045. Uncannily, these events mirror those of Macbeth's own rise to power. When his cousins killed his father for the Mormaership of Moray in 1020, Macbeth survived and, twelve years later, returned to slay his surviving cousin, seize the mormaership and take his cousin's wife. Macbeth displayed a surprising inability to learn from his own experiences.

Duncan's eldest son, Malcolm, escaped, firstly to Cumbria, where he arrived in the first year of Edward the Confessor's reign, sometime between June 1042

Edward the Confessor, sitting in majesty on a backless throne or stool, with crown and sceptre. (The Bayeux Tapestry – eleventh century. By special permission of the City of Bayeux)

and June 1043. Malcolm then joined his uncle in Northumbria: 'wishing to follow the advice of Earl Siward in all his actions there, [Malcolm] made his way to him, and acting immediately on his advice and under his escort he sought an audience with King Edward . . . and was gladly admitted to his friendship and the assistance he had promised.' As Edward 'knew that he [Malcolm] had been unjustly deprived of the dignity of king, he gladly welcomed him to his allegiance and special service'.[55] The nature of Malcolm's service at Edward's Court is unclear, but it implies that he swore fealty to Edward, perhaps in return for English support. The dependent nature of the relationship is further attested by Edward's grant to Malcolm of the rich manor of Corby in Northamptonshire. It would be surprising if Edward and/or Siward had not attempted to exploit Malcolm's presence in England to advance their own interests in Scotland. By supporting Malcolm's attempt to overthrow Macbeth, Edward and Siward may have sought to install their own puppet king over Scotland.

Siward was reportedly provoked into taking action after Macbeth broke the terms of a treaty between them, although details of the treaty or its breach are unknown.[56] The existence of an agreement is uncorroborated, but it is conceivable that a settlement was reached after the Northumbrian invasion of 1046 was repelled. This may explain the apparent absence of warfare between Scotland and Northumbria until 1054. Alternatively, this may simply have provided a (retrospective?) pretext for a Northumbrian offensive.

Malcolm was presumably influential in the planning and timing of any invasion. By 1054, Malcolm was in his twenties, mature enough to be a credible contender for the kingship. Fordun's account of the events surrounding Malcolm's return to Scotland is heavily mythologised.[57] He relates in detail how the mythical MacDuff was persecuted by Macbeth but escaped, landing at 'Ravynsore' (Ravenscar, North Yorkshire). He then reported to Malcolm that 'the greater part of the chiefs of the kingdom' had sworn their allegiance to Malcolm, beseeching him to return to Scotland. Malcolm, fearing a plot, tested MacDuff's loyalty by claiming to be unfit for the kingship because of his sinful life. MacDuff tried to persuade Malcolm to return, citing parallels of historical kings who had committed similar sins, but eventually gave up with great reluctance, thus convincing Malcolm of his trustworthiness.

Once persuaded, Malcolm sent MacDuff back to Scotland with a message to his supporters that they were to prepare secretly for Malcolm's imminent return: 'Malcolm went into the presence of King Edward at the earliest opportunity, humbly petitioning him that he would graciously deign to permit certain of the nobles of England, who were willing of their own accord to set out with him for Scotland to win back his kingdom. The King kindly gave his immediate assent to his request and granted full licence to anyone who wished. Moreover he graciously promised that he himself would come to his aid with his military might, if it were necessary.'[58] Fordun also claims that, of all the English lords willing to help, Malcolm accepted assistance only from Siward. Although Malcolm may have been expected to seek support from his uncle in the first instance, the implication is that Malcolm was attempting to minimise English involvement in the campaign. Malcolm already appears to have been thinking about his relationship with the English Crown after gaining the kingship of the Scots and, conscious of the risks of becoming an English client king, limited English support to that of his Northumbrian relatives.

Alternatively, Fordun himself may have deliberately underrated the extent of English involvement for reasons of later Scottish national pride. Fordun criticises English chroniclers such as William of Malmesbury who, he claims, 'ascribes everything to Siward, depriving Malcolm of all glory in the victory, when in actual fact Malcolm alone with his own men and standard-bearer was responsible for the whole victory'.[59] Such sensitivities are understandable. In a letter to Pope Boniface VIII in 1301, Edward I attempted to justify his claimed overlordship of Scotland by fabricating historical precedents, one of which was that 'St Edward, the King of England, gave the kingdom of Scotland to Malcolm, to be held of him'.[60] English medieval chroniclers claimed that Malcolm became King of Scots 'by gift of King Edward', did homage to the English king and that 'Siward . . . appointed Malcolm king, as the King [Edward] had commanded'.[61] The most blatant example of this is in Langtoft's early fourteenth-century *Chronicle*:

> On the day of Pentecost, at Burgh in Lindsey,
> Is announced to the king at his dinner
> That duke Siward has in his custody
> Macbeth king of Scotland, who sought to betray
> The king of England of his lordship.
> Macbeth is deprived of life and kingdom;
> Malcolm of Cumberland is king of Scotland
> By gift of king Edward, and invested and seised,
> And does his homage, binds himself by fealty.[62]

Although Malcolm may not have accepted military assistance from any English noble other than Siward, the Northumbrian casualties included an unspecified number of the king's housecarls.[63] Housecarls originally formed an élite army that served as a royal bodyguard to the Danish kings of England, but they were soon adopted by the nobility, including Siward. Their presence indicates Edward's personal commitment to, and active support of, Siward's invasion. Edward's direct involvement may also be supported by claims in English medieval chronicles that Siward invaded Scotland 'at the king's command'.

Siward's Anglo-Danish forces comprised 'an army of cavalry and a powerful fleet'.[64] The routes followed by his twin-pronged attack, by land and sea, are unrecorded, but would have been dictated by strategic and tactical considerations and were probably similar to those followed by invading armies from Roman times onwards. By land, the best route was up the east coast, through Lothian, crossing the River Forth near Stirling, its lowest fordable point, and then north into the historic core of the Scottish kingdom. Wyntoun, probably drawing on earlier sources, provides the only description:

Þan withe þaim of Northumbyrlande	Then with them from Northumberland
Þis Malcome enteryt in Scotlande,	This Malcolm entered Scotland,
And past oure Forthe, doun straucht to Tay,	And past over Forth, down straight to Tay,
Vp þat wattyr þe hie waye	Up that water the high way
To þe Brynnane to gedyr haille.	Then to Birnam to gather whole.
Þar þai bade and tuk consale.	There they bade and took counsel.[65]

The naval forces, which presumably provided support to cover the army's extended supply lines, would have kept close to the Lothian coast, crossed the Firth of Forth and then sailed around Fife and up the Firth of Tay.

Although Wyntoun's is a late account, the reference to Birnam is of interest. This presages the mythological motif of the moving wood, but why Birnam? And were only Northumbrian forces mustered there? Birnam lies not south of Dunsinane, the direction from which a Northumbrian army might be expected to have advanced, but to the north-west. Perhaps significantly, Birnam lies only 3.5 km south-east of Dunkeld, on the opposite side of the River Tay. This may indicate that Dunkeld was still a focus of opposition to Macbeth, nine years after Crinán's defeat and death, and that Siward and Malcolm rendezvoused with supporters there.

Siward's campaign culminated in a single battle, but a large and bloody one. The scale of the Northumbrian invasion of 1054 and the ensuing battle clearly impressed contemporary Anglo-Saxon chroniclers: 'Earl Siward went with a great raiding-army into Scotland, and made great slaughter of Scots and put them to flight; and the King [Macbeth] escaped. Also many fell on his [Siward's] side, both Danish and English, and also his own son.' And: 'Earl Siward travelled forth with a great raiding-army into Scotland, both with raiding ship-army and with raiding land-army, and fought against the Scots, and put to flight the King Macbeth, and killed all that was best there in the land, and led away from there such a great war-booty as no man had ever got before; but his son, Osbern, and his sister's son, Siward, and some of his housecarls and also the king's, were killed there on the Day of the Seven Sleepers [27 July].'[66]

A later account claims that the dead numbered 'many thousands of Scots',[67] but a contemporary record suggests that losses were high on both sides: 'A battle between the men of Scotland and the Saxons in which fell 3000 of the Scots and 1500 of the Saxons, including Dolfinn son of Finntor'.[68] It is always

The Battle of Dunsinane, a romanticised nineteenth-century depiction by John Martin. As the Northumbrian army, led by Malcolm and Siward, marches on Dunsinane from Birnam Hill, the three sisters appear before Macbeth. Macbeth is depicted in the dress of an eighteenth- or nineteenth-century Highland clan chief. (National Galleries of Scotland)

difficult to assess the accuracy of such body counts but, even allowing for some exaggeration, these sources are consistent in depicting a hard-fought battle.

The fatalities comprised not only common foot soldiers; some casualties were eminent enough to merit individual death notices. The losses on Macbeth's side included 'all the Normans whom we mentioned before';[69] Osbern Pentecost and Hugo, the Norman castellans who had sought refuge at Macbeth's Court two years earlier, were killed fighting for their new lord. Dolfinn is unidentified, but may have been a supporter and perhaps a relative of Malcolm's; a great-grandson of Crinán's bore the same name.[70]

More significantly, the dead included Siward's nephew, also called Siward, and son, Osbern. Siward's reaction to this loss personified the heroic ideals of a war-leader, according to the *Chronicle of Huntingdon* in an episode ultimately incorporated in Shakespeare's *Macbeth*: 'Siward, the powerful Earl of Northumbria . . . sent his son on an expedition into Scotland. He was slain in the war, and when the news reached his father, he inquired: "Was his death-wound received before or behind?". The messengers replied, "Before". Then said he: "I greatly rejoice; no other death was fitting either for him or me".[71] Whereupon Siward led an army into Scotland, and having defeated the King and ravaged the whole kingdom, he reduced it to subjection himself.' After defeating Macbeth, Siward returned to Northumbria and died in York the following year. A warrior to the end, Siward spent his final hours in his armour on the city walls, rather than on his deathbed.

Although the precise date of this battle and something of its casualties are known, its site is not recorded in contemporary sources. As a result, it is most accurately referred to as the 'Battle of the Seven Sleepers', from the festival on which it was fought. The first reference to its location is not until the early fifteenth century, when Wyntoun tersely describes how Siward's army sped from Birnam to Dunsinane under its leafy camouflage, where it 'passed against' Macbeth.[72] On this evidence alone, the Battle of the Seven Sleepers appears to have been at or around Macbeth's fortress at Dunsinane.[73] Despite the source's late date, this location is widely accepted and has never been challenged convincingly. Indeed, Dunsinane is a very plausible site. It is situated within the

Dunsinane Hill (centre), according to medieval chronicles the location of Macbeth's fortress and his defeat in battle by an Anglo-Scandinavian army led by Malcolm and Siward. This picture of the southern end of the Sidlaw Hills, viewed from the west, also shows the King's Seat (left) from which, according to local tradition, Macbeth threw himself to his death after the battle. (The Author)

historic core of the Scottish kingdom, only 12 km north-east of Scone, and may
have been an early medieval royal fortress. Northumbrian strategy appears to
have been to strike at the heartland of Macbeth's kingdom, presumably with the
objective of eliminating Macbeth and/or proceeding to Scone and installing
Malcolm as king. However, the proximity and strength of Macbeth's army left
Malcolm and Siward no alternative but to join battle and fight it out.

Clearly, the invasion and ensuing battle did not go entirely to plan; although
Macbeth and his army were routed, Macbeth escaped, Northumbrian losses were
heavy and Scotland was only partially conquered. Fordun, puzzlingly, does not
mention the battle, but provides a plausible explanation for the incomplete
nature of Malcolm and Siward's victory: 'Malcolm . . . had not yet crossed the
border of the kingdom, when he heard that the whole population of the kingdom
was in turmoil, and divided into factions between Macbeth and MacDuff.
MacDuff as he was going ahead had spread the news [of his coming] . . . So
Malcolm with his soldiers increased his speed, and did not rest until he had
assembled a strong army with contingents joining in from all sides.'[74] Malcolm
and Siward had not only lost the element of surprise but the effectiveness of their
army was degraded by having to join battle immediately after a forced march of at
least 200 km. Macbeth's army, fighting on familiar terrain and prepared for the
Northumbrian advance, was able to inflict heavy casualties.

Against this background, Siward's victory in the Battle of the Seven Sleepers is
all the more impressive. Northumbrian success may be attributed to a
combination of sheer strength of numbers and the quality of the troops involved,
such as the housecarls of Siward and Edward the Confessor. Increasing support for
Malcolm within Scotland was probably also a factor; Fordun remarks that
Malcolm's support grew as Macbeth's ebbed away. Although Fordun elevates
Malcolm's role in the invasion at Siward's expense, it is clear that this battle was
not simply a case of English versus Scottish, but a coalition of Northumbrian
forces and Malcolm's Scottish supporters, supported by Edward the Confessor,
which took on Macbeth and his army, which included a Norman element.

The Battle of the Seven Sleepers smashed Macbeth's grip on the Scottish
kingship and split Scotland in two. Malcolm's territorial gains are usually claimed
to have been restricted to southern Scotland: Lothian, Cumbria and Strathclyde.
However, this would have provided a poor springboard from which to conquer the
area north of the Forth–Clyde isthmus, comprising the greater part of Scottish
territory and the kingdom's historic core, only three years later. It seems more
likely that the area under Malcolm's jurisdiction extended at least as far north as
the scene of his victory. If this was at Dunsinane, which seems probable, the

Malcolm III and his queen, later saint, Margaret, as depicted in the sixteenth-century *Seton Armorial*. (National Library of Scotland Acc. 9309, no. 5/ by courtesy of Sir Francis Ogilvy, Bart)

territory conquered would have included Scotland's heartland with its historic royal centres, upon which control of the kingship rested. But Malcolm's power may have stretched much further north, probably as far as the Mounth. This is supported by Fordun's romantic, but misleading, picture of how: 'Macbeth, perceiving that his might was diminishing daily, while Malcolm's was increasing, suddenly left the southern regions and made for the north, where he thought he could defend himself more securely in the narrow defiles and hidden depths of the forests.'[75] But Macbeth was not on the run; he had withdrawn beyond the Mounth into his Moray fastness, where his tenacity and strength of support ensured that his kingship survived for another three years. Gruoch's fate is unrecorded.

Malcolm's difficulty in exploiting his victory may also be attributable to the other priorities he faced after the Battle of the Seven Sleepers. These would have been to consolidate his hold over southern Scotland and establish the legitimacy of his rule there. The latter would have been particularly important because Macbeth's survival and retention of a residual northern kingdom cast doubt on the legitimacy of Malcolm's kingship. Malcolm, however, held the trump card – the political and historic heartland of the Scottish kingdom, including the royal centre at Scone. The possession of Scotland's royal powerbases was fundamental to acquiring and maintaining the kingship. Malcolm's inauguration at Scone according to traditional practice would have demonstrated unambiguously that he was the rightful King of Scots.

There seems little doubt that Malcolm was inaugurated King of Scots after the Battle of the Seven Sleepers in 1054. The *Chronicle of Melrose* records that Siward installed Malcolm in the kingship after Macbeth's defeat, which it conflates with his death three years later.[76] But as Siward died in 1055, Malcolm's inauguration must have taken place after the battle, not after Macbeth's death.

The reason for the absence of corroborating texts for these events is clear. The incomplete nature of Malcolm's victory has produced an enduring anomaly in Scottish regnal history. Both medieval chroniclers and modern historians invariably date the start of Malcolm's reign not from his (albeit partial) victory over Macbeth in 1054 but from Macbeth's death in 1057 or, following Marianus' *Chronicle*, from the death of Macbeth's successor, his stepson Lulach, in 1058.[77] Fordun, for example, states that Malcolm was not inaugurated at Scone until after Macbeth and Lulach had been killed and Malcolm had 'overthrown or brought into his peace all his enemies everywhere'.[78] Following his misdating of Lulach's death, Fordun claims that Malcolm was inaugurated at Scone on St Mark's Day (25 April), 1057; the same date in 1058 is presumably intended.

The original reasons for this discrepancy are apparent. Although it incorporated great cultural and linguistic diversity, Scotland had been a unified kingdom since the absorption of the Picts by the Scots in the mid-ninth

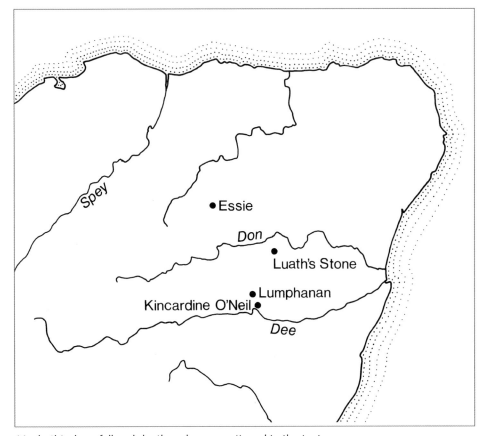

Macbeth's downfall and death – places mentioned in the text.

century. The indivisibility of kingdom and kingship was central to the concept of Scotland. In keeping with this, medieval chroniclers were reluctant to accept the reality that Scotland was briefly split between two rival kings, favouring instead a conventional linear succession, with Malcolm assuming the kingship on Lulach's death. This orthodoxy is perpetuated by historians to this day.

Malcolm, presumably conscious that his father had been killed by Macbeth beyond the Mounth, bided his time before striking northwards into Moray. He waited for three years before taking the war beyond the Dee, into Macbeth's residual kingdom. Macbeth's presence near the southern limit of the territory under his control provided the opportunity Malcolm was seeking and, in 1057, 'Macbeth . . . was killed in Lumphanan by Malcolm'.[79] Other sources add that this occurred 'in battle' and that 'Malcolm cut him [Macbeth] off by a cruel death'.[80] Fordun describes how: 'Malcolm by a quick march unexpectedly pursued him [Macbeth] over the mountains and as far as Lumphanan, and there suddenly intercepted him in a light skirmish, and killed him along with the few who resisted . . . For all the people that Macbeth led out to battle knew full well that Malcolm was their true lord; therefore they refused to fight a battle against him, and fled away and deserted the field of battle at the first sound of trumpets.'[81] Malcolm appears to have mounted a successful surprise attack. Fordun, however, not only misdates Macbeth's death, but attributes the encounter to Malcolm's pursuit of Macbeth immediately after the Battle of the Seven Sleepers. Here Fordun conflates events, telescoping the chronology to link directly Macbeth's flight and death.

It is unclear whether Macbeth prolonged the war in the north after 1054, perhaps by mounting raids south of the Mounth. Certainly, Macbeth did not cower in the security of his royal centres on the Moray Firth, as the location of his death reveals. Macbeth's presence at Lumphanan may have been linked to its proximity to routes across the Mounth, as Fordun infers. Lumphanan lies only 5 km north of the principal pass through the Mounth at Kincardine O'Neil, on the River Dee, and its strategic significance is perhaps indicated by the Peel of Lumphanan, a thirteenth-century motte and bailey castle. Malcolm's pursuit of Macbeth over the Mounth may have been in the aftermath of an unsuccessful raid by Macbeth, or a larger attack intended to recover his kingdom.

Macbeth died in August, on 'the same Mass of St Mary' on which Duncan met his death;[82] 16 August 1057 is probably intended. Macbeth was killed seventeen years to the day since he slayed Duncan. This 'dark synchronicity'[83] may have been no coincidence, but a deliberate and successful attempt by Malcolm to avenge his father's murder on a symbolically significant date. The uncertainty that surrounds so many aspects of Macbeth's life also follows him after death, with alternative traditions about his burial place.

It is difficult to assess the achievements of Macbeth's reign. Although Macbeth is widely portrayed by both medieval chroniclers and modern historians as a wise and good king and his reign as a prosperous one, these conclusions do not appear to be based on historical evidence, but attest the mythologising of Macbeth. However, his pilgrimage to Rome clearly distinguishes him as a king who was international in his outlook and experience. This contrasts with all previous and many later Scottish kings. Indeed, Macbeth was the only Scottish king ever to go on pilgrimage to Rome. Macbeth's other achievement was his sheer tenacity. His seventeen-year reign was reasonably long by the standards of early medieval

The Peel of Lumphanan, a thirteenth-century motte and bailey castle. The flat top of the artificial earthen mound (the motte) would have been occupied by a timber castle, while the surrounding enclosure (the bailey) was probably defended by a turf rampart rather than the more usual timber palisade. The wall visible around the summit of the motte is a product of late eighteenth-century landscaping. (Cambridge University Collection of Air Photographs: copyright reserved)

Scotland in general, but even more so given the circumstances in which he gained the kingship. This same resoluteness is also apparent following his defeat in the Battle of the Seven Sleepers; Macbeth not only survived, but escaped to retain his kingship over a diminished northern kingdom for a further three years.

LULACH'S BRIEF REIGN

Even after Macbeth's death, Malcolm did not gain control of Moray immediately. Instead, Macbeth was succeeded by his stepson, Lulach. Although this supports the theory that Macbeth had no children of his own, it also reflects the continued significance attached to the descendants of Boite, the sometime *tanaise* of Malcolm II and Lulach's maternal grandfather. It was on this descent, not his relationship to Macbeth, that Lulach's claim to the Scottish kingship presumably rested. This is reflected in Lulach's description in terms of his relationship to Boite through the male line: 'Lulach, nephew of the son of Boite'.[84]

Like Macbeth, his father's cousin, Lulach belonged to the hereditary aristocracy of Moray; his father, Gillacomgain, was mormaer from 1029, until killed by Macbeth in 1032. As Macbeth's adopted son, Lulach may have held prominent office during Macbeth's reign. But it cannot be considered significant that the *Annals of Tigernach* describe Lulach as King and Macbeth as High-King of Scotland.[85] This does not imply that Lulach was a king under Macbeth's high-kingship, but simply reflects Irish perceptions and terminology. Given his pedigree, Lulach is more likely to have been Mormaer of Moray during Macbeth's kingship and was probably also Macbeth's *tanaise*.

After Macbeth's death notice in Marianus' *Chronicle*, a marginal note records that 'Lulach succeeded' to the kingship.[86] Fordun claims that: 'Immediately after the death of Macbeth certain members of his family . . . took his kinsman Lulach . . . to Scone, placed him on the royal throne and made him king. For they expected that the people would gladly obey him as their king. No one however wished to obey him or to have any part in what they had done.'[87] Yet it is inconceivable that Lulach could have acquired the kingship without such support. It seems more likely that Lulach was King of Scots in name only. Indeed, his 'kingdom' probably comprised no more than the province of Moray, which Macbeth had retained after 1054.

Against this background, it is highly unlikely that Lulach was inaugurated at Scone, as this region had been under Malcolm's control since the Battle of the Seven Sleepers. Instead, the eagerness of medieval chroniclers to formalise the lineal succession of a unitary kingship may have resulted in the perception of Lulach as a 'proper' King of Scots, leading Fordun to assume that he was inaugurated at Scone in accordance with ancient tradition. This passage simply reflects the chronicler's expectations, based on historical precedent. But it is interesting, and reassuring, that the chroniclers did not attempt to make their task easier by erasing Lulach from the historical record; Lulach's inclusion attests their assiduousness.

There is no evidence to support claims that Lulach and Malcolm 'were fellow conspirators [against Macbeth] who fell out', becoming 'rival claimants' for the kingship in 1057–8.[88] There was no competition; Malcolm had held the kingship and most of Scotland for three years, enabling him to consolidate his position, while Lulach had recently inherited a peripheral province from his step-father. Lulach did not possess the qualities and experience that enabled Macbeth to seize and retain the kingship. Indeed, Fordun even implies that Lulach may not have actively sought the kingship, but that he was propelled to the throne by Macbeth's relatives, eager to fill the void created by Macbeth's death. Lulach became 'king' only because Malcolm was unable to capitalise on his victory over Macbeth at Lumphanan in 1057 by immediately following it up with the conquest of Moray. Malcolm's forces may have been overstretched and/or hampered by the onset of winter in the Grampians.

Lulach's survival was shortlived. Indeed, his reign was the briefest of any Scottish king, before or since. A marginal note in Marianus' *Chronicle* records that 'Lulach reigned from the Nativity of St Mary to the Mass of St Patrick, in the month of March'.[89] Although influenced by the confusion surrounding the precise date of Macbeth's death, this indicates that Lulach reigned only from 16 August 1057 to 17 March 1058. As *Duan Albanach* states: 'After Macbeth . . . seven months in the reign of Lulach'.[90]

The sources give no details of Lulach's reign, but it was so brief and his authority so limited in extent that it would be surprising if he made any notable achievements. Indeed, Lulach's reign is overshadowed by his death, which is better recorded. The regnal lists frequently exaggerate the shortness of his reign, assigning it between four-and-a-half months and as little as one month, so short that one list gives four years in error for four months.[91] The regnal lists also record that 'Lulach the stupid (*fatuus*) . . . was killed in Essie, [near Rhynie] in Strathbogie', while a more detailed and sympathetic account states: 'The unfortunate Lulach was king for three months: he fell by the arms of the same Malcolm. The man met his fate at Essie, in Strathbogie; thus, alas! through lack of caution, the hapless king perished.'[92]

Malcolm, presumably emboldened by his success against Macbeth at Lumphanan seven months earlier, this time struck further into Moray, slaying Lulach. Strathbogie was of great strategic significance, comprising a major route into Moray through the Mounth. That Lulach met his death within Moray probably indicates the limited extent of his authority and/or his poor military skills and strength. The nature of the encounter is unclear; the *Annals of Ulster*[93] records that Lulach was slain in battle by Malcolm, although Fordun was aware of conflicting traditions: 'Malcolm . . . sent out his thanes in all directions to track him [Lulach] down, but for four months their efforts were expended in vain, until as they were searching in the higher regions, he was found in . . . Essie in . . . Strathbogie, and they killed him along with his followers, or as some report, Malcolm came upon him by accident in the same place and killed him.'[94] The reference to Lulach's 'lack of caution' suggests that he was surprised or tricked by Malcolm. The latter is substantiated by the *Annals of Tigernach*, which record that Malcolm killed Lulach 'by treachery',[95] and may be reflected in Lulach's nickname, 'the stupid'. Alternatively, as one of history's losers, perhaps a later scribe could not resist the temptation to attach posthumously a derisory nickname to such a transient king.

As with the last three years of Macbeth's kingship, the nature of Lulach's kingship has caused some problems of interpretation, originating with those medieval chroniclers who perceived Scotland and its kingship to be indivisible and therefore sought to portray a neat, lineal succession. Accordingly, Lulach is recognised as a King of Scots by medieval chroniclers and modern historians alike, his brief reign in 1057–8 standing out as an anomaly against the 'official' accession of Malcolm III in 1057. Indeed, it was probably the medieval perception of Lulach as King of Scots that led Fordun to assume that Lulach was inaugurated at Scone and to claim that Malcolm was only installed after Lulach's death.

As with Macbeth, there are conflicting traditions about Lulach's burial place, with medieval regnal lists and chronicles all stating Iona and local tradition maintaining that he was buried in Essie. With Lulach died the aspirations of the Mormaers of Moray for the Scottish kingship. However, his death did not mark the end of the hereditary Mormaership of Moray or the periodic violence that existed between Moray and the Scottish kings.

CHAPTER 4

The Making of the Myth

The historical Macbeth described in the previous chapters will be unfamiliar to many readers acquainted with Shakespeare's *Macbeth*. Macbeth murdered Duncan for the Scottish kingship and was defeated, though not killed, by a Northumbrian army under Malcolm and Siward, but there the similarities end. The historical and dramatic Macbeths, though clearly related, are very different figures. How did the historical Macbeth become the personification of ambition and evil famously portrayed by Shakespeare? And why?

The answers lie in the various myths that developed around the historical Macbeth. This process probably began during Macbeth's reign and was certainly underway during that of his successor, Malcolm III. Although there are gaps, particularly in the earlier stages of its development, the evolution of the mythological Macbeth can be traced through many medieval and later Scottish sources. It is to this sequence of myths, telling and retelling the story of Macbeth, that the transformation of the historical figure into the character of Shakespeare's tragedy may be attributed. But although Shakespeare's *Macbeth* represents the culmination of the myth in its most famous form, its evolution did not stop there. Since the eighteenth century, the myth has appeared in an expanding range of artistic media, while ostensibly historical studies have continued to generate new and recycle old myths.

The mythical Macbeth could be studied thematically, tracing the appearance, development and literary parallels of characters, events and motifs through time. But instead of focusing on individual elements divorced from their historical and literary contexts, this chapter takes a chronological approach, examining each successive surviving form of the myth. This enables the evolution of the myth to be followed over the past 900 years, from Macbeth's lifetime to the present day. It also facilitates the interpretation of the appearance of new elements within the myth.

ORIGINS OF THE MYTH

As contemporary Anglo-Saxon and Irish annals attest, the manner in which Macbeth acquired and lost the Scottish kingship attracted considerable attention. Within Scotland, these events presumably aroused even greater interest and probably inspired the composition of poems or tales concerning Macbeth and his exploits. The background to this literature lies in the tradition of courtly and heroic poetry that is found throughout medieval Europe. In Scotland, most of this poetry would have been composed and transmitted orally in Gaelic, as both literacy and writing materials were restricted to learned clerics and some royal officials. Only as a result of being committed to writing at a later date, usually in an ecclesiastical context, was this oral literature preserved. Little is known about the forms this courtly tradition took during the eleventh century because of the poor survival of early medieval Scottish texts. However, some clues exist.

Although it survives mostly in later manuscripts, the courtly or bardic literature of early medieval Ireland is much better preserved than that of Scotland. It includes royal genealogies, elegies (laments), eulogies (praise poems), and satires. The Irish bardic poet or *fili* (pl. *filid*) was: 'a professor of literature and a man of letters, highly trained in the use of a polished literary medium, belonging to a hereditary caste in an aristocratic society, holding an official position therein by virtue of his training, his learning, his knowledge of the history and traditions of his country and his clan. . . . He was often a public official, a chronicler, a political essayist, a keen and satirical observer of his fellow-countrymen'.[1] The *filid* combined the roles of poet, historian, mythologist and royal propagandist. Early Irish law tracts attest the hierarchical grading of poets and their high social status; a poet of the most superior grade possessed the same rank and privileges as a petty king (*rí tuaithe*) and sat at the top table, opposite the king and queen, in the king's hall.

The existence of a similar élite of professional poets in eleventh-century Scotland may be inferred from *Duan Albanach*, which is addressed to 'all the learned ones of Scotland', the Scottish *filid*. Moreover, traces of a Scottish courtly tradition survive in the regnal lists, royal genealogies, chronicles and historical poems. This literature was the product of royal patronage, while the dedication to Macbeth of a mythological poem about the Picts indicates that it was composed under Macbeth's patronage. Fordun's description of the inauguration of Alexander III reveals that the position of the King's poet survived in Scotland until at least 1249, when the poet played a prominent role in this important state occasion,² while a hereditary bardic order survived in Gaelic Scotland until after the Middle Ages.³

The earliest poetry concerning Macbeth would have been composed within this bardic tradition, during Macbeth's reign and by his own Court poet. By analogy with Irish and later Scottish bardic examples, this poetry probably included eulogies, perhaps praising Macbeth's crushing of his opponents, his seizing of the kingship, his regal qualities and the benevolence of his reign. Although none of these poems have survived in their original form, some verses from just such a poem are preserved in a later source.

IN PRAISE OF MACBETH: THE *PROPHECY OF BERCHÁN*

The *Prophecy of Berchán* takes its name from an Irish saint whose prophecies it claims to record. Although Berchán's identity is debatable, he was probably the founding abbot of the monastery of Clonsast, Co. Offaly, in the late seventh century. But despite its title, the *Prophecy* is neither a genuine prophecy poem nor the work of Berchán, on whom it was 'fostered' at a later date. Instead, the *Prophecy* is a composite work, created by more than one poet during the eleventh century, but survives only in later manuscripts. Its fourth section is a verse history of Scottish kings from the mid-ninth to the late eleventh centuries.

The *Prophecy* attests the close cultural links between Scotland and Ireland during the eleventh century. It is in Middle Irish and employs Irish terminology, as evidenced by its references to the 'high-kingship' of Scotland, and was presumably composed in Ireland. But the *Prophecy* also displays a close knowledge of Scottish kings and the geography of eastern Scotland, reflecting the poet's travels or the provenance of the earlier poetry it incorporates. Acknowledging this dual nature, the *Prophecy* may be described as 'Hiberno-Scottish'.

Cryptic in nature, the *Prophecy* refers to kings not by name but by sobriquets, distinguishing features or key events from their reigns. Although much of this information is unique, making the *Prophecy* an important source of information about early Scottish kings, these events are often difficult to interpret or reconcile with other material. Moreover, the inclusion of several apparently factual errors has led to persistent doubts about its historical value. Macbeth is the subject of three stanzas:

> After that the red king will take sovereignty, the kingship of noble
> Scotland of hilly aspect; after slaughter of Gaels, after slaughter of
> Vikings, the generous king of Fortriu will take sovereignty.

The red, tall, golden-haired one, he will be pleasant to me among them; Scotland will be brimful west and east during the reign of the furious red one.

Thirty years over Scotland, a high-king ruling; in the middle of Scone he will spew blood on the evening of a night after a duel.[4]

Macbeth, however, reigned for seventeen years and was killed at Lumphanan. Although this suggests that the *Prophecy* is fundamentally flawed as a historical source, an alternative interpretation underlines its importance for the study of Macbeth and the origins of the mythology surrounding him.

The *Prophecy* is unambiguously favourable to Macbeth, describing him as 'generous' and possessing regal good looks. The title 'king of Fortriu' is a deliberate archaism emphasising the legitimacy of Macbeth's kingship. The rulers of the Pictish province of Fortriu, which comprised Strathearn, Gowrie and Angus, had been the dominant political force south of the Mouth and may have periodically extended their authority northwards.[5] Indeed, from the late seventh century the kingship of Fortriu was synonymous with that of the Picts as a whole. Even after the Picts disappeared, the title retained a strong political symbolism; Fortriu was still the power base of the Scottish kings, just as it had been of the Pictish kings before them. The poet was bestowing on Macbeth the legitimacy conferred by a Pictish past.

Macbeth's reign is also described positively, as a time of abundance. This echoes concepts of early, originally pagan, Celtic kingship, in which the king guaranteed the fertility of his kingdom and his continued kingship by possessing various sacral powers and observing both practical and ritual obligations and proscriptions.[6] This was a popular theme in early Irish literature, where it appears as *fír flathemon*, the 'prince's truth'; the just rule of a righteous king. According to the seventh-century *Audacht Morainn* (*Testament of Morann*):

It is through the prince's truth that abundances of great tree-fruit of the great wood are tasted.
It is through the prince's truth that milk-yields of great cattle are maintained.
It is through the prince's truth that there is abundance of every high, tall corn.
It is through the prince's truth that abundance of fish swim in streams.
It is through the prince's truth that fair children are well begotten.[7]

The *Prophecy*'s description of Macbeth's reign as a prosperous one – 'Scotland will be brimful west and east during the reign of the furious red one' – mirrors this theme, unambiguously expressing his right to the throne as a just king.

But Macbeth did not rule by right alone. His 'taking' of the kingship is referred to twice, praising Macbeth's boldness and courage and emphasising the significance attached to this action from an early date. The 'slaughter of Gaels', if not describing Duncan's defeats by the Orkney Vikings, may refer to the violence that accompanied Macbeth's seizing of the kingship. Macbeth's description as 'the furious red one' is a reference to his battle fury and praises his prowess on the battlefield. In keeping with the character of early medieval kingship, the *Prophecy* portrays Macbeth as a war leader; Macbeth the warrior king.

This consistently positive portrayal of Macbeth indicates that these verses originally belonged to a praise poem composed for, and probably commissioned by, Macbeth himself. This interpretation is reinforced by the poet's statement that he expects Macbeth to be 'pleasant' to him, presumably in reward for composing such a fine eulogy. The *Prophecy*'s verses about Macbeth must have been composed during Macbeth's own lifetime. This explains some otherwise anomalous passages. In particular, Macbeth's 'thirty years over Scotland' may now be interpreted as the poet's way of wishing Macbeth a lengthy reign, disguised as prophecy. Thirty years was a very long reign by early medieval Scottish standards and, significantly, one year longer than the reign of Malcolm II, Macbeth's probable grandfather. The poet was praising Macbeth by predicting that he would occupy the kingship for longer than any Scottish king within living memory. Rounded reign lengths are also a poetic convention that recurs throughout the *Prophecy*. The information about Macbeth's death is inaccurate because these verses were composed during his lifetime.

In contrast, the *Prophecy* states accurately that Duncan reigned for only 'five years with a half', revealing that these verses were composed *after* his death.[8] In addition, the overtly negative description of Duncan as 'a king whose name is the many maladies' suggests that these verses also belonged to, or were derived from, the same praise poem to Macbeth. Such sentiments are unlikely to have prevailed if these verses had been composed during the reign of Malcolm III, Duncan's son.

The reference to Macbeth's fate is also prophetic. Emphasising Macbeth's bravery and providing a fitting end for a warrior king, the verses foretell Macbeth's death while defending his kingship, possibly in single combat. Symbolically, these prophesied events were set at Scone, the royal inauguration centre. The poet's 'mistake' is paralleled by the stanzas on Malcolm III, which predict that he will die in Rome, presumably on pilgrimage.[9] In fact, Malcolm died attacking Northumbria without ever reaching Rome.

The *Prophecy*'s treatment of Macbeth and his reign is characterised by its consistently positive representation and the apparent errors concerning his reign length and death. Only by interpreting these verses as a previously unidentified praise poem (or part of one) composed for Macbeth do they make sense. They are therefore of the greatest significance, providing a direct link with the historical Macbeth, King of Scots. These stanzas preserve a eulogy to Macbeth and attest the former existence of an otherwise lost body of bardic praise poetry. This poetry, or perhaps the *Prophecy* itself, exerted a profound influence on the mythological tradition concerning Macbeth which can be traced throughout the Middle Ages to the present day.

THE MYTH DIVERGES: *DUAN ALBANACH*

A different tradition emerges in another eleventh-century verse history, *Duan Albanach*. Literally meaning the *Scottish Poem*, it is also known as *A Eolcha Alban Uile* (*O all You Learned Ones of Scotland*), after its dedicatory first line. Based on a Scottish regnal list turned into Middle Irish verse, *Duan Albanach* is a history of Scottish kings from the mythological and eponymous Albanus to Malcolm III. Unlike the *Prophecy of Berchán*, *Duan Albanach* does not display a knowledge of Scottish geography and refers to the Scottish kings 'from the east', indicating that it was composed in Ireland, presumably by an Irish poet.

Duan Albanach ends with Malcolm III, its penultimate stanza confirming that it was composed during his reign:

> Malcolm is king now,
> the son of Duncan the handsome, of lively aspect;
> his duration no one knows
> but the Learned One who is Learned.[10]

Duan Albanach is sympathetic to Malcolm and his lineage, describing Duncan, Malcolm's father, as 'pure wise', 'handsome, of lively aspect' and 'of princely visage'. The contrast with the *Prophecy of Berchán*'s 'king whose name is the many maladies' could not be greater.

This favourable disposition towards Duncan is not accompanied by a hostility to Macbeth. Instead, he is referred to simply as 'Macbeth the famed'. Although this indicates the poet's awareness of traditions concerning Macbeth, these are conspicuous by their absence. Other than this, it only gives Macbeth's reign length, accurately, as seventeen years. *Duan Albanach*'s terse treatment of Macbeth contrasts markedly with that of the *Prophecy of Berchán* and reflects their different contexts of composition and intended audiences. The 'learned ones' to whom *Duan Albanach* is addressed may have included Malcolm's own Court poet(s), thus ensuring that Malcolm and his father were treated with due respect. At the same time, the poet bore no grudge against Macbeth, with the result that he receives only a laconic and neutral reference.

The *Prophecy of Berchán* and *Duan Albanach* are of great importance in tracing the origins and evolution of the mythological Macbeth. They reveal not only that the mythologising of Macbeth was already underway during his own lifetime, but also that two contrasting mythological traditions had emerged within a generation of his death. The first, based on a praise poem to Macbeth and incorporated in the *Prophecy of Berchán*, depicts Macbeth and his reign positively, while maligning Duncan. The second, represented by *Duan Albanach*, is sympathetic towards Duncan and, though neutral, anticipates Macbeth's negative portrayal in later sources. These sources illustrate the contrasting portrayals of the mythological Macbeth during the eleventh century and may be attributed to their different historical and political contexts of composition.

Duan Albanach marks the beginning of the transformation of Duncan into a national martyr. But it is simplistic to conclude that subsequent forms of the myth were dictated by the pro-Duncan bias of the later poets and chroniclers commissioned by the House of Atholl to damn Macbeth's memory. Instead, various strands are detectable within successive versions of the Macbeth myth, some of them favourable to Macbeth, others critical of Duncan;[11] several accounts portray *both* kings unfavourably. Poets and chroniclers were constrained, to varying degrees, by the sources they drew upon and the influence of earlier versions of the myth is apparent in the perpetuation of some early mythological themes.

'FRUITFUL SEASONS': THE *VERSE CHRONICLE*

Only a single, laconic mythological reference to Macbeth survives from the next three centuries. The *Verse Chronicle*, also known as *Liber Extravagans*, is a Scottish king list, in Latin couplets, to which has been added relevant annalistic entries. The *Chronicle* begins with Kenneth mac Alpin and ends with the death of William ('the Lion') in 1214, indicating that it was originally composed during the reign of Alexander II (1214–49), although it was extended at least twice during the thirteenth century. It was then copied into the margins of the *Chronicle of Melrose*, probably before 1264. Nevertheless, the *Verse Chronicle* is sometimes mistakenly attributed to Ailred (1109?–66), Abbot of Rievaulx, who was at the Court of David I during the 1130s.

The *Verse Chronicle* is the first source to portray Macbeth's reign as illegitimate: 'Duncan, King of the Scots died, and Macbeth usurped his kingdom'.[12] In contrast, 'Malcolm, the son of Duncan, succeeded to the kingdom of Scots by hereditary right'. But the *Chronicle* incorporates divergent mythological traditions. Implicitly reiterating Macbeth's status as a righteous ruler, it states that 'Macbeth was King of Scots for seventeen years and in his reign there were fruitful seasons'. First observed in the *Prophecy of Berchán*, the portrayal of Macbeth's reign as a period of abundance and prosperity is the most enduring element of the Macbeth myth.

THE FOUNDATION OF THE MYTH: FORDUN'S *CHRONICLE*

Little is known of John of Fordun. He probably came from Fordoun, Kincardineshire, while the continuer of his chronicle describes him as 'chaplain of the church of Aberdeen', suggesting that he was a chantry priest in Aberdeen Cathedral.[13] Fordun ambitiously attempted to compile a history of Scotland from the earliest times to the present day, the first chronicler to do so. Although he had only reached the death of David I (1153) when he died, probably sometime between 1371 and 1377, Fordun had completed the first five books and left extensive notes in preparation for the remainder.

The *Chronicle of the Scottish People* (*Chronica Gentis Scotorum*), written in Latin prose, was based on extensive documentary research, which perhaps began as early as 1363. In pursuit of his research, Fordun travelled 'in the meadow of Britain and among the oracles of Ireland, through cities and towns, through universities and colleges, through churches and monasteries, talking with historians and visiting chronographers'.[14] Fordun faced numerous problems in constructing a continuous historical narrative from diverse and frequently contradictory sources. Nevertheless, his *Chronicle* attests his skill and diligence as a researcher and writer of history and reveals him to have been 'a careful compiler drawing upon material not otherwise known to have been preserved'.[15]

Fordun's *Chronicle* marks a key stage in the evolution of the Macbeth myth. For the first time, the myth appears in a developed form, displaying a considerable elaboration on the embryonic forms discussed above. But it is unclear if this is attributable to Fordun's abilities as a chronicler or to the poor survival of earlier versions of the myth. In Fordun's *Chronicle*, Macbeth emerges for the first time as a murderer, usurper and tyrant. Embellishing earlier annalistic records, Fordun is the first medieval chronicler to accuse Macbeth of murdering Duncan; Duncan 'was killed through the wickedness of the family of the murderers of both his grandfather and great-grandfather, chief among whom was Macbeth son of Findlaech, by whom he was fatally wounded in secret at Bothgofnane'.[16] Fordun stresses the illegitimacy of Macbeth's kingship; he is described as an 'unlawful king', regarded by his subjects as 'a man of no higher rank than themselves'.[17]

Under Macbeth, the Scots were 'oppressed under a tyrannous regime, neither able nor daring to rise in revolt, but always brooding over the cruel death of their king [Duncan] in their hearts and the unjust banishment of his heir [Malcolm] over such a long period of time'.[18] Macbeth:

condemned to various punishments many of the magnates who were bound by a vow of conspiracy and especially those whom he knew were close friends of Malcolm. Some of them he consigned to execution, some he thrust into squalid prison, others he reduced to extreme poverty by confiscating all their goods. Several also fearing the ferocious sentence of the king fled from the kingdom, leaving behind their lands and their children and their wives as well.[19]

MacDuff, Malcolm's principal supporter and 'the excellent, noble and loyal thane of Fife', makes his first appearance in the myth.[20] After MacDuff fled Scotland to persuade Malcolm to return, Macbeth reacted by: 'laying siege to all MacDuff's castles and forts, he captured lands and estates. Whatever was valuable or seemed desirable he commanded its confiscation and, carrying off all MacDuff's property, he ordered it to be placed forthwith in his own treasury. Moreover he caused him to be publicly proclaimed . . . an exile for ever, stripped of all his estates and all the rest of his possessions.'[21] But Macbeth's oppression and MacDuff's existence are uncorroborated by contemporary sources. Moreover, Macbeth's tolerance of Crinán as Abbot of Dunkeld until 1045 is hardly the hallmark of a tyrant.

Fordun was presumably influenced by earlier sources, but his motivation in portraying Macbeth so negatively was also political. Compiling the first complete narrative history of Scotland, Fordun emphasised the continuity of Scottish kingship to counter English claims of historical overlordship. Macbeth was perceived to have violently interrupted an otherwise unbroken and ancient pattern of royal succession, killing Duncan and usurping the kingship. Macbeth, of course, was not unique in acquiring the kingship by murdering his predecessor but the central issue was his ineligibility for the kingship; this attracted the chroniclers' hostility. As Bower, Fordun's continuer, states: 'up to this time, thank God, the posterity of this unconquered king [Malcolm II] have happily reigned in succession [in Scotland], except that during certain corrupt periods Macbeth and the idiot Lulach, Donald Ban [1093–7] [II] and Duncan [1094] in turn usurped the kingdom for short periods of time.'[22]

Fordun's *Chronicle* established the framework of the mythology surrounding Macbeth. Its portrayal of a murderous and tyrannical Macbeth had an enduring influence on both medieval chroniclers and later historians, ensuring Macbeth's unfavourable portrayal throughout the Middle Ages and beyond.

DEMONISING MACBETH: WYNTOUN'S *ORYGYNALE CRONYKIL*

Andrew of Wyntoun (*c.* 1355–1422) was probably born in Portmoak parish, beside Loch Leven, Kinross-shire, and educated in St Andrews. A canon regular of the Augustinian priory in St Andrews, he became prior of the dependent priory on St Serf's Island in Loch Leven in 1395, an office he held until 1413. It was on St Serf's Island that Wyntoun composed his *Orygynale Cronykil of Scotland*, a metrical history of Scotland from the Creation until the accession of James I (1406). Its rhyming couplets and Scots language give the *Orygynale Cronykil* a distinctive style: 'The quality of the verse is quaint, and often perfunctory rather than in any way inspired, but at its best it is eminently quotable and often provides memorable references to incidents both well-known and little-known.'[23]

The *Orygynale Cronykil* is an important source because Wyntoun drew on earlier, possibly oral, traditions that no longer survive. These sources may have been preserved in the now lost *Register* of St Andrews and perhaps included a mid-thirteenth-century chronicle of Scotland to Malcolm III by Veremondus, possibly a monk of St Andrews. Wyntoun's unique reference material makes the *Orygynale Cronykil* the earliest surviving source of a great deal of information concerning Macbeth and his reign.

The Loch Leven connection has prompted claims that Macbeth's gifts to the Culdees there would have ensured a lasting interest in the King within the monastic community and that this would have ensured Wyntoun's direct access to reliable and unique historical information concerning Macbeth. This is important because Wyntoun's Macbeth bears a discernible resemblance to Shakespeare's Macbeth: 'If . . . Wyntoun was drawing on genuine recollections of the man himself [Macbeth] which had been preserved in Loch Leven tradition since the eleventh century, then the monstrous character of Shakespeare's construction can be said to contain at least some trace, however distorted, of the personality of its historical original.'[24] But the claimed existence of such a tradition is undermined by Wyntoun's failure to refer to the gifts, although he does mention Macbeth's more general generosity to the Church.[25] Either Wyntoun was unaware of Macbeth's historical association with Loch Leven or he did not wish to publicise it. Perhaps significantly, the relevant documents had been removed from the community before Wyntoun became prior. There is no evidence that the Loch Leven link provided Wyntoun's sources on Macbeth.

Wyntoun was not dependent on local information but was widely read. Over half the *Orygynale Cronykil* (five out of nine books) does not concern Scotland and displays Wyntoun's extensive knowledge of classical and continental sources, including Marianus' *Chronicle*, from which Wyntoun derived his description of Macbeth's pilgrimage. Also aware of the earliest stratum of mythology concerning Macbeth, Wyntoun explicitly links the prosperity of Macbeth's reign with the justice of his rule:

All his tyme wes gret plente	All his time was great plenty
Habundande bathe on lande and se.	Abundance both on land and sea.
He was in [iustice] richt lauchfull	He was in justice right lawful

Another manuscript version states that:

in his tyme þar wes plente	in his time there was plenty
Off gold and siluer, catall and fee.	Of gold and silver, cattle and sheep.[26]

But despite portraying his reign favourably, the *Orygynale Cronykil* is unambiguously hostile to Macbeth. In particular, Macbeth's murder of Duncan is depicted as an act of the most heinous treachery. Conflating Macbeth's cousin, Duncan, with his (probable) grandfather, Malcolm II, Wyntoun accuses Macbeth of betraying the 'uncle' who fostered him so tenderly, murdering him in Elgin and usurping his kingship.[27]

Comparison with Fordun's *Chronicle* suggests that Wyntoun sometimes embellished passages found in earlier sources, presumably for literary effect. For example, Wyntoun adds two key elements to the MacDuff episode.[28] MacDuff's wife, appearing for the first time, taunts Macbeth that her husband has escaped but might return to cause Macbeth 'gret payn'; MacDuff duly returns and slays Macbeth. In contrast, some incidental details, such as the location of Macbeth's fortress and the battle at Dunsinane, are more plausible. This information is not essential to the narrative and there is no apparent reason why Wyntoun should have fabricated it, suggesting that it is derived from earlier sources that no longer survive. Wyntoun does, however, make some errors; the description of Macbeth as Duncan's nephew and Gruoch as Duncan's widow attest the conflating of characters and the telescoping of a narrative, in which Gillacomgain drops out and his role is subsumed by Duncan. Wyntoun, like other medieval chroniclers, was attempting to synthesise and rationalise disparate and sometimes conflicting information to form a continuous narrative and this inevitably resulted in some errors.

The most strikingly original element of Wyntoun's version of the Macbeth myth is its deeply and darkly supernatural nature. Macbeth is now transformed into a powerful demonic character, the devil's child. Walking in the woods one day, Macbeth's mother met what appeared to be a handsome man, the couple had sex and Macbeth's mother became pregnant:

Fra þis person wiþe hir had playide,	For this person with her had played,
And had þe iourne wiþ hir don,	And had the journey with her done,
Þat he had gottyn on hir a son,	That he had gotten on her a son,
And he þe dewil was þat hym gat	And he the Devil was him that got[29]

The supernatural theme is maintained by three prophecies, which are related out of sequence. The first occurs during Macbeth's childhood or youth, when three 'weird sisters' appear in a dream to reveal to Macbeth his royal destiny. Here, 'weird' is used in its original sense of 'fate' or 'destiny':

Qwhen he murtherist his awyn eme	When he murders his own uncle
Be hop þat he had in a dreyme,	By hope that he had in a dream,
Þat he saw qwhen he was ynge,	That he saw when he was young,
In housse duellande wiþe þe kynge.	In a house dwelling with the king.
A nycht he thoucht in his dremynge	One night he thought in his dreaming
He saw thre women [by] gangande,	He saw three women going by,
And þa women þan thoucht he	And those women then thought he
Thre werd systeris mast lyk to be.	Three weird sisters most like to be.

Þe fyrst he herd say gangande by:	The first he heard say going by:
'Lo, yondyr þe thayne of Crwmbathy!'	'Lo, yonder the thane of Cromarty!'
Þe toþir woman said agayn:	The other woman said again:
'Off Mwrray yondyr is þe thayn'.	'Of Moray yonder is the thane'.
Þe thrid þan said: 'I se þe kynge'.	The third then said: 'I see the king'.
Al þis he herde in his dremynge.	All this he heard in his dreaming.[30]

'Cromarty' may be an error for the historical thanage of Cromdale in Moray, while Moray itself was not a thanage but a province and medieval earldom. The significance of these titles is that they attest Macbeth's progression through the social hierarchy, from thane or *toísech*, to mormaer and ultimately king. There is no reference to Glamis and Cawdor, which were later substituted by Boece and make little sense in terms of Macbeth's political aspirations.

Macbeth was soon driven to action:

Son eftyr þat, in his youthade,	Soon after that, in his youth,
Off þir thayndomys he thayn was made;	Of these thanedoms he thane was made;
Syne next he thoucht for to be kynge,	Since next he thought for to be king,
Fra Dunkanys dayis had tane endynge.	For Duncan's days were then ending.
Þe fantasy þus of þis dreyme	The fantasy thus of this dream
Mowit hym mast to sla his eme.	Moved him must to slay his uncle.

The second prophecy, that the then unborn Macbeth will be an important and wealthy man and will not be slain by any man of woman born, was made to Macbeth's pregnant mother by the Devil:

said þat hir son suld be	said that her son should be
A man of gret state and bounte,	A man of great state and bounty,
And na man sulde [be] born of wif	And no man should [be] born of wife
Off powar to reiff hym his lif.	Of power to take from him his life.[31]

As the Devil's son, Macbeth can only be killed by someone of 'unnatural' birth.

The source of the third and final prediction is not revealed. Malcolm and Siward, mustering their forces before advancing on Macbeth's fortress, receive a report concerning Macbeth's dependence on supernatural prophecies, including one that he will remain undefeated until Birnam Wood comes to Dunsinane Hill:

Sen þai herde þat Makbethe ay	Then they heard that Macbeth always
In fantoun fretis had gret fay,	In phantom prophecies had great faith,
And trowit had in sic fantasy,	And had belief in such fantasy,
Be þat he trowit stedfastly	By which he believed steadfastly
Neuir discomfyt for to be	Never discomforted for to be
Qwhil wiþe his eyne he sulde se	While with his eyes he should see
Þe wode be broucht of Brynnane	The wood be brought from Birnam
Til þe hil of Dunsynnane.	To the hill of Dunsinane.[32]

The latter prophecies lead Macbeth into a false sense of security, but Malcolm and Siward's forces take foliage from Birnam Hill to camouflage their advance on Dunsinane:

Off þat wode þan ilka man	Of that wood then every man
In til his hande a busk tuk þan;	Into his hand a bush took then;
Off al his ost was na man fre	Of all his host was no man free
Þan in his hande a busk bur he.	Then in his hand a bush bore he.
Til Dunsynnane þan alssa fast	To Dunsinane then all so fast
Agaynnis þis Makbethe þai past;	Against this Macbeth they passed;
For þai thoucht wiþe swylk a wylle	For they thought with such a while
Þis Makbeth for to begile,	This Macbeth for to beguile,
Swa for to cum in prewate	So for to come in secrecy
On hym or he sulde wyttride be.	On him or he should warned be.[33]

So disturbed was Macbeth at the sight of the 'flittande wode' (moving wood) from his fortress that he fled over the Mounth to Lumphanan, where an unidentified knight summarily despatched him to the Devil:

Bot a knycht þat in þat chasse	But a knight that in that chase
Til þis Makbethe þan nerrast was,	To this Macbeth then nearest was,
Makbeth turnyt hym agan,	Macbeth turned to him again,
And said: 'Lurdan, þou prekis in wayn;	And said: 'Lord, you stab in vain;
For þou may noucht be he, I trow,	For you may not be he, I pledge,
Þat tile dede sal sla me now.	That to death shall slay me now.
Þat man is noucht born of wiff	That man is not born of wife
Off powar to reff me my liff'.	Of power to take from me my life'.
Þe knycht said: 'I was neuir born,	The knight said: 'I was never born,

Bot of my modyr wayme was schorn.	But from my mother's womb was shorn.
Now sal þi tresson here tak ende,	Now shall your treason here take end,
And til þi fadyr I sal þe sende'.	And to your father I shall you send'.[34]

Wyntoun's *Orygynale Cronykil* is the earliest known source to invest the Macbeth myth with a supernatural dimension. This fundamental development in the evolution of the myth would characterise Macbeth's portrayal by later chroniclers and by Shakespeare. But where did this theme originate? Was it a product of Wyntoun's imagination?

Many of the more fantastic elements found in Wyntoun's account of Macbeth occur widely in folklore but may be traced to early Norse and Celtic mythology.[35] The three weird sisters are analogous to the Norns or Fates of Norse mythology – three prophetic women who dwelled at the root of Yggdrasil, the world tree, and shaped the destinies of men. The recurrence of the number three – weird sisters, prophecies, titles held by Macbeth – is characteristic of both Celtic and Norse mythology. Many of the episodes related by Wyntoun belong to types of Celtic mythological tales, standard elements of the *fili*'s repertoire, including otherworldly conceptions and births (*coimperta*), dreams and visions (*físi*), invasions (*tochomlada*), battles (*catha*), and violent deaths (*aideda*).[36] For example, Macbeth's otherworldly conception distinguishes him as a 'fatherless' hero of the type foundly widely in early Irish and Welsh mythology. Similarly, Macbeth's demise echoes the mythological death tales of some early Irish kings, in which the monarch is doomed by his inability to observe the conflicting injunctions that ensured his continued well-being and meets his inevitable end by the three-fold death of transfixion, burning and drowning.[37] Macbeth is 'the best-known of Celtic kings lured to their death by the false security of contradictory promises'.[38]

The presence of these supernatural motifs in the *Orygynale Cronykil* reflects Wyntoun's use of earlier sources. Indeed, Wyntoun attributes his account of Macbeth's conception to 'sum storys', which were probably in Gaelic and transmitted orally. These unspecified stories must have belonged to an otherwise lost body of traditional Scottish mythology that circulated in the centuries after Macbeth's death. These tales appear to have told the story of Macbeth's life according to the traditional conventions of the *fili*'s repertoire, incorporating several elements of great antiquity that occur widely in Celtic literature. Familiar with these traditions, Wyntoun incorporated them in his *Orygynale Cronykil* to form a composite myth that was very different from its predecessors. This also explains the origins of both the supernatural elements and the unique incidental detail in his chronicle. But there is a temptation here to over-emphasise literary parallels at the expense of historical context. Why did the supernatural Macbeth appear at this time?

Although the 'weird sisters' have no physical presence, appearing only in a dream, they are clearly witches; their 'fantoun fretis' initiated a chain of violent and tragic events, indicating their evil intent. Moreover, in addition to Macbeth's diabolic conception, MacDuff accuses Malcolm of being descended from the Devil when he initially fails to persuade Malcolm to return to Scotland.[39] The prominence accorded to these themes reflects Wyntoun's anxieties about witchcraft and diabolism.

Although witchcraft in Scotland is most commonly associated with the seventeenth century, this represented a recrudescence of earlier concerns. Between 1375 and 1435 the number of witchcraft trials and the proportion of them involving diabolism increased steadily in western Europe, reflecting more zealous inquisitorial practices and the social stresses created by the Black Death.[40] The *Orygynale Cronykil* belongs to a period that saw the increasingly vigorous persecution of witches and expresses contemporary concerns. Although drawing on elements from Celtic and Norse tradition, it is to Wyntoun's personal interests and anxieties and the intellectual and moral climate of his age that the supernatural character of his Macbeth may be attributed. Moreover, the continuation of the witch-hunts into the early modern period ensured that Wyntoun's emphasis on the supernatural had an enduring influence on many subsequent versions of the myth.

PERPETUATING THE MYTH: BOWER'S *SCOTICHRONICON*

Born in Haddington, East Lothian, Walter Bower (*c.* 1385–1449) studied in Scotland and Paris and was probably a canon of the Augustinian Priory of St Andrews before becoming Abbot of Inchcolm, an island abbey in the Firth of Forth, in 1418. An active supporter of the Stewart monarchy, Bower was one of the commissioners appointed to collect money firstly for the ransom and then the dowry of James I, in 1424 and 1433 respectively. Probably compiled from about 1440, Bower based his *Scotichronicon* on the completed books of Fordun's *Chronicle* and the notes Fordun left at his death, extending the period covered until 1437. Like Fordun's *Chronicle*, *Scotichronicon* is a national history, although its patriotic tone is stronger.

Bower's *Scotichronicon* follows Fordun's account of the reigns of Macbeth and Lulach very closely. There is no supernatural dimension. The negative portrayal of Macbeth may now be attributed to Bower's pro-Stewart views. The Stewart dynasty, founded by Marjorie, eldest daughter of Robert I ('the Bruce'), and Walter the Steward (or Stewart), held the Scottish kingship from 1371 and could trace its ancestry back through Duncan to the earliest Scottish kings. Having violently interrupted this ancient and auspicious royal lineage, Macbeth was guaranteed a negative treatment. Bower's account of the Macbeth myth articulated contemporary political views.

But Bower's account also incorporates a positive element. Perpetuating one of the most ancient strands of the myth, Bower states that 'In the time of Macbeth there was great fertility in Scotland'.[41] This theme is repeated in some appended Latin verses which are not in Fordun's *Chronicle*:

> For eighteen years Macbeth ruled Scotia.
> In his reign it was a time of fertility.
> Duncan's son Malcolm by name
> Killed him at Lumphanan by a cruel death.
>
> The luckless Lulach was king for three months.
> He was slain by the sword of the same Malcolm.
> The man met his fate in Essie in Strathbogie
> where the unhappy king was rashly slain.[42]

The sympathetic tone, lamenting the cruel and unlucky deaths of Macbeth and Lulach respectively, contrasts with that expressed within the body of *Scotichronicon*. These verses may be derived from an earlier, probably Gaelic, elegy to Macbeth and Lulach, which was presumably composed shortly after their deaths.

CONDENSING THE MYTH: MAJOR'S *HISTORY*

John Major, or Mair (1470–1550), was born at Gleghornie, near North Berwick, and studied at Cambridge and Paris before being appointed Professor of Theology at Glasgow in 1518. After spells at St Andrews (1522–5) and Paris again (1525–33), Major returned to St Andrews, where he became Provost of St Salvator's College.

During his first stay in Paris, Major completed his punningly titled *Historia Majoris Britanniae*; either the *History of Greater Britain* or *Major's History of Britain*. Published in Paris in 1521, Major's *History* represents a landmark in

Scottish historiography. For the first time, a Scottish chronicler concentrated not just on Scotland's past but, treating Scotland as an integral part of Britain, produced a history of both England and Scotland. Major was less gullible than many of his predecessors and contemporaries and did not indulge in the fantastical elaboration that characterised most later, and some earlier, Scottish chronicles. The supernatural element is also absent. Instead, Major condensed Fordun's account of the Macbeth myth.

Unusually, Major's account of Macbeth's reign begins by criticising the inaction of Duncan and his predecessors:[43]

> those kings showed a grave want of foresight, in that they found no way of union and friendship with the opposing faction [Macbeth's]: for either they should have banished them from the land of their fathers as disturbers of the common peace and welfare; or, if this opposite faction was carrying on its designs in secret, and was unknown to the king, he should not at least have taken measures against it without a large army at his back: for to gain a kingdom many a wicked act is done. . . . Give them but the chance – and those men are few indeed who will not risk their all for a crown – though their title to it may be far from clear.[44]

This may be an oblique reference to the political intrigues during the minority of James V (1513–28) and another example of the Macbeth myth being tailored to convey contemporary political messages. Indeed, Major's *History* expresses the political philosophy that authority was not vested in kings, but was derived from the people.

THE EMBELLISHED MYTH: BOECE'S *HISTORY*

Hector Boece (*c.* 1465–1536), who is sometimes known by his Latinised name, Boethius, was born in Dundee and studied at St Andrews and Paris, where he was a Regent or Professor of Philosophy at Montaigu College (1492–8). He returned to Scotland at the invitation of William Elphinstone, Bishop of Aberdeen, to take up the appointment of Regent Master in Arts at King's College, Aberdeen's newly founded university, and subsequently became its first principal. Boece was made a canon in Aberdeen Cathedral at the same time.

Although published only six years after Major's *History*, Boece's *Scotorum Historiae* (*History of the Scots*) is very different in style. Composed in Latin verse, Boece's *History* appeared in Paris in 1527. In compiling his *History*, Boece relied extensively on earlier Scottish chronicles, primarily those of Fordun and Wyntoun, although he also incorporated some material that is not preserved in any other source. However, Boece combined extreme credulity with 'an eye for marvels', with the result that his *History* is characterised by 'colourful narration rather than analysis and interpretation'.[45] After Major's *History*, this represented a considerable backwards step in Scottish historiography. Nevertheless, Boece's lively literary style and rich descriptions of characters and events ensured that his *History* became highly influential in the Scots' perception of their past. James V demonstrated his approval by awarding Boece a pension until Boece became Vicar of Tullynessle in 1528.

The wide dissemination and enduring appeal of Boece's *History* was assisted by its translation into Scots. The year after its publication, James V – who, according to tradition, knew no Latin – commissioned both prose and verse translations. The prose translation, *Croniklis of the Scots*, by John Bellenden (d. 1587), was completed between 1530 and 1533 and published in 1536. The verse translation, *The Buik of the Croniclis of Scotland*, by William Stewart, a priest, possibly of Quothquan in Lanarkshire, was undertaken between 1531 and 1535. Bellenden was rewarded by James V with a pension of £50 Scots a year between 1527 and 1534, before being appointed Parson of Fyvie. He later became Archdeacon of Moray and Canon of Ross, but his opposition to the Reformation led to his fall from favour and self-imposed exile in Rome, where he died. Bellenden and Stewart followed Boece's format closely, although both included some material that is not in Boece's *History*.

Boece further embellished the Macbeth myth.[46] He relates how Macbeth was the son of Doada, second daughter of Malcolm II, and 'Synell' (mistakenly derived from Fordun's 'Finele'), Thane of Glamis. Macbeth was initially loyal to Duncan and 'appeared most able to have governed a realm, were not his strength mixed too much with cruelty'. The latter was evident in Macbeth's crushing of Duncan's enemies in the Western Isles, where he gained the reputation for being a 'cruel and bloody monster'. Boece is the first chronicler to portray Macbeth as one of Duncan's generals, leading a battalion against the Norwegians at Culross, in Fife.

Boece also introduced several new incidents and characters, many of which subsequently became integral to the myth. Banquo, Thane of Lochaber, makes his first appearance, initially physical, after his murder at Macbeth's orders, and later spectral. A purely mythical character, Banquo was introduced as 'the beginner of the Stewarts in this realm, from whom our King now present [James V] by long and ancient lineage is descended'.[47] Invented to interest and please Boece's patron by providing an ancestor for the Stewart dynasty, Banquo

Macbeth as medieval despot. Macbeth, newly created King of Scots, orders the executions of Banquo and Fleance, as portrayed by George Cattermole (1800–68). This image, more than any other, reflects romantic perceptions of Macbeth as a dark and deeply disturbed character. (Victoria & Albert Museum/Bridgeman Art Library, UK)

was soon accepted as a genuine, historical figure, the progenitor of the Stewart kings. Elsewhere, Boece's version of the myth diverges from earlier accounts, for example, in portraying Duncan's death by poisoning at Macbeth's hands.

Boece also elaborated on the supernatural elements introduced by Wyntoun. The weird sisters no longer appear to Macbeth in a dream, but as physical beings, play a more prominent role and are referred to as witches for the first time. The witches initially appear to Macbeth and Banquo on the moor near Forres, where they address Macbeth by different titles to those used by Wyntoun's weird sisters: Thane of Glamis, Thane of Cawdor and King of Scots. This weighs heavily on his mind: 'Macbeth, revolving all things as they were said by the witches, began to covet the crown'. The character of Macbeth's wife, who is not named, is developed by Boece, transformed from her minor role in Wyntoun's *Cronykil* into the ambitious and unscrupulous woman who is instrumental in driving Macbeth to his terrible course of action:

His wife, impatient of long delay . . . gave him great exhortation to pursue the prophecy that she might be a queen, often calling him a feeble coward and not desirous of honour, since he dare not attempt with manhood and courage that which is offered to him by the benevolence of fortune, although various others exposed themselves to the most terrible jeopardy knowing no certainty to succeed thereafter . . . Macbeth, at the instigation of his wife . . . went to Inverness, where he slew king Duncan.[48]

In apparent contrast, Macbeth is also portrayed as a 'righteous king' who actively protected his subjects.[49] Macbeth 'set . . . to govern the realm in justice and to punish the cruelties and great oppressions done in the time of King Duncan through his feeble administration'. This involved the slaying of seditious and tyrannical thanes, and the bringing to justice of all miscreants, oppressors and thieves, so that Macbeth 'was holding the sure shield of innocent and pure people, and [a] most diligent punisher of injuries done against the common good'. Macbeth also 'made such laws for the common good of Scotland that he was worthy to be numbered among the noble kings, if he had succeeded to the crown by just title, his laws were found profitable'. The laws concerned protected women and children in warfare, enabled daughters to inherit property as well as sons and limited the size of women's

A woodcut illustration from Holinshed's *Chronicles* (1577) that shows Macbeth's pursuit of justice: 'When these theiues, barrettours, & other oppressours of the innocent people were come to darreigne batell in this maner of wise (as said is) they were streight wayes apprehended by armed men & trussed up in halters on gibbets, according as they had justly deserved.'

dowries. But rather than Macbeth's legislation, these belong to the traditional bardic law of Gaelic Scotland.

But after he had 'governed the realm [for] ten years in good justice', Macbeth 'returned to his innate cruelty, and became furious'.[50] Charting this descent into tyranny and terror, Boece relates how Macbeth plotted to slay Banquo and Fleance after inviting them to a banquet, killed those nobles who broke his laws and appropriated their lands, and murdered Lady MacDuff and her child after MacDuff's escape. Boece offers no explanation for this change in character. It seems more likely that he was attempting to reconcile two contradictory mythological traditions, one portraying Macbeth as a righteous king and the other as an oppressive usurper, by accommodating them both within Macbeth's reign.

With the exception of the *Verse Chronicle*, each version of the Macbeth myth contains a kernel of historical truth, usually specific events surrounding Macbeth's rise and fall; his murder of Duncan, seizing of the kingship, defeat by Malcolm and ultimate death. Many of these can be corroborated by eleventh-century sources. These are the key, historically attested events in Macbeth's reign, the factual pegs on which the cloak of mythology hangs. In contrast, other aspects of Macbeth and his reign exhibit a less historical treatment, with each successive account attesting their increasingly mythological quality. This was a product of the chroniclers' technique, synthesising earlier sources, many of them already mythological in nature, to construct what was believed to be a more complete and accurate narrative. Chroniclers also sought to increase the appeal of their work to their patrons by making the narrative more exciting and by reflecting contemporary concerns and tastes. As a result, the myth was embellished at practically every stage in its recording. These continuous processes of elaboration and transformation can be traced in the evolution of the myth from the late eleventh to the mid-sixteenth centuries.

The works of Boece and his translators represent the culmination of the mythological narrative. Nevertheless, two late sixteenth century Latin histories of Scotland are of interest. John Leslie's *On the Ancestry, Customs and Achievements of the Scots* (*De Origine, Moribus et Rebus Gestis Scotorum*), published in Rome in 1578, is notable for portraying the weird sisters as devils disguised as women who tell Macbeth that Banquo's descendants would be kings.[51] Its also illustrates the Stewart dynasty as a genealogical tree, with their kings as the fruit descended from the root of Banquo.

George Buchanan was a distinguished scholar, neo-Latin dramatist and tutor to the young James VI.[52] His *History of Scotland* (*Rerum Scoticarum Historiae*), published in Edinburgh in 1582, assessed Macbeth as 'a man of penetrating

The genealogical tree of the Scottish monarchy from John Leslie's *De Origine, Moribus et Rebus Gestis Scotorum* (1578). It shows the monarchy's claimed descent from Banquo, Thane of Lochaber (at the base), to James VI and I (at the crown).

genius, a high spirit, unbounded ambition, and, if he had possessed moderation, was worthy of any command however great; but in punishing crimes he exercised a severity, which, exceeding the bounds of the laws, appeared oft to degenerate into cruelty'.[53] Most presciently, Buchanan also commented about Macbeth that 'some of our writers relate a number of fables, more adapted for theatrical representation . . . than history'.[54]

By this time some English chroniclers were also showing an interest in Scottish history; the Macbeth myth was about to reach a wider audience and enter a new phase.

THE ILLUSTRATED MACBETH: HOLINSHED'S *CHRONICLES*

Raphael (or Ralph) Holinshed (d. 1581?) was born at Bramcott in Warwickshire and arrived in London early in Elizabeth's reign. There he worked as a translator for Reginald Wolfe, a printer and publisher who was already compiling a 'chronicle of universal history'. Holinshed continued this and his *Chronicles of England, Scotland and Ireland* covered the history of each country from the Creation until 1575, 1571 and 1547 respectively. The first edition was published in three volumes (but in two separately bound books) in 1577, the histories of pre- and post-Conquest England in volumes one and three respectively, separated by the histories of Scotland and Ireland in volume two. Holinshed's *Chronicles* immediately ran into problems with the authorities, leading to the deletion of politically controversial passages. A second, expanded and updated, edition appeared in 1587, again with offending passages removed. For his *Historie of Scotland*, Holinshed relied heavily upon Bellenden's translation of Boece's *History*. Also reflecting greater English interest in Scotland's past, Boece's *History* was translated into English for the first time by William Harrison and published in two volumes in 1587.

Like earlier Scottish chroniclers, Holinshed portrayed Macbeth as a man of mixed qualities: 'a valiant gentleman, and one that if he had not beene somewhat cruell of nature, might haue beene thought most woorthie [of] the gouernement of a realme'.[55] The character of Macbeth's wife emerges clearly: after Macbeth heard the prophecy 'his wife lay sore upon him to attempt the thing, as she that was verie ambitious, burning in unquenchable desire to beare the name of a queene'. A notable feature of Holinshed's account of Macbeth's reign is that it digresses to give a lengthy genealogy of 'the originall line of those kings, which have descended from . . . Banquo', ending with James VI and I (1567–1625).

A woodcut illustration from Holinshed's *Chronicles* (1577) that shows Macbeth and Banquo encountering the three sisters: 'It fortuned as Makbeth & Banquho iourneyed towarde Fores, where the king as then lay, they went sporting by the way togither without other companie, save only themselves, passing through the woodes and fieldes, when sodenly in the middes of a lande, there met them iii women in strange & ferly apparell, resembling creatures of an elder worlde'.

Holinshed made the works of Scottish chroniclers accessible to an English readership for the first time. His *Chronicles* occupy a significant place in the development of the mythical Macbeth, providing the link between the Macbeth portrayed in the Scottish chronicles and the myth's culmination in Shakespeare's *Macbeth*. Holinshed's *Chronicles* gave Shakespeare access to a rich vein of Scottish chronicles, myth and history interweaved, that went back through Bellenden and Boece to Wyntoun, Fordun and beyond.

Holinshed's *Chronicles* is notable for another, frequently overlooked, reason. The first edition was illustrated with a set of enchanting woodcuts, although these were dropped from the second edition. These, the earliest pictorial representations of the myth, illustrate four scenes from the narrative, depicting Macbeth and other characters in Elizabethan costume.

A DRAMATIC TRANSFORMATION: SHAKESPEARE'S *MACBETH*

William Shakespeare's famous tragedy is undoubtedly the most familiar form of the Macbeth myth.[56] Indeed, Shakespeare's *Macbeth* is so well known that the

131

THE TRAGEDIE OF
MACBETH.

Actus Primus. Scœna Prima.

Thunder and Lightning. Enter three Witches.

1. When shall we three meet againe?
In Thunder, Lightning, or in Raine?
2. When the Hurley-burley's done,
When the Battaile's loft, and wonne.
3. That will be ere the fet of Sunne.
1. Where the place?
2. Vpon the Heath.
3. There to meet with *Macbeth*.
1. I come, *Gray-Malkin*.
All. *Padock* calls anon: faire is foule, and foule is faire,
Houer through the fogge and filthie ayre.   *Exeunt.*

Scena Secunda.

*Alarum within. Enter King Malcome, Donal-
baine, Lennox, with attendants, meeting
a bleeding Captaine.*

King. What bloody man is that? he can report,
As feemeth by his plight, of the Reuolt
The neweft ftate.
Mal. This is the Serieant,
Who like a good and hardie Souldier fought
'Gainft my Captiuitie : Haile braue friend;
Say to the King, the knowledge of the Broyle,
As thou didft leaue it.
Cap. Doubtfull it ftood,
As two fpent Swimmers, that doe cling together,
And choake their Art: The mercileffe *Macdonwald*
(Worthie to be a Rebell, for to that
The multiplying Villanies of Nature
Doe fwarme vpon him) from the Wefterne Ifles
Of Kernes and Gallowgroffes is fupply'd,
And Fortune on his damned Quarry fmiling,
Shew'd like a Rebells Whore : but all's too weake :
For braue *Macbeth* (well hee deferues that Name)
Difdayning Fortune, with his brandifht Steele,
Which fmoak'd with bloody execution
(Like Valours Minion) caru'd out his paffage,
Till hee fac'd the Slaue :
Which neu'r fhooke hands, nor bad farwell to him,
Till he vnfeam'd him from the Naue toth'Chops,
And fix'd his Head vpon our Battlements.

King. O valiant Coufin, worthy Gentleman.
Cap. As whence the Sunne 'gins his reflection,
Shipwracking Stormes, and direfull Thunders :
So from that Spring, whence comfort feem'd to come,
Difcomfort fwells : Marke King of Scotland, marke,
No fooner Iuftice had, with Valour atm'd,
Compell'd thefe skipping Kernes to truft their heeles,
But the Norweyan Lord, furueying vantage,
With furbufht Armes, and new fupplyes of men,
Began a frefh affault.
King. Difmay'd not this our Captaines, *Macbeth* and
Banquoh?
Cap Yes, as Sparrowes, Eagles;
Or the Hare, the Lyon :
If I fay footh, I muft report they were
As Cannons ouer-charg'd with double Cracks,
So they doubly redoubled ftroakes vpon the Foe :
Except they meant to bathe in reeking Wounds,
Or memorize another *Golgotha*,
I cannot tell : but I am faint,
My Gafhes cry for helpe.
King. So well thy words become thee, as thy wounds,
They fmack of Honor both : Goe get him Surgeons.

Enter Roffe and Angus.
Who comes here?
Mal. The worthy *Thane* of Roffe.
Lenox. What a hafte lookes through his eyes?
So fhould he looke, that feemes to fpeake things ftrange.
Roffe. God faue the King.
King. Whence cam'ft thou, worthy *Thane*?
Roffe. From Fiffe, great King,
Where the Norweyan Banners flowt the Skie,
And fanne our people cold.
Norway himfelfe, with terrible numbers,
Affifted by that moft difloyall Traytor,
The *Thane* of Cawdor, began a difmall Conflict,
Till that *Bellona's* Bridegroome, lapt in proofe,
Confronted him with felfe-comparifons,
Point againft Point, rebellious Arme 'gainft Arme,
Curbing his lauifh fpirit : and to conclude,
The Victorie fell on vs.
King. Great happineffe.
Roffe. That now *Sweno*, the Norwayes King,
Craues compofition :
Nor would we deigne him buriall of his men,
Till he disburfed, at Saint *Colmes* ynch,
Ten thoufand Dollars, to our generall vfe.
King. No

The Tragedie of Macbeth. The opening page of the play in Shakespeare's First Folio (1623).

historical Macbeth has been almost completely eclipsed by his dramatic counterpart. To many, the distinction between the historical, mythical and dramatic Macbeths is lost; the Macbeth of modern consciousness is almost invariably Shakespeare's Macbeth. And where archaeologists and historians have been unable to provide answers, artistic imagination has boldly filled the void.

Although known universally as *Macbeth*, the earliest surviving text of the play, in Shakespeare's First Folio of 1623, is entitled *The Tragedie of Macbeth* and this is presumably its original and full title. The earliest recorded performance of *Macbeth* took place in the spring of 1611, but reflections in other plays reveal that *Macbeth* was first performed in 1606. Shakespeare therefore probably began writing *Macbeth* in the autumn of 1605.

James VI interrogating witches. *Newes from Scotland* (*c.* 1591) reported that, during the interrogation, Agnes Samson allegedly repeated 'the very words which passed between the King's Majesty and his Queen [Anne of Denmark] at Oslo in Norway [on] the first night of their marriage'.

Despite agreement over its dating, the circumstances of, and motives behind, *Macbeth*'s composition are more controversial. Discussion has focused on Macbeth's status as a 'topical' or an 'occasional' play. Advocates of *Macbeth*'s topicality argue that the play reflects its general historical context of composition in a range of references, direct or oblique, to events and characters of the period 1603–6, such as the Gunpowder Plot of 1605 and its conspirators.[57] Proponents of *Macbeth*'s occasional status attribute the play directly to more specific historical circumstances, namely the unprecedented accession of a Scottish king to the English throne, when James VI of Scotland became James I of the united kingdoms in 1603.[58] Without this, they claim, Shakespeare is unlikely to have written *Macbeth*. More precisely still, others have claimed that *Macbeth* was written for, and first performed at, a specific event or occasion, the state visit of Christian IV of Denmark, James' brother-in-law, in July and August 1606.

A woodcut in *Newes from Scotland* (c. 1591) depicts the Devil preaching to the witches of North Berwick. The background portrays a storm allegedly raised by witches against the ship carrying James VI and his bride back to Scotland from Norway.

Of relevance here are James' personal interests in kingship, the responsibilities of monarchs and their subjects, and witchcraft. James wrote three treatises on these subjects in two years, *The True Lawe of Free Monarchies* (1598), *Basilikon Doron* (1599, revised 1603) and *Daemonologie* (1598). His interest in witchcraft may have been inspired by accusations that his cousin, Francis Stewart, Earl of Bothwell, was in league with witches who were said to have raised a storm around the ship carrying the King and his new bride back from Denmark in 1590. James took a close personal interest in the ensuing trials, which stimulated his wider interest in witchcraft.[59] Was Shakespeare pandering to James' interests in writing *Macbeth*?

Macbeth is undeniably a product of the social and political climate of late Elizabethan and early Stuart England in general and of the opinion prevailing in the aftermath of the Union of the Crowns in 1603 in particular. This momentous political event focused English popular attention on Scotland, specifically its kings, kingship and royal succession. A play based on or incorporating these themes was therefore an appealing proposition, both artistically and commercially, for English playwrights and acting companies. *Macbeth* was not the first play to address these issues. Within eighteen months of James' accession, the King's Men, a London theatrical company, performed *The Tragedie of Gowrie*. Although now lost, this almost certainly dramatised the alleged conspiracy, led by the Earl of Gowrie, to assassinate James in 1600.[60] Gowrie and his brother were killed at the scene, resulting in some scepticism about James' version of events and motives.

Elizabethan and Stuart dramatists and actors had to work within rigorous censorship laws, which prevented the performance of plays referring to a living monarch or to religious issues; *The Tragedie of Gowrie* was soon banned. Dramatists could only address these subjects by incorporating them in historical dramas. Again, *Macbeth* was not the first play to do this, although none of the four earlier English tragedies about Scottish kings survive. The earliest was *The Tragedie of the Kinge of Scottes* (1567–8); the king concerned is unidentified. The others belong to a seven-year period straddling James' accession to the English throne; *Robart the Second Kinge of Scottes Tragedie* or *The Scottes Tragedie* (1599), *Malcolm Kynge of Scottes* (1602) and *The Tragedie of Gowrie*. Moreover, a play about Macbeth, since lost, may have existed during Elizabeth's reign. Will Kemp, the leading comic actor, implies in *Nine Daies Wonder* (1600) the existence of a ballad featuring Macbeth and 'prophetesses'. Matthew Gwinne's *Tres Sibyllae* (*Three Sibyls*), a short tableau performed to welcome James to St John's College, Oxford, in 1605, is also relevant. Although now lost, this may have been based on Holinshed's account of the encounter between Macbeth and the three sisters and also reflected James' belief that he was descended from Banquo.

Macbeth clearly belongs to a wider dramatic tradition. Tragedies concerning Scottish kings became increasingly popular with English audiences from the late sixteenth century. The earliest of these predate the Union of the Crowns and could not have been composed in response to the accession of James I. Shakespeare was following a fashion for such plays, although James' accession must have greatly increased their appeal to dramatists, actors and audiences alike. Furthermore, there is no evidence that *Macbeth* was written expressly for, or performed before, James, either during the visit of Christian IV or on another occasion. By addressing the issues raised in *Macbeth*, it can hardly be claimed that Shakespeare was specifically pandering to James' interests; concerns about kingship, government and witchcraft were widespread in England during this period, as contemporary books, pamphlets and witchcraft trials demonstrate. Indeed, kingship, magic and the supernatural feature prominently in several Shakespearean plays.[61] Although many of *Macbeth*'s historical points of reference may be identified, the specific social and political contexts of its composition and earliest performances are now lost.

Shakespeare's principal source in writing *Macbeth* was the second (1587) edition of Holinshed's *Chronicles*,[62] which in turn was based closely on Bellenden's translation of Boece's *Scotorum Historiae*. Shakespeare used not only Holinshed's account of Macbeth's reign, but also drew on those of other early Scottish kings, primarily Duff.[63] This was the origin of both the murder and the witches. Duff had hanged several relatives of Donwald, a 'capteine of the castell' of Forres, for conspiring with witches against him. Donwald's wife incited him to seek revenge by killing Duff the next time he stayed at the castle. When the king was asleep and his chamberlains were in a drunken stupor, Donwald and his servants cut the King's throat and removed his body from the castle. When the alarm was raised the next morning, Donwald flew into a rage and, accusing them of having the opportunity to murder Duff and dispose of his body, killed the King's two chamberlains.

Shakespeare[64] also drew on Holinshed's description of the calamitous events that followed Duff's murder:

> For the space of six moneths togither, after this heinous murther thus committed, there appeered no sunne by day, nor moone by night in anie part of the realme, but still was the skie couered with continuall clouds, and sometimes such outragious windes arose, with lightenings and tempests, that the people were in great feare of present destruction . . .

Monstrous sights also that were seen within the Scottish kingdome that yeere were these: horsses in Louthian, being of singular beautie and swiftnesse, did eate their owne flesh, and would in no wise taste anie other meate. In Angus there was a gentlewoman brought foorth a child without eies, nose, hand, or foot. There was a sparhawke also strangled by an owle . . . But all men understood that the abhominable murther of king Duffe was the cause heereof.[65]

This is another manifestation of the ancient concept of sacral kingship. But instead of the righteous king whose reign brings fertility, this represents an inversion, the unrighteous king whose misrule precipitates disorder and who brings disease, defeat, disaster and death on his kingdom and people.

Holinshed may also have inspired the appearance of Banquo's ghost in Macbeth.[66] Holinshed describes how Kenneth II poisoned Duff's son, Malcolm, in order to ensure his own succession and was afterwards struck with remorse.[67] One night, a mysterious voice warned Kenneth of the everlasting infamy of his name and the death of his descendants, so that others would inherit the kingship. In addition, Holinshed's[68] genealogy of Banquo's descendants may have inspired the 'show of kings' in Macbeth.[69] Shakespeare selected mythical episodes concerning several Scottish kings from Holinshed's Chronicles, combining and transforming them into the dramatised myth about Macbeth we know today.

Shakespeare may also have borrowed from other sources, including any of the tragedies about Scottish kings mentioned above. The works of Boece, and its translations by Bellenden and Stewart, Leslie, Buchanan and William Camden's Remains Concerning Britain (1605) have all been proposed as possible sources used by Shakespeare. Moreover, the sisters' prophetic greeting to Macbeth[70] closely resembles that made by a 'Sibylla' to Queen Elizabeth at Kenilworth Castle, as reported in The Whole Woorkes of George Gascoigne (1587). The range of available source material, confirmed and possible, proves that Shakespeare had no need to visit Scotland to gather material for Macbeth. Alleged similarities between 'the traditions in the neighbourhood of Dunsinnan Castle . . . and the celebrated play' do not provide evidence that 'our great dramatist was upon the spot himself, and was inspired with such uncommon poetical powers from having viewed the places, where the scenes he drew were supposed to have been transacted'.[71]

Shakespeare's other source was, of course, his imagination. Macbeth departs from Holinshed's account on several occasions, altering or omitting episodes for dramatic effect or economy. For example, Shakespeare portrays Duncan as an old and revered king, accentuating the evil of Macbeth's crime. Other elements, such as Lady Macbeth's sleepwalking and suicide, are Shakespeare's own inventions. Shakespeare reinvigorated the Macbeth myth, transforming it from an obscure tale about a flawed hero who became a tyrannical king into a complex drama about unbridled ambition, treachery, evil, murder and madness. Shakespeare successfully introduced the Macbeth myth to a much wider audience, giving it a new form and an enduring appeal and relevance. But the evolution of the myth did not end with Shakespeare.

THE DISSOLUTE MACBETH: *THE SECRET HISTORY OF MACKBETH*

The final version of the myth before Macbeth became a subject of modern historical enquiry was published in London in 1708 as *The Secret History of Mackbeth, King of Scotland*. The anonymous author claimed that it was 'Taken from a very Ancient Original Manuscript'. The *Secret History* is a rambling romantic novel and features an unfamiliar Macbeth:

> His person was tall, and exactly proportion'd, a Masculine Beauty fate Enthron'd in his Face, and from his Eyes such a haughty and commanding Spirit shone out, as discover'd a Challenge of Sovereign sway. But his Manners were every way engaging to all he Convers'd with, never assuming to himself above his Company; Affable and Complaisant to all, and openly an Enemy to none. This won him the Hearts of all the Men of the Court, whilst his Person and Address, made an easy way for him to the Hearts of the Ladies.[72]

The latter was Macbeth's great weakness. According to the story's narrator, Macbeth's now repentant retainer, the Thane of Angus: 'Love chiefly employ'd our Industry; Intrigues with the Ladies took up more of our time than Intrigues of State'. He then describes Macbeth's amorous exploits. The *Secret History* contains some memorable language. For example, when admonished for his womanising, Banquo replies: 'I have been a Latitudarian in love . . . yet I was never so unreasonable as to desire the Brother to pimp for me to his Sister'. All the action revolves around the bedchamber, leading to some novel variations on the story. Banquo, for instance, is killed by Lady Macbeth in self defence and, predictably, in bed.

But the *Secret History* also has a political dimension. The reference to 'rogues and villains [who] had swallowed up the Court and surrounded the King' hints at the political circumstances in which it was written, while Angus is cast as a revolutionary: 'It was no new thing with us to remove one king and set up another as we have judged it conducive to the public good; and mankind indeed seems to have a right of doing this on just occasions'. The author expounds his political philosophy in a sermon in which the Thane of Argyll warns the newly crowned Malcolm:

> not to fall into the Errors of your Predecessour. . . . Society is the Institution of Heaven . . . the Prince therefore of any People shou'd reflect, that he is chose, and exalted to that high Post, not to indulge his Appetite . . . and make ev'ry thing subservient to his Will, as if he were the Lord, not Ruler, of his People, and they his Slaves, not Subjects. . . . What Mad and prophane Flaterers are those then, who wou'd persuade Monarchs, that they are free from all Bounds but their Will, when God himself has confin'd himself to certain Laws in his Administration, which he has assur'd us he never will transgress? My lord, Let the Public be your Council . . . the Publick will give you faithful Advice . . . know that your Office is constituted for the Good of the People, and not they for your Will and Pleasure.[73]

The *Secret History* is partly political treatise, disguised as historical romance, in which Macbeth draws attention to the excesses of kings, perhaps a reference to Stuart absolutism. The most likely context is provided by the Test Act of 1681, an attempt to curb resistance to the royal will that aroused widespread opposition in Scotland. Indeed, the real the hero of the story is Archibald, ninth Earl of Argyll,[74] who was executed in 1685 for his opposition to the Test Act and the succession of the Catholic James VII and II. In the *Secret History*, his namesake, Archibald, Thane of Argyll, distinguishes himself as a 'hater of tyrants' and 'leader of the patriots' against Macbeth.

But the *Secret History*'s appeal may have lain more in the rising popularity of the novel and increased interest in the performance and characters of Shakespeare's *Macbeth* during the eighteenth century. The *Secret History*'s appeal is evident from the appearance of further editions in 1741 and 1768 (both London), 1828 (Peterhead) and 1841 (Edinburgh). In each case the story was claimed to have been based on an ancient manuscript, although the provenance of the alleged sources differed in every edition. Presaging modern myths, the outrageous intention of the 1768 edition was to redress the influence of Shakespeare's *Macbeth*, which, it claimed, may 'misguide the judgement of an inattentive spectator or reader, by substituting implicitly the matter in the play for the genuine history of the times and persons represented'.

It is unclear if the *Secret History* is a literary fake or simply a work of 'historical' fiction, although it must have fooled at least some of those involved in its publication; Peter Buchan, who published the 1828 edition, was otherwise a distinguished publisher of ballads and local history. The authors' patrons were presumably among the gullible; the 1768 edition was dedicated to the Duchess of Hamilton, a descendant of 'the two most illustrious characters in the performance', while the 1828 edition was dedicated to the Earl of Fife, appealing to his ego by referring to him as the Thane of Fife.

MODERN MYTHS

As the *Secret History* demonstrates, the Macbeth myth continued to evolve after the appearance of Shakespeare's *Macbeth*. Indeed, renewed interest in Macbeth, stimulated by the play and combined with the scarcity of eleventh-century sources, has ensured the continued development of the myth to this day. As a result of differing approaches adopted over the past two centuries, the mythical Macbeth now takes several divergent forms. These modern myths belong to two loose groups: modern retellings of Shakespeare's *Macbeth*, which are considered below, and the influence of the myth on ostensibly factual historical analyses.

The Macbeth myth has had a pervasive influence on the study of the historical Macbeth. Since the late eighteenth century, many Scottish histories have derived their accounts of Macbeth and his reign directly, selectively and uncritically from the chronicles, with the inevitable result that they perpetuate medieval myths. Two mythological strands may be identified.

Some historians have emphasised the evil, violence and tyranny of Macbeth's reign and the perceived illegitimacy of his kingship; Macbeth the usurper, 'snorting with the indigested fumes of the blood of his sovereign'.[75] Respected historians of the present day are not immune from such perceptions; Professor Geoffrey Barrow claims that 'a harsh, brutally violent Iron Age quality characterized the struggles of these warlike mormaers [of Moray]', presumably including Macbeth.[76] This modern perception of Macbeth, epitomised by Bob Stewart's *Macbeth, Scotland's Warrior King* (1988), is a strong one. Macbeth's murder of Duncan dominated these perceptions and formed the point of reference against which Macbeth was viewed and judged, regardless of the fact that many early Scottish kings were murdered by their successors. This narrow perspective, uninformed of the wider context of early medieval kingship, inevitably leads to distorted interpretations: 'Macbeth . . . seems to have been haunted by a poignant consciousness of guilt. To soothe the anguish of his spirit, he was liberal to the poor, he gave largesses to the clergy, and caused ample distributions to be made at Rome. To the Culdees of Lochleven he conveyed valuable lands.'[77] Macbeth's pilgrimage simply becomes a quest for papal absolution for his crime, his grants to the Culdees charitable acts made out of contrition.

Other writers adopted a less judgmental, more sympathetic stance and their revisionist approach has exerted a profound influence on popular perceptions of Macbeth. Their stated objective was 'to discover the real Mac Beth as opposed to the figure of tradition', attempting to distinguish history from myth, fact from fiction.[78] But few of them even attempted an appraisal of the relevant source material and none felt able to concede that, in the study of Macbeth,

Macbeth as a Celtic warrior king. Growing awareness that Macbeth reigned not during the high Middle Ages but the eleventh century has led to an increasing perception of Macbeth as a primitive war leader. (Illustration by James Field, from Bob Stewart's *Macbeth: Scotland's Warrior King* (1988). © Firebird Books)

the distinction between myth and history is frequently very blurred.

Although some historians professed neutrality, most pursued the subject from a preconceived agenda. Their aim was 'to rescue the good name of the historical MacBeth' from 'the fabulist school of fawning sycophants who invented their lies centuries after his death' and 'the later romancers [who] laid the crimes of others to his charge, so that now he stands before the world branded with "every sin that has a name"'.[79] Again, more recent and respected historians adopt a similar approach; Professor Edward Cowan's 'attempt to redeem' Macbeth's reputation 'begin[s] at the very dawn of Scottish history in order to refute Shakespeare's claim that MacBeth was a tyrant and a foul usurper'.[80] But rather than producing objective historical analyses, these commentators had reached their verdict at the outset: 'to talk of Shakespeare's Macbeth as the MacBeth of historical reality is . . . to malign a ruler who stands head and shoulders above the feuds and petty squabbles which ravaged the kingdoms of Europe in the eleventh century'.[81]

This historical revisionism was intended to expose a perceived miscarriage of justice, right a historical wrong and exonerate Macbeth from the charges levelled against him over the centuries, thus enabling him to occupy his proper place in history. But behind this attempted rehabilitation sometimes lay a thinly veiled nationalism, attempting to restore the blackened reputation of a good Scottish king from the libels of an English dramatist. Other motives were personal, as John MacBeth's dedication reveals: 'To the memory of the much-maligned MacBeth, the crowned head of my father's ancient and far-scattered clan'.[82]

The revisionist approach simply rejects one mythological tradition, that of Macbeth as murderer, tyrant and usurper, in favour of another. The now ascendant tradition, portraying Macbeth and his reign positively, can be traced back to the *Prophecy of Berchán*. This tradition acclaims Macbeth as a 'righteous king': able, excellent, efficient, valorous, vigorous, popular, just, equitable, kind to the poor and generous to the Church, his reign a time of peace, prosperity, abundance, good government and even happiness. All these assessments are unsubstantiated by contemporary historical sources, while others are pure fantasy; Macbeth had 'pleasing manners', while Gruoch was 'painted as by nature a sunny little woman, bright, dainty, graceful, tender, with a strong and clear intellect which she felt, but did not recognise, and that never prevented her from winning the affection of those around her'.[83] The latter interpretation reflects nineteenth-century stage portrayals of more feminine and wifely Lady Macbeths, most famously that of Ellen Terry, in contrast to increasingly violent and evil Macbeths.[84]

Some historians sought to reconcile these divergent traditions by interpreting Macbeth's good reign as a deliberate strategy: 'He endeavoured to conciliate the minds of his subjects, and to make them forget, if possible, the enormities by which he had paved his way to the throne, by a beneficent though vigorous administration'.[85] Others attributed Macbeth's downfall to his benevolence: 'If a king makes fertile seasons, it must be by promoting agriculture, and diffusing among his people the blessings of peace. Had he paid more attention to his own interests, and less to those of his subjects, the crown might have remained in his family. But neglecting the practice of war, he fell a martyr to his own virtues.'[86]

Such perceptions led to Macbeth's reign being viewed as a golden age, 'that period of national prosperity and fabulous wealth', 'the best reign in early Scots history', in what was otherwise perceived to be a dark and undistinguished 'period of constant battle and sudden death'.[87] Mrs Stopes extolled 'the good old days of King Macbeth, a king so powerful, so prosperous, so faithful, so hospitable, and . . . *so national*'.[88] Another popular modern perception of

Macbeth is as the last great Celtic King of Scots, although what this means and its significance is never defined. Macbeth was not only perceived to belong to a golden age, but a *Celtic* golden age, before increased anglicising influences altered Scottish kingship and society for ever. Yet again, the interpretation of Scottish history is coloured by romantic nationalism.

These preconceptions also affected the interpretation of contemporary historical sources, sometimes in a most anachronistic manner. For example, Siward's return home 'with booty such as no man had before obtained' after the Battle of the Seven Sleepers was viewed as 'a remarkable testimony to the excellence of Macbeth's government and the soundness of whatever economic policy he may have followed'.[89] These claims rest solely on selected mythological sources and fail to take into account biases in the evidence, specifically the prominence accorded to Macbeth and his reign by both medieval chroniclers and modern historians. The revisionist 'history' of Macbeth and his reign simply perpetuates one strand of medieval mythology and cannot be substantiated. There is no evidence to indicate that Macbeth's reign was any more prosperous than those of other eleventh-century Scottish kings.

The modern mythology of Macbeth comprises not only recycled medieval myths but also works of historical fiction. The underlying premise of Dorothy Dunnett's *King Hereafter* is that Macbeth and Thorfinn, *Jarl* of Orkney, were the same person. Far-fetched though this may seem, it was anticipated a century earlier by the historian William Skene: 'The authorities for the history of Macbeth know nothing of Earl Thorfinn and his conquests. On the other hand the Sagas equally ignore Macbeth and his doings.'[90] Macbeth and Thorfinn went on pilgrimage to Rome at about the same time, prompting the suggestion that they travelled together.[91] It does not take much imagination to infer that, rather than two people travelling together, they were actually the same person.

But Macbeth *does* feature in the *Orkneyinga Saga*, while the date of Thorfinn's pilgrimage is problematical. There is no evidence that Macbeth and Thorfinn were in Rome the same year and, even if there was, there is nothing to suggest that they accompanied each other, let alone that they were the same person. Instead, this reflects the importance attached to the pilgrimage to Rome by insular kings during the mid-eleventh century. Royal pilgrimage was a high-profile activity, involving long-distance travel, visiting important ecclesiastical centres, meeting ecclesiastical dignitaries and possibly kings and competing with status-conscious monarchs to make the most impressive entrance to the Eternal City. Neighbouring rulers may have competed more intensely, with the result that Macbeth and Thorfinn would have made unlikely travelling companions.

Another modern myth concerns Macbeth's alleged association with the Stone of Destiny, on which Scottish kings were inaugurated at Scone. Doubts have been expressed about the Stone's authenticity since the late eighteenth century and a persistent tradition maintains that Edward I was fooled into taking a substitute stone in 1296 after the real Stone was hidden for safekeeping.[92] An anonymous letter in *The Times* of 1 January 1819 reported the discovery of what was reputed to be the real Stone on Dunsinane Hill. Rather than the monks of Scone Abbey hiding the Stone before Edward's arrival in 1296, Macbeth was claimed to have been responsible. This ignores the fact that Fordun records the Stone's presence at Scone two centuries after Macbeth's death, at the inauguration of Alexander III in 1249. In a contrived attempt to resolve this discrepancy, it was claimed that: 'Macbeth, from an implicit faith in the sacred character of the stone, and that the possession of it would insure the continuance of his sovereignty, transferred it to a close concealment in his fortress, substituting in its place a similar stone, which has ever since been accepted as the real one.'[93]

Despite its inherent implausibility, this tradition has been resurrected recently.[94] Although these claims are popular in Scotland, there is no evidence to support them and the 'Dunsinane Stone', if it ever existed, disappeared soon after its alleged rediscovery in 1819. Instead, the 'Dunsinane Stone' tradition represents the conflation of two powerful Scottish myths, Macbeth and the Stone of Destiny, which overlap in the popular imagination because of their common theme of early Scottish kingship and the proximity of Dunsinane and Scone. There is no reliable evidence to link Macbeth with the Stone of Destiny. Macbeth *may* have been inaugurated on the Stone, but he is most unlikely to have removed it from Scone and hidden it.

THE APPEAL OF MACBETH

The continuous evolution of the myth over the past millennium is a powerful testimony to an enduring and widespread fascination with Macbeth. But to what does the myth owe its appeal? Why has the tale of an eleventh-century Scottish king proved so consistently popular, making Macbeth the most famous Scottish monarch, his name and story known around the world?

The longevity of the Macbeth myth is attributable to its repackaging to suit changing political and historical circumstances and social and cultural tastes.

This has occurred on many occasions, thereby ensuring the myth's ongoing relevance. Despite their dark undertone, the verses in the *Prophecy of Berchán* praise a powerful king and heroic war leader, prophesising his death at the royal inauguration centre of Scone at the end of a long kingship. Here the appeal is specific and direct; the verses are derived from a eulogy in traditional heroic style, presumably intended to flatter Macbeth himself.

But later sources cast Macbeth in a very different role. The medieval Scottish chronicles had a strong ideological motive in emphasising the antiquity and genealogical continuity of the Scottish kingship in the face of English claims of overlordship. The chroniclers' nationalistic approach to the writing of history is reflected in their negative portrayal of Macbeth, who was believed to have usurped the Scottish kingship and interrupted this royal continuity. Despite this, elements of an older and more favourable tradition, reflecting ancient beliefs in the sacral powers of kings, survived embedded in some versions of the myth.

Although the medieval Scottish chroniclers were consistently hostile towards Macbeth, the manner in which they portrayed him changed over time. This is particularly evident in Wyntoun's *Orygynale Cronykil*. Wyntoun introduced darkly supernatural elements to the myth and literally demonised Macbeth by portraying him as the Devil's son. This transformation gave the myth an added relevance by both expressing and exploiting contemporary concerns about witchcraft, diabolism and the power of evil. The strong supernatural dimension also proved to be of lasting interest to later chroniclers and is central to Shakespeare's *Macbeth*.

Drawing heavily on Holinshed's *Chronicles*, Shakespeare successfully transformed the Macbeth myth into a drama, broadening and updating its appeal and introducing it to a much wider audience. *Macbeth* was popular with Jacobean audiences partly because it addressed contemporary concerns in an accessible and entertaining manner. Those concerns arose specifically from the accession of James VI of Scotland to the English throne and included (specifically Scottish) kingship, royal succession, the king's evil and witchcraft, issues in which James VI and I himself was deeply interested. *Macbeth's* topicality ensured its success, but its appeal was more enduring.

Shakespeare's *Macbeth* has enthralled audiences over four centuries. The tragedy's allure is evident from the frequency of its performance, the extensive literary and dramatic criticism it has attracted[95] and its translation into many languages. The Macbeth myth lends itself to the stage and the play's long-lasting success rests on the diversity of its appeal as dramatic entertainment.

This is evident from about 1660, when professional acting resumed at the Restoration of Charles II. As Samuel Pepys noted in 1667, *Macbeth* 'appears a play most excellent in all respects, but especially in divertisement, though it be a deep tragedy; which is a strange perfection in a tragedy, it being most proper here and suitable'.[96] The play became even more popular from the mid-eighteenth century, when the traditional over-acted and over-declamatory style attacked by Garrick in 1744 was eclipsed by his own talented and well-researched performance.[97] Garrick, perhaps the only actor to have truly mastered the part, became the standard against which later performances would be judged.

Macbeth is a play of fast-moving action and high drama, containing several peaks of theatrical tension, heroic but flawed characters, strong supernatural elements and a violent climax. The pace is maintained by frequent changes of scene (29 scenes in 5 acts) and the play's short length (about 2,108 lines), making it the third shortest in the First Folio. These qualities are attractive to audiences and actors alike, enabling the play to grasp and retain the audience's attention. Indeed, the theatrical challenges posed by the staging and interpretation of *Macbeth* have consistently drawn the leading actors of the age, resulting in many notable performances. The list of those who have played Macbeth and Lady Macbeth reads like a roll-call of the most eminent names of the British stage, from David Garrick/Hannah Pritchard and John Philip Kemble/Sarah Siddons in the eighteenth century, through William Charles Macready/Helen Faucit and Sir Henry Irving/Ellen Terry in the nineteenth, to Laurence Olivier/Vivien Leigh (in Glen Byam Shaw's 1955 Stratford Memorial Theatre production) and Ian McKellen/Judi Dench (in Trevor Nunn's 1976–8 Royal Shakespeare Company production) in the twentieth century. As one theatre critic observed, 'the play cannot work without a magnetic central pair: it is much more a star vehicle than a company show'.[98]

Macbeth's impressive pace, many changes of scene and sword-fights present difficulties, even dangers, to its performers. These, combined with the play's strong supernatural theme, have inspired several theatrical superstitions and given *Macbeth* its own unique 'curse'.[99] *Macbeth*'s reputation is all the more remarkable given the superstitious nature of the acting profession. The superstitions surrounding Macbeth are a prominent element of its appeal to both actors and audiences. But in one respect, *Macbeth* might well be considered as cursed.

In a world sustained by violence, the only way in which firstly Macbeth and then Malcolm can express their opposition is through aggression.[100] Violence is integral to *Macbeth*, a key element of the play's dramatic appeal, and it is perhaps unsurprising that this has sometimes been mirrored by its audiences. Indeed, the potential of the play to whip audiences into an aggressive frenzy may occasionally have been exploited by theatre managers or actors. For example, when the rebuilt Covent Garden Theatre reopened on 18 September 1809, Kemble chose *Macbeth* for the first night, probably to attract a full house and generate publicity. The new prices charged resulted in the 'O.P.' (Old Price) disturbances, lasting seventy days. Although *Macbeth* is not the only Shakespearean play to have caused a riot, it holds the unenviable record for having sparked the worst. The cause was the directly competing interpretations of the part by Macready and the American actor Edwin Forrest. A very public, antagonistic and nationalistic rivalry between the two actors and their supporters climaxed in the Astor Place riot in New York on 10 May 1849. A crowd of 10,000 took to the streets, leaving 31 people dead and over a hundred wounded.[101] Few plays can have aroused such extreme reactions or resulted in such fatal consequences.

Productions of *Macbeth* provide many insights into contemporary theatrical, and therefore also popular, perceptions of the myth as well as on the play's shifting social and political significance. It was usual for *Macbeth* to be played in contemporary dress until the mid-eighteenth century, when it became more common to emphasise the 'primitiveness' of *Macbeth* through the wearing of traditional Highland dress, medieval armour or an imaginative combination of both. Macbeth's portrayal as a contemporary Highlander would have played on English prejudices in the wake of the failed Jacobite rebellion of 1745–6, which reinforced English stereotypes of the Highland Scots as untrustworthy and violent. Such was the contemporary political significance of *Macbeth* that, after the Jacobite victory at Falkirk in 1746, 'The king

Macbeth as a Highland warrior – a caricature of William Charles Macready, the English actor-manager, as Macbeth in the Princess's Theatre production, 1845. He sought to capture Macbeth's 'primitive' and war-like character by combining Highland dress with medieval armour. Macready used his 'heroic truncheon' to good effect on wayward fellow actors and rioting audiences alike; the truncheon even broke on at least one of these occasions. (Victoria & Albert Museum, UK/Bridgeman Art Library)

[George III] was advised to go to the theatre and to command the *Tragedy of Macbeth*', which was then performed.[102] Reinforcing the play's political significance, some Highland clans – the MacKinnons, MacMillans and MacQuarries – claimed descent from Macbeth.[103] Although improbable,[104] this mythological ancestry symbolised their independence from firstly the Scottish and later British crowns.

The enduring relevance of the themes of ambition, temptation, supernatural and evil explored in the play are fundamental to its continued appeal. Its portrayal of vaulting ambition – and, indeed, coining of the phrase – and the pursuit and exercise of power has fascinated statesmen, perhaps mindful of the salutary lessons it contains. For example, at the height of the American Civil War Abraham Lincoln declared: 'I think nothing equals *Macbeth*. It is wonderful'.[105] And the often unseen influence of a woman behind an evil or despotic head of state is still likened to that of Lady Macbeth over her husband. In an increasingly competitive age, *Macbeth* presents an unambiguous lesson on how to claw oneself to the top. But although Cranfield School of Management has recently begun to use Shakespeare's plays to teach leadership skills, it has chosen to focus on the more positive lessons gained from *Henry V* and *Julius Caesar*, rather than *Macbeth*.[106]

The power of *Macbeth* to stimulate the creative imagination is apparent from its adaptation to many different media. *Macbeth* appealed particularly to the Romantic movement of the late eighteenth and nineteenth centuries. Many distinguished artists, including Sir Joshua Reynolds, Henry Fuseli, Dante Gabriel Rossetti and John Singer Sargent, depicted the most dramatic scenes from *Macbeth*, particularly the witches, Banquo's ghost and Lady Macbeth. The earliest operatic adaptation, Guiseppe Verdi's *Macbeth* (1847, revised 1865), based on an Italian verse adaptation by Giulio Carcano, also belongs to the Romantic Age.[107] Richard Strauss' symphonic poem, *Macbeth* (1890), and Dmitry Shostakovich's opera *Lady Macbeth of the Mtsensk District* (1934), based on an 1865 story by Nikolai Leskov, are the other significant musical works inspired by *Macbeth*.

Shakespeare's *Macbeth* has also inspired many twentieth-century dramatic, cinematic and literary retellings, in various genres. The plays include Gordon Bottomley's *Gruach* (1921), Barbara Garson's *MacBird!* (1967), Charles Marowitz's *A Macbeth* (1971), Eugène Ionesco's *Macbett* (1972) and Tom Stoppard's *Dogg's Hamlet, and, Cahoot's Macbeth* (1979). Modern literary reworkings of the myth include historical novels, such as Nigel Tranter's *MacBeth the King* (1978) and Dorothy Dunnett's *King Hereafter* (1982), and mystery thrillers, including Marvin Kaye's *Bullets for Macbeth* (1976), Ngaio Marsh's *Light Thickens* (1982) and Nicolas Freeling's *Lady Macbeth* (1988).

Illustrating that the play may be approached on different levels, Shakespeare's *Macbeth* itself has sometimes been assigned to the 'whodunnit' genre, for example, by the woman in James Thurber's 'The Macbeth Murder Mystery'.[108] Seeing the Penguin edition of *Macbeth*, she concludes that it must be a crime thriller: 'I got real comfy in bed that night and all ready to read a good mystery story and here I had *The Tragedy of Macbeth* – a book for high-school students. Like *Ivanhoe*'. And applying the logic and conventions of detective stories, she concludes that the murderer must be, not Macbeth, but MacDuff. A distinctive feature of several of these plays and novels is their translation of the Macbeth

Orson Welles' expressionistic portrayal of an evil and primitive Macbeth (in thigh-length leather boots) in the title role of his film version of *Macbeth* (1948). (Republic, courtesy the Kobal Collection)

myth, its characters and themes, to other periods and places. Reinforcing *Macbeth*'s contemporary relevance, several of these have a modern setting.

One of the most successful media for which *Macbeth* has been adapted is film. Cinematic versions of *Macbeth* have a long and distinguished history;[109] a brief sequence depicting the duel scene[110] dates from as early as 1905. Silent film versions include Sir Herbert Beerbohm Tree's *Macbeth* (1916), based on his 1911 theatrical production.[111] Similarly, Orson Welles' expressionistic portrayal of an evil and primitive *Macbeth* (1948) drew on his 1936 New York stage production.[112] Although controversial at the time, the most highly acclaimed screen adaptation remains Roman Polanski's brutal, bloody and surreal *Macbeth* (1971). Other notable film versions are George Schaefer's *Macbeth* (1960), Trevor Nunn's (1976) adaptation for television, and even an animated version, directed by Nikolai Serebirakov (1992), in the *Shakespeare: the Animated Tales* series.[113] Although each offered its own unique interpretation of *Macbeth*, these films more or less closely follow the plot and high medieval setting of Shakespeare's *Macbeth*. Diverging from this in a quest for 'Dark Age' authenticity, Cromwell Productions' *Macbeth* (1996), in *The Definitive Shakespeare* series, sought to 'give it a truly Caledonian hallmark', steeped 'in the Celtic flavour of eleventh century Scotland'.[114]

Macbeth in medieval armour: Jon Finch plays the title role of Roman Polanski's film version of Macbeth (1971). Macbeth is widely perceived and played as a monarch of the high Middle Ages, rather than the dawn of the medieval period. (Columbia, courtesy the Kobal Collection)

Other films have transposed the tragedy in space and time. Indeed, cinematic settings of *Macbeth* span the past millennium and include three continents. Ken Hughes' *Joe Macbeth* (1955) and William Reilly's *Men of Respect* (1990) are set in contemporary criminal underworlds in the USA. Michael Bogdanov's (1997) television adaptation is set in a contemporary war zone; Macbeth and the cast appear in combat fatigues, brandishing automatic weapons. Most striking of all is Akiro Kurosawa's complex adaptation, *Kumonosu-ju* (1957), a film of great formality and powerful imagery. Released with subtitles as *Throne of Blood*, but literally meaning *The Castle of the Spider's Web*, this translated the tragedy to medieval Japan.[115] Yukio Ninagawa's theatrical productions (Edinburgh Festival, 1985, and the National Theatre, London, 1987) also set *Macbeth* in feudal Japan.[116]

Macbeth's influence is so strong that it is difficult to overestimate its cultural and historical significance: 'So great a masterpiece draws to itself so much learning, so much reasoning, so much speculation, that it becomes a nodal point in the history of man's awareness of himself'.[117] Not surprisingly, *Macbeth* is frequently referred to in superlatives. August Wilhelm Schlegel, the Romanticist who translated Shakespeare's plays into German, asked of *Macbeth*: 'who could exhaust the praise for this sublime work? Since *The Furies* of Aeschylus [the Athenian tragic poet, 525–456 BC], nothing so grand and terrible has ever been composed'.[118] In keeping with this, *Macbeth* has attracted the attention of some of the world's greatest thinkers. Sigmund Freud's fascination with the play is apparent from his assessment of Macbeth and Lady Macbeth: 'Together they exhaust the possibilities of reaction to the crime, like two disunited parts of a single psychical individuality, and it may be that they are both copied from a single prototype'.[119]

For almost 400 years, the myth's appeal has been due almost exclusively to Shakespeare's compelling tragedy. *Macbeth* is one of the most popular dramas, in

Macbeth translated to medieval Japan: Toshiro Mifune as Washizu (the Macbeth figure) and Isuzu Yamada as Asaji (the Lady Macbeth figure) in Akiro Kurosawa's *Kumonosu-ju* (*Throne of Blood*) (1957). The blood-spattered walls contrast with the stark simplicity and geometrical formality of the set. (Toho, courtesy the Kobal Collection)

any language, of all time, capturing the imagination of successive generations of actors, critics and audiences alike and inspiring artists, dramatists, film-makers and novelists. It is these continuous processes of retelling in different media and translation to various – but especially contemporary – settings, that ensure *Macbeth*'s enduring relevance and favour. This is a lasting testament, not only to Shakespeare's brilliance as a dramatist, but also to the frequently overlooked chroniclers on whose writings Shakespeare based his play. But the play is also a tribute to the courage and determination of the historical Macbeth, King of Scots, whose bold but bloody deeds have both repulsed the sensitivities and inspired the creativity of successive generations.

CHAPTER 5

In Search of Macbeth

The Macbeth myth, in all its forms, displays a strong sense of place, associating many events and characters with specific locations. Shakespeare's tragedy, for example, opens in the aftermath of a battle in Fife in which Macbeth had distinguished himself against the Norwegians. The action then moves north, to the moor near Forres and Macbeth's castle at Inverness, before switching south to its denouement at Dunsinane. Topographical references occur throughout: Sweno, the Norwegian king, pays the Scots at Inchcolm to retrieve his dead; Duncan is buried on Iona; Macbeth, and later Malcolm, are enthroned at Scone; while Malcolm and Siward advance on Macbeth's fortress from Birnam Wood. The Scottish chroniclers, who knew Scotland better than Shakespeare did, refer to additional places in their versions of the myth. And with thanes of Cawdor, Glamis, Lochaber, Fife, Lennox, Ross, Menteith, Angus and Caithness, the cast itself reads like a gazetteer of Scotland. The Macbeth myth is fixed in the Scottish landscape and has, in turn, generated a rich body of topographical mythology.

In contrast, the historical Macbeth is firmly linked with very few places, although his association with others may be inferred. This makes it difficult for archaeology to contribute directly to the study of Macbeth. And although archaeology presents the greatest potential source of information about early medieval Scotland, it is of limited value when studying specific reigns. The absence of precise dating evidence currently makes it impossible to assign artefacts or buildings to Macbeth's reign, let alone identify those with which Macbeth himself was associated. Nevertheless, exploratory excavations conducted at some Scottish royal centres have led to the tentative identification of archaeological 'events', usually phases of destruction or burning, with historically recorded incidents.[1] Such excavations have the potential to contribute to the study of Macbeth and his reign, even if only indirectly.

MONUMENTS, MYTHS AND MACBETH

In the absence of more reliable information, mythology *may* assist the identification of some sites associated with Macbeth. Yet few of these places appear in sources earlier than Boece's *History*, while others feature only in later folklore. This indicates that Macbeth's links with most, if not all, of these locations are wholly mythological. Nevertheless, these places and their traditional associations with Macbeth comprise another, largely neglected, dimension of the Macbeth myth. These sources illustrate how various monuments were invested with meaning and value through their links with the mythological Macbeth. This chapter identifies those places linked with Macbeth, historically and/or mythologically, outlines their archaeology and history and assesses the nature of their association with Macbeth.

The myth's topographic content has stimulated attempts to identify those places associated with Macbeth and any surviving remains there. The earliest recorded example of this may be Wyntoun's identification of Dunsinane as Macbeth's fortress and the scene of his battle against Malcolm and Siward.

The hogback tombstone on Inchcolm, on the Firth of Forth. A tenth- or eleventh-century funerary monument in the form of a stylised house, now exhibited in the visitor centre on the island. Despite being badly eroded, the stylised roofing slates are still visible. Although this form of monument is of Viking origin and inspiration, it was adopted widely in northern England and Scotland. This example is therefore more likely to mark the grave of a member of the early monastic community on Inchcolm, rather than that of a passing Viking seafarer. (Crown copyright: Royal Commission on the Ancient and Historical Monuments of Scotland)

Although Wyntoun had access to earlier sources that no longer survive, the possibility that Dunsinane's impressive defences, prominent location and proximity to Scone may have inspired its mythological association with Macbeth cannot be excluded. If so, this would be the earliest example of Macbeth's mythological association with a monument.

With this possible exception, the attribution of monuments to events within the Macbeth myth did not begin until the sixteenth century. Relating how, during Duncan's reign, a Danish army under Sweno was defeated by Macbeth and Banquo at Kinghorn, on the south coast of Fife, Boece could point to the physical legacy of this battle: 'The Danes who fled to their ships gave great sums of gold to Macbeth to suffer their nobles who were slain . . . to be buried at Saint Columb's Inch. In memory thereof many ancient sepulchres are sited in the said Inch, engraved with the arms of the Danes.'[2] This episode, which was incorporated in later chronicles, evidently formed the basis of Shakespeare's reference to Inchcolm.[3] An example of a distinctive form of tombstone, in the form of a stylised house and known as a hogback, survives on Inchcolm and may have inspired this reference.[4] Although belonging to a class of monument of

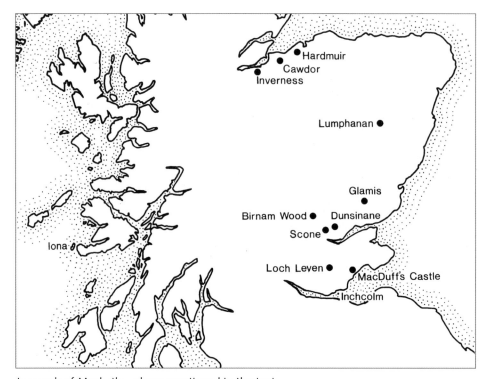

In search of Macbeth – places mentioned in the text.

Anglo-Scandinavian origin, this is unlikely to have been the work of passing Danish raiders during Duncan's reign. Instead, it probably marks the mid-tenth-century grave of a member of Inchcolm's monastic community.

Reflecting its strong links between incidents, characters and places, the Macbeth myth is not confined to a literary medium but also occurs as topographical mythology. These myths were recorded from the 1770s. This period saw a growing fascination with the study of Scotland's past, reflecting a renewed sense of national identity and the rise of antiquarianism, and increasing interest in Shakespeare's *Macbeth*. This was the Romantic Age and places reputedly associated with Macbeth attracted Scottish antiquarians and English travellers alike. Several visitors recorded their observations and impressions, and sometimes the traditions concerning these locations. These were oral traditions, collected from local people, although they are unlikely to have been transmitted by word of mouth since the mid-eleventh century. Instead, this folklore was ultimately derived from literary sources, predominantly the chronicles of Boece and his translators. This, in turn, sometimes stimulated the local elaboration of myths, adding more locations and events to the narrative. In some cases, local traditions may even have been prompted by visitors' own enquiries, which were also based on the Macbeth portrayed in the chronicles. This chapter follows in the footsteps of those antiquarians and travellers.

THE MOOR NEAR FORRES

> BANQUO   How far is't called to Forres? What are these,
> So withered and so wild in their attire,
> That look not like th'inhabitants o'th'earth,
> And yet are on't?
>
> *Macbeth* Act 1, Scene 3

Macbeth first encountered the witches 'in the middest of a laund' as he and Banquo 'iourneyed towarde Fores, where the king as then laie . . . passing through the woodes and fieldes', as Holinshed relates.[5] Shakespeare transformed this setting into the more dramatic 'blasted heath'.[6] According to local tradition:

> The Hard Moor, to the westward of Forres . . . is the traditional region where Macbeth met the witches. . . . Such is the wonderful power of Shakespeare that out of a few meagre and uncertain legends he has riveted the imagination

of thousands to this locality. It is indeed a 'hard moor' and 'blasted heath' even at this present, and well befits the imaginary sense of such a supernatural meeting. A knoll . . . crowned with a group of dark old pines is pointed out where the interview was held.[7]

This is Macbeth's Hillock (National Grid Reference NH 959568), in Hardmuir Wood, 7 km west-south-west of Forres, Morayshire.

Despite its isolation, the legendary association with Macbeth and the witches attracted visitors to this desolate spot. James Boswell and Dr Samuel Johnson passed it on their tour of Scotland in 1773. Johnson recorded that 'We went forwards . . . to Fores, the town to which Macbeth was travelling, when he met the weird sisters in his way. This to an Englishman is classic ground. Our imaginations were heated, and our thoughts recalled to their old amusements'.[8] Boswell's account reveals just how inspired Johnson was: 'In the afternoon, we drove over the very heath where Macbeth met the witches, according to tradition. Dr Johnson again solemnly repeated . . . a good deal more of Macbeth. His recitation was grand and affecting, and . . . had no more tone than it should have. It was the better for it. He then parodied the "All-hail" of the witches to Macbeth, addressing himself to me.'[9] Johnson was more restrained the following day. After staying overnight in Forres, he and Boswell 'next morning entered upon the road, on which Macbeth heard the fatal prediction; but we travelled on not interrupted by promises of kingdoms'.[10]

So great was the moor's fame that it reportedly attracted the enquiries of an unnamed US president during the 1880s.[11] During the same decade, the moor was also visited by one of the most famous stage couples to play Macbeth and Lady Macbeth: 'When Henry Irving and Ellen Terry visited the Blasted Heath, in the summer of 1887, Irving enquired of the driver whether there were still any witches, and he was much mystified with the answer he got, that they had disappeared "at the time of the flood" . . . the great Moray Flood of 1828.'[12] Their visit was presumably linked to the opening the following year of Irving's new and critically acclaimed interpretation of *Macbeth*. Irving and Terry evidently took their background research seriously.

GLAMIS AND CAWDOR

LADY MACBETH   Great Glamis, worthy Cawdor,
                    Greater than both by the all-hail hereafter
                                        Macbeth Act 1, Scene 5

Glamis and Cawdor are Scotland's most famous thanages, immortalised by their traditional association with Macbeth. Although now inseparably linked in the popular imagination, they are geographically distant; Glamis is 9 km south-west of Forfar, Angus, while Cawdor, 8 km south-west of Nairn, Nairnshire, lies some 125 km to the north-west, on the other side of the Mounth. The Thanage of Glamis is first recorded in 1264 and a Thane of Cawdor (or Calder) in 1295, with the latter title remaining in use well into the sixteenth century. The earlier histories of Glamis and Cawdor are obscure, although their recorded status as thanages by the thirteenth century suggests that they may have been the administrative centres of royal estates for possibly some centuries before. Glamis' royal associations are supported by the murder of Malcolm II there in 1034.

Although Glamis and Cawdor were both historic thanages, there is no evidence to link the historical Macbeth with either of them. Instead, his relationship with Glamis and Cawdor is mythological and late, first appearing in Boece's *History*. The chroniclers mistakenly believed that Macbeth had inherited the thanage of Glamis from his father, who had reputedly killed Malcolm II. This enabled the chroniclers to portray Macbeth as belonging to a family of regicides. Macbeth, however, belonged to the hereditary Mormaers of Moray. This may make his association with Cawdor, which lies within the historic province of Moray, more plausible, although there is no corroboratory evidence. Although Cawdor Castle 'probably occupies the site of a more ancient place of strength',[13] there are no traces of early medieval fortifications at either site. However, these may have been obscured or obliterated by the construction of the later castles.

Glamis and Cawdor were both medieval baronial seats. Cawdor

Cawdor Castle, Nairnshire. The great fifteenth-century tower dominates the castle, which evolved over the following centuries. Although Macbeth is styled Thane of Cawdor in later versions of the myth, and most famously in Shakespeare's *Macbeth*, there is no evidence that this site was fortified in the eleventh century. (Crown copyright: Royal Commission on the Ancient and Historical Monuments of Scotland)

Glamis Castle, Angus. The sixteenth-century L-plan tower house was remodelled and extended from the seventeenth century to create a grand baronial palace, the hereditary seat of the Earls of Strathmore and Kinghorne. (Crown copyright: Royal Commission on the Ancient and Historical Monuments of Scotland)

Castle (NH 847498), the seat of the Earls of Cawdor, dates from 1454, when William, Thane of Cawdor, was granted a royal licence 'to build his castle of Cawdor and fortify it with walls, moats, and iron portcullis, and furnish the same with turrets and other defensive equipment'.[14] Its earliest element comprises the great turreted tower house, while the adjoining ranges date from between the sixteenth and nineteenth centuries.[15] The origins of Glamis Castle (NO 386480), the seat of the Earls of Strathmore and Kinghorne, are obscure, but by the late sixteenth century it comprised an L-plan tower house which was extensively added to and altered at a later date.[16]

Although built over four-hundred years after Duncan's murder, both castles are inseparably associated with Macbeth in popular tradition: 'The castle of Glamis probably enjoys a wider fame than almost any other Scottish building, associated as it is all over the world with the tragedy of "Macbeth" . . . the shadowy Thane of Glamis is the predominating figure which rises before the mind's eye as one gazes on its quaint and antique towers'.[17] Cawdor Castle could boast some colourful mementoes of the violent deeds with which it was popularly associated: 'Some red stains on the floor of what was called "King Duncan's Room" . . . used to be shown as "King Duncan's blood"'.[18] Exhibited there was: 'the identical four-posted bed in which the murder of King Duncan was committed. . . . The room,

The vaulted basement in the central tower at Cawdor Castle, Nairnshire. The chest may once have held what was claimed to be 'King Duncan's chain-armour'. A curious feature is that the basement has been built around the trunk of a hawthorn tree.

and the bed within it, were both burned by an accidental fire in 1815, thereby depriving all future visitors of so very interesting an exhibition.'[19] 'King Duncan's chain-armour', which was kept in the vaulted basement, appears to have escaped damage. These appear to be late traditions – Boswell and Johnson, who visited Cawdor Castle, say nothing of them – and they have no historical basis.

INVERNESS

DUNCAN   This castle hath a pleasant seat; the air
         Nimbly and sweetly recommends itself
         Unto our gentle senses.

Macbeth Act 1, Scene 6

Conflicting accounts of the locations of Duncan's murder and Macbeth's castle appear in different versions of the Macbeth myth. The earliest sources and

Fordun place the murder at *Bothgouanan*, near Elgin, while Boece and the later chroniclers claim that Macbeth killed Duncan at Inverness. Unable to reconcile these traditions, Holinshed gives both locations. Macbeth's castle does not appear in any of these accounts. Shakespeare was the first to set the murder within Macbeth's castle, partly for dramatic effect and to emphasise the treasonable nature of the deed, but also reflecting the merging of Holinshed's accounts of the murders of Duff and Duncan. Of the two locations for Duncan's murder, Shakespeare chose the mythical one, Inverness. Despite this, Macbeth's portrayal as Thane of Cawdor has led to Cawdor being popularly identified as the scene of the crime.

The recorded origins of Inverness as a fortified royal centre may go back to the sixth century, when St Columba visited the fortress of Bridei (or Brude), a 'most powerful King of the Picts', on his mission to convert the Picts to Christianity. According to Adomnán's *Life of Columba*, Bridei's fortress was near the River Ness. Artefacts and radiocarbon dates from Craig Phadraig (NH 640453), an Iron Age vitrified fort 2.4 km west of Inverness, attest its reoccupation during the sixth and seventh centuries.[20] There is, however, no evidence of later occupation.

Craig Phadraig, Inverness-shire. An elongated hillfort, defended by two ramparts of vitrified stone, occupies the hilltop. The hillfort, probably constructed during the fifth or fourth centuries BC, was reoccupied by the Picts during the sixth and seventh centuries AD. (Crown copyright: Royal Commission on the Ancient and Historical Monuments of Scotland)

Alternatively, Bridei's fortress may have been at Inverness,[21] strategically sited near the mouth of the Ness, where the Beauly and Moray Firths meet. A plausible location for an early medieval fortress is the site later occupied by Inverness Castle. This formerly stood on Castle Hill (NH 667451), on the east bank of the Ness and the western edge of the medieval burgh, dominating the town and an adjacent ford. Although traditionally reputed to have been built by Malcolm III after he had killed Macbeth,

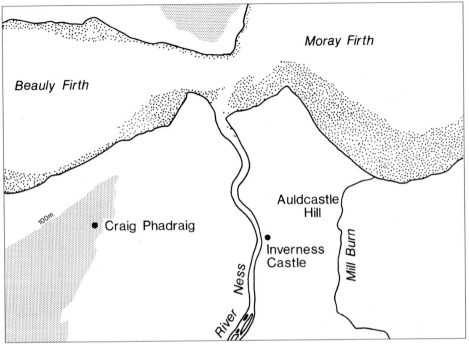

Inverness, detailing the locations of early medieval and medieval fortifications mentioned in the text.

Inverness Castle appears to have originated as a motte and bailey fortification associated with the foundation of the royal burgh of Inverness in the mid-twelfth century. The earliest masonry castle on the site dates only from 1412, when Alexander Stewart, Earl of Mar, was appointed governor, and the Earl of Huntly added a substantial stone tower house after becoming sheriff of Inverness in 1508.

Inverness Castle also featured on Boswell and Johnson's itinerary. Boswell describes how:

We then went to Macbeth's castle. I had a romantick satisfaction in seeing Dr Johnson actually in it. It perfectly corresponds with Shakespeare's description . . . Just as we came out of it, a raven perched on one of the chimney tops, and croaked. Then I repeated:

'. . . The raven himself is hoarse,
That croaks the fatal enterance of Duncan
Under my battlements.'[22]

Inverness Castle, from across the River Ness. Although occupying the site of the medieval (though not necessarily the eleventh-century) castle of Inverness, the present buildings on Castle Hill date only from the nineteenth century. (Crown copyright: Royal Commission on the Ancient and Historical Monuments of Scotland)

Johnson was also impressed, if less vocal: 'Here is a castle, called the castle of Macbeth, the walls of which are yet standing. It was no very capacious edifice, but stands upon a rock so high and steep, that I think it was once not accessible, but by the help of ladders, or a bridge.'[23]

But Boswell and Johnson may have let their imaginations get the better of them. Converted into Fort George after the Jacobite rebellion of 1715, Inverness Castle was destroyed by the Jacobites in 1746. By 1791, of this 'irregular fortification', 'nothing now remains . . . but rubbish', although part of the eastern curtain wall was said to be standing in 1835.[24] Although still known as Inverness Castle, the castellated sheriff court building now occupying the site dates only from 1834.

Moreover, Boswell and Johnson may have visited the wrong site. According to local tradition, Macbeth's Castle was on the eastern side of Inverness.[25] This earlier fortification reputedly stood on Old Castle (or Auldcastle) Hill in the Crown area of Inverness (NH 674457), between the River Ness to the west and the Mill Burn and Moray Firth to the east: 'The Thane of Calder's [Cawdor's] castle was built on the eastern extremity of the hill. It was razed to the ground by Malcolm, in detestation of the murderer of his father .... There is not a vestige of this castle to be seen . . . [except] Fragments of bricks at times are turned up by the plough.'[26] As masonry castles were unknown in eleventh-century Scotland, the 'bricks' are unlikely to have belonged to a fortification linked with Macbeth.

Inverness was an important power centre during the Middle Ages but, like other places within Moray, there is no archaeological or historical evidence to support the presence there of a fortress associated with Macbeth.

SCONE

ROSS	Then 'tis most like The sovereignty will fall upon Macbeth.
MACDUFF	He is already named and gone to Scone To be invested.

Macbeth Act 2, Scene 4

Scone is referred to briefly on only two occasions in the Macbeth myth but plays a significant role as the place where firstly Macbeth, and later Malcolm, were made king. This reflects Scone's historic role as the inauguration place of Scotland's medieval kings and, until it was captured by Edward I of England in 1296, the location of the famous Stone of Destiny, upon which the Scottish kings were made.[27] Although the installation of Alexander III in 1249 is the earliest to have been recorded in any detail, Scone's origins as a royal inauguration place are probably much earlier. Fordun anachronistically records the 'coronations' at Scone of Giric in 875 (actually 878) and his successor, Donald II, in 892 (actually 889).[28] Although uncorroborated, these references at least reflect the medieval perception of Scone as a royal induction site of considerable antiquity. Fordun described Scone as 'the place where both the Pictish and the Scottish kings from ancient times had established the chief seat of their kingdom'.[29] Although ignoring the reality of peripatetic kingship, this suggests that Scone originated as a Pictish royal centre and investiture site, perhaps of the province of Gowrie before becoming the royal inauguration centre of the Pictish kingdom as a whole. The Scots probably then appropriated Scone in the mid-ninth century, drawing on the antiquity of the site and its ritual associations to legitimise their newly extended kingship over Alba.

Scone retained some of its significance as a royal centre throughout the Middle Ages and sometimes beyond: the last kings crowned there were James I in 1424 and Charles II in 1651; the Thanage of Scone, recorded by 1234, attests its status as the administrative centre of a medieval royal estate; royal charters signed there record both the presence of kings and Scone's function as a legislative centre; while the nearby Gallows Knowe indicates the dispensing of justice.

Scone was also a significant ecclesiastical centre. Alexander I founded an Augustinian priory there in 1114, when Scone was 'the chief seat of government' (*in superiore sede regni Scona*).[30] In doing so, 'the church of Scone was given over to canons', indicating that the priory was based on a pre-existing, probably Culdee, community.[31] The priory was elevated to the status of an abbey in 1164 but was destroyed in 1559 by reformers from Perth, incited by an inflammatory speech made by John Knox.

A major royal centre both before and after the eleventh century, Scone almost certainly retained that role during Macbeth's reign. This is supported by the *Prophecy of Berchán*'s prediction that Macbeth would die 'in the middle of Scone'. That Scone was considered an appropriate setting for Macbeth's death emphasises its significance during his reign, probably pointing to its contemporary status as the pre-eminent royal centre and inauguration place of the Scottish kings. The origin of this source, in a praise poem composed for Macbeth, attests Macbeth's direct links with Scone; he was probably inaugurated and had a palace there.

On the east bank of the River Tay (NO 113265), 2 km north of Perth, Scone occupies a slight eminence on an elevated terrace overlooking a bend in the Tay and its confluence with the River Almond. There is little to suggests Scone's former status. The most imposing structure is the neo-Gothic Scone Palace, the seat of the Earls of Mansfield, which was built between 1803 and 1812. The grounds were extensively landscaped at the same time, explaining why there are so few upstanding remains, although excavation may be productive. Scone's only visible link with its royal past is Moot (or Boot) Hill, a large, possibly artificial, flat-topped earthen mound. Successive Scottish kings were inaugurated on or in front of Moot Hill, most famously Alexander III in 1249. Within the context of Malcolm II's reign, but perhaps referring more generally, Fordun described the mound as 'the moothill on which stood the royal seat at Scone where the kings sitting on the throne in royal attire are accustomed to proclaim judgements, laws and statutes to their subjects'.[32] At its centre stands a small neo-Gothic chapel, which probably incorporates the fabric of the old parish church, first recorded in 1624.

Scone and its Moot Hill performed symbolic and functional roles of fundamental importance to the early Scottish kingship. As king and kingdom

Scone Palace, Perthshire. It occupies the site of the Scottish royal centre and the medieval abbey, although the neo-Gothic baronial residence, the seat of the Earls of Mansfield, dates only from the early nineteenth century. (The Author)

were closely identified in early medieval Scotland, the royal inauguration place was the symbolic centre of the kingdom, around which the affairs of state revolved. This comprised not only the ritual installing of kings, but also the exercise of royal authority. Macbeth, therefore, is likely to have spent a significant part of his reign at Scone.

LOCH LEVEN

Macbeth's association with Loch Leven is, unusually, historically recorded. The lands endowed by Macbeth and Gruoch to the Culdees of Loch Leven indicate that they took a close personal interest in the community there and it seems likely that Macbeth and his queen knew and visited the monastery.

St Serf's Island, in Loch Leven, Kinross-shire, was an early and important ecclesiastical centre.[33] There are two conflicting accounts of its foundation. The island was given to God, St Serf (or Servanus) and the Culdees dwelling and serving God there by Brude, the last Pictish king, who died in 843, according

The Loch Leven charter, *c.* 1150, in which David I granted St Serf's Island to the Augustinian canons of St Andrews. The island was bestowed on the Augustinians for them to establish an order of canons regular and the charter gave the canons permission to expel any Culdees who refused to conform. This marked the end of the Culdee community of Loch Leven.

to a tradition preserved in the Loch Leven notes recorded in the St Andrews *Register*.[34] But the *Life of St Serf* (*Vita Sancti Servani*)[35] describes how the saint was given the island by Adomnán, St Columba's hagiographer and successor as Abbot of Iona, who died in 704.[36] St Serf is an early but obscure saint and the authenticity of these much later foundation myths is unconfirmed. One of them, at least, is clearly unreliable.

Although the character of the early monastery on Loch Leven is unclear, it had become a Culdee community by the mid-tenth century. Its island setting and contemporary descriptions of the Loch Leven Culdees as 'hermits' indicates that it belonged to the ascetic category of Culdee foundation. However, the donation of churches to the monastery by bishops of St Andrews during the eleventh century suggests that the community included not only cloistered monks, but also clerics who ministered to the surrounding population or aristocracy. Loch Leven is a good example of an 'offshore church . . . providing pastoral care by establishing mainland stations for preaching and other ministrations to the local populace'.[37] The principal church belonging to the monastery was at Portmoak, on the eastern shore of Loch Leven.

From the mid-tenth century, Loch Leven came under the influence of the increasingly powerful royal ecclesiastical centre of St Andrews. In about 950, the Culdees under Abbot Ronan granted their land to Fothath, Bishop of

St Andrews, in return for food, clothing and protection.[38] Attesting its importance and royal connections, grants of land were made to the community of St Serf by Scottish monarchs, including Macbeth, and bishops of St Andrews between about 1040 and 1107.[39] In about 1150, David I granted the island to the Augustinian canons of St Andrews for them to establish an order of canons regular and expel any Culdees who refused to conform.[40] Soon after, Robert, Bishop of St Andrews, conferred St Serf's Priory on the Augustinian priory attached to St Andrews Cathedral. Loch Leven's declining significance was sealed by the diocesan reorganisation of the twelfth century, which saw it incorporated into the diocese of St Andrews.

Despite its eclipse by St Andrews, Loch Leven was an important centre of monastic learning throughout the Middle Ages and was not abandoned until the Reformation. It may be the 'bishops' island' (*insula pontificum*) where Adomnán's *Life of Columba* was copied on the instructions of Alexander I (1107–24),[41] while Andrew of Wyntoun, Prior of Loch Leven from 1395 to 1413, composed his *Orygynale Cronykil* there. The monastic library, containing sixteen books, was transferred to St Andrews when the Augustinian priory there acquired St Serf's Priory. This included an 'old book written in the ancient idiom of the Scots' (i.e. Gaelic) in which grants of land to the community and the foundation myth were recorded.[42] This may have been an illuminated gospel book containing marginal *notitiae* recording grants of land, perhaps similar to the *Book of Deer*.

St Serf's Island (NO 160005), near the south-eastern shore of Loch Leven, is the largest island in Loch Leven. It should not be confused with the more famous island on which Loch Leven Castle stands and from which Mary, Queen of Scots, escaped in 1568. Although St Serf's Island is now around 40 ha in area, it was less than half this size before 1829–30, when the water level in the loch was lowered by 1.4 m.[43]

A description of St Serf's Island in 1766 reported that: 'The middle or highest part of it is covered with ruins. The foundations are visible enough, and it seems to have been a very large building. The whole is divided into a great many little squares, from which it appears . . . that not only a church . . . but a monastery had stood in it.'[44] The 'little squares' are possibly monastic cells.

The only visible remains of the monastery are the ruins of a small church and the disturbed foundations of the medieval ranges. The church was converted for use as a shepherd's bothy in 1834, but the surviving masonry and Romanesque mouldings, particularly of the blocked west arch, are of good quality and date to the twelfth century.[45] During agricultural improvements on the island in 1830, disturbance of the ground to the south and west of the church revealed the

The ruined church on St Serf's Island, Loch Leven, Kinross-shire. This nineteenth-century engraving shows the twelfth-century church after its conversion into a shepherd's bothy. The blocked Romanesque doorway is indicated by darker shading. (Crown copyright: Royal Commission on the Ancient and Historical Monuments of Scotland)

presence of a cemetery. Excavations were conducted on St Serf's Island at various times between the 1850s and 1870s.[46] Although poorly recorded, these indicate that extensive remains of the medieval monastery, including the footings of stone buildings, survive. The buildings of its early medieval predecessor are more likely to have been of timber and detectable only under modern standards of excavation. Nevertheless, traces of the early medieval monastery, including the one patronised by Macbeth, may await discovery beneath the later ruins.

MACDUFF'S CASTLE

MACBETH   The castle of MacDuff I will surprise;
        Seize upon Fife; give to th'edge o'th'sword
        His wife, his babes, and all unfortunate souls
        That trace him in his line.

Macbeth Act 4, Scene 2

MacDuff's castle is the scene of one of the most shockingly violent incidents in the Macbeth myth. On finding that MacDuff has betrayed him and fled to join the

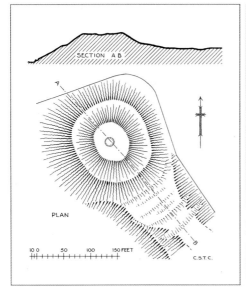

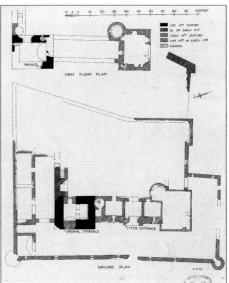

The Maiden Castle, Dunipace Hill, Kennoway, Fife. According to tradition, the motte, probably of twelfth-century date, was occupied by the MacDuff Earls of Fife. (Crown copyright: Royal Commission on the Ancient and Historical Monuments of Scotland)

Plan of MacDuff's Castle, East Wemyss, Fife. (Crown copyright: Royal Commission on the Ancient and Historical Monuments of Scotland)

exiled Malcolm in England, Macbeth flies into a rage and either murders, or orders the killing of, MacDuff's defenceless wife and son. This episode is another later embellishment, first appearing in Boece's *History*,[47] although MacDuff's castle also features in earlier versions of the myth as the place where Macbeth challenges MacDuff's treachery.

Although this episode is mythological in nature and the earliest masonry castles in Scotland were not built until the twelfth century, at least three candidates for MacDuff's castle have been proposed. Reflecting MacDuff's thanage, all are in Fife. Wyntoun, the earliest to provide a location, places MacDuff's castle at Kynnaghty or Kennawchty (Kennoway).[48] This is probably Maiden Castle (NO 349015), a motte on Dunipace Hill.[49] Enclosed by seven ramparts and seven ditches, this was occupied by MacDuff's descendants, according to Boece,[50] while local tradition reported that 'Some pretend it was a seat of M'Duff, Earl of Fife'.[51] But a better candidate for the builder of Maiden Castle is probably Merleswain, who was endowed with lands in Kennoway by Alexander I.

Confusingly, the castle which is most commonly associated with MacDuff was previously called Kennoway Castle or Thanes Castle, but is now more widely

The ruined towers of MacDuff's Castle, East Wemyss, Fife. Although traditionally attributed to MacDuff, the Thane of Fife persecuted by Macbeth, the earliest phase of the castle belongs to the late fourteenth-century. MacDuff's Castle probably takes its name from the medieval Earls of Fife. (Crown copyright: Royal Commission on the Ancient and Historical Monuments of Scotland)

known as MacDuff's Castle or, after its location, East Wemyss Castle (NO 344971). Although 'said to have been built by MacDuff',[52] construction probably did not begin until the late fourteenth century, while the tower and front range are later than 1530.[53]

A third tradition places MacDuff's castle further west, near Culross: 'upon the banks of [the Firth of] Forth is Castlehill, antiently called Dunnemarle Castle . . . a fort or strong hold of the MacDuffs, Thanes of Fife . . . According to tradition, it was here that the cruel murder of Lady MacDuff and her children, by order of Macbeth . . . was perpetrated. The castle is in ruins; but a finer situation for a house can hardly be imagined.'[54]

This confusion about the location of MacDuff's castle probably arises from the number of castles held by the MacDuff medieval Earls of Fife and is reflected in Fordun's and other chroniclers accounts of how Macbeth besieged all MacDuff's castles and strongholds.[55] However, all these castles, including those traditionally associated with the MacDuff who features in the Macbeth myth, are later, and frequently much later, than the eleventh century.

FROM BIRNAM WOOD . . .

THIRD APPARITION   Macbeth shall never vanquished be until
Great Birnam Wood to high Dunsinane Hill
Shall come against him.

Macbeth Act 4, Scene 1

The north-eastern slopes of Birnam Hill, Perthshire. Since its plantation with conifers in the nineteenth century the vegetation has given way to mixed coniferous and broad-leaved woodland. (The Author)

Macbeth, of course, did not visit Birnam Wood; it came to him. The famous 'flittand wode', first referred to by Wyntoun, is unlikely to have moved to Dunsinane, even with the aid of Siward's army.[56] Instead, the moving wood is a mythological motif, symbolising Malcolm's conquest of the Scottish wilderness and, by implication, of Macbeth himself, while its approach towards Dunsinane signals Macbeth's impending and unavoidable doom. The mythological status of this motif is confirmed by its appearance in several medieval sources, although its origins are of much greater antiquity.[57]

As one of the most memorable images of the Macbeth myth, Birnam Wood deserves closer attention. Where is, or was, Birnam Wood and what is its significance? The present Birnam Wood (NO 0439) occupies the eastern slopes of Birnam Hill and the King's Seat, some 2 km south-east of Birnam village and 18 km north-west of Dunsinane Hill. But this is not the ancient Birnam Wood.

From the first century AD, when Roman writers wrote of the vast and impenetrable Caledonian forest,[58] Scotland, particularly highland Scotland, has often been depicted as a heavily wooded and hostile country. As late as 1590, William Camden described Atholl as not only 'infamous for witches and wicked women' but also

Birnam Wood, Perthshire, as depicted in William Roy's military survey of 1747–55 (sheet 17.3, detail). Although still a sizeable natural or semi-natural broad-leaved wood, much of the ancient Birnam Wood had already disappeared, leaving Birnam Hill denuded and surviving woodland restricted to the floor of Strath Tay (centre). (By permission of the British Library, Maps, C, P, B. Sheet 17 PTS 5/2–5/3)

the location of 'that Wood Caledonia, dreadfull to see to for the sundry turnings and windings in and out therein, for the hideous horror of darke shades, for the Burrowes and dennes of wilde bulles with thicke manes'.[59]

Real or mythical, most of this native Caledonian forest had disappeared by the mid-eighteenth century. Yet General Roy's Military Survey of Scotland (1747–55) and James Stobie's map of Dunkeld (1780) reveal that substantial areas of natural or semi-natural woodland then survived in Atholl, particularly in Strath Tay. Much of this woodland, mostly of oak or mixed oak and birch, was managed in a sustainable manner by coppicing every twenty to twenty-five years. But, by the late eighteenth century, many semi-natural broad-leaved woodlands were being converted to more lucrative coniferous plantations.[60]

During the mid-eighteenth century, the north-western slopes of Birnam Hill (NO 0240) were one of three main areas of relict natural woodland in the Dunkeld district. This was all that remained of the ancient Birnam Wood, which previously covered a more extensive area and was a royal hunting reserve until the fifteenth or early sixteenth centuries.[61] During the nineteenth century, agricultural improvements, particularly on the nearby Murthly estate (NO 0739), frequently unearthed large oak trunks, the remains of this ancient forest.[62]

Inspired by its traditional association with Macbeth, Birnam Wood attracted the attention of antiquarians and travellers, although few trees survived. Thomas Pennant, the antiquarian, naturalist and traveller, visited Birnam Wood in 1769 and quipped that it 'seems never to have recovered [from] the march which its ancestors made to Dunsinane'.[63] Birnam Hill is denuded in the accompanying engraving, although the remnants of Birnam Wood are visible as a sizeable broad-leaved wood, probably of coppiced oaks, alongside the River Tay.

The area around Birnam Hill was planted during the late eighteenth and early nineteenth centuries. During his Scottish tour of 1829, the composer

'View of Dunkeld, Birnam Hill and Dunsinane at a distance', engraved by Mazell, after a painting by Charles Steuart. Birnam Hill is clearly treeless, although extensive broad-leaved woods are shown in the valley below. (Pennant 1790 edn, Vol. 3, pl. 6)

Felix Mendelssohn sketched a coniferous plantation on the lower slopes with a mixed broad-leaved and coniferous plantation in the valley floor.[64] By 1843, extensive areas within the barony of Murthly, including Birnam, had been planted, mostly with fir and coppiced oak.[65] In 1857, it was recorded that 'thriving plantations of larch are getting up in many parts of the hill, while the skirts of the north and west of the hill are getting covered with natural birch'.[66] And by 1883, as part of a more extensive plantation of 1620 ha, Birnam Hill was 'thickly covered with thriving plantations . . . worthy of the reputation of "Great Birnam Wood"'.[67] Birnam Wood, as it exists today, is a modern coniferous plantation.

But what became of the ancient Birnam Wood of Macbeth's day and before? By 1843 only two trees were claimed to survive: 'There are two very large trees near the church, on the bank of the Tay, and said to be the remains of the once celebrated forest of Birnam; the one is oak, the other plane-tree, and each about 18 feet in circumference. They are objects of curiosity to strangers, and are interesting from their antiquity, being the twin survivors of a numerous family long ago departed.'[68] In 1883, these trees, the most famous of old Birnam Wood's 'few gigantic living specimens', were believed to be a thousand years old

Above: a scene from the Gundestrup cauldron (inner plate E), Denmark, which dates from about the second century BC. The antiquity of the motif of the moving wood is demonstrated by this scene of armed warriors carrying a tree or branch. (National Museum of Denmark, Copenhagen); left: the tree that did not go to Dunsinane. The last surviving oak from the ancient Birnam Wood. Its ancient boughs are so weak that they have to be supported by upright timbers. (The Author)

and attracted 'tourists and students of Nature from all parts of the world'.[69] One of these, 'the tree that did not go to Dunsinane', survives. It allegedly 'looks medieval', and still draws visitors.[70]

. . . TO DUNSINANE HILL

MENTEITH	What does the tyrant?
CAITHNESS	Great Dunsinane he strongly fortifies.

Macbeth Act 5, Scene 2

Mythology

Dunsinane occupies a pre-eminent place in the mythology of Macbeth. Not only is it the location of 'Macbeth's castle', but it is also the scene of his bloody battle against Malcolm and Siward and his death. But although Macbeth's association with Dunsinane is a strong one, it is also late. The earliest source to link Macbeth with Dunsinane is Wyntoun's *Orygynale Cronykil*, but although composed in about 1410 it is based on earlier sources, some of which no longer survive. According to Wyntoun, Macbeth built a 'gret housse' of 'tymbyr . . . and stane' 'apon þe hicht of Dunsynnane'.[71] This was Macbeth's royal Court, where he was called by his marshal to eat with his thanes and knights assembled in the hall there one night. Dunsinane is portrayed as a royal residence and although Wyntoun does not describe it as being fortified, this is implied. Later versions of the myth consistently refer to Dunsinane as a place of strength. Boece states that Macbeth 'biggit ane strang castell in þe hicht of Donsynnane' ('built a strong castle on the height of Dunsinane') and this portrayal of Dunsinane was incorporated in Shakespeare's *Macbeth* via Holinshed.[72]

Macbeth levied oxen from throughout Angus and Fife to assist the construction of Dunsinane, according to the chroniclers. The weakness of oxen

Macbeth's castle on Dunsinane Hill, as depicted in contemporary architectural style in a woodcut in Holinshed's *Chronicles* (1577). 'Further to the ende he might the more sickerly oppresse his subjectes with all tyranlike wrongs, he buylded a strong Castell on the top of an high hill cleyed Dunsinnane'.

provided by MacDuff provoked Macbeth into threatening to put the Thane of Fife himself under the yoke, prompting MacDuff to flee to England and seek Malcolm's return. This incident may have been introduced to explain why Macbeth rebuked MacDuff and the latter fled. Dunsinane is a symbol of Macbeth's oppression, built so 'þat he mycht invaid þe pepill with mair tyranny'.[73] In Shakespeare's *Macbeth*, Dunsinane symbolises Macbeth's physical isolation and denial of his impending doom: 'Hang out our banners on the outward walls; / . . . Our castle's strength / Will laugh a siege to scorn'.[74]

Is Dunsinane just a literary motif, a mythical place? Or, like Birnam Wood, does it have a basis in physical reality? If so, was it ever Macbeth's fortress and royal Court?

The Hillfort

Dunsinane is certainly real enough. An outlying summit at the south-western end of the Sidlaw Hills (NO 214317), 13 km north-east of Perth, Dunsinane

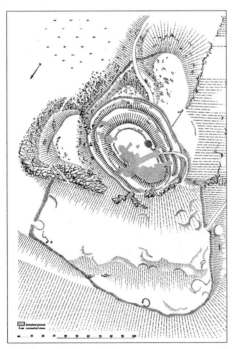

A plan of the hillfort, Dunsinane Hill, Perthshire. The shaded areas, concentrated within the interior of the citadel, indicate ground disturbed by late eighteenth- and nineteenth-century excavations. (Crown copyright: Royal Commission on the Ancient and Historical Monuments of Scotland)

Hill rises 308 m above sea level and affords commanding views across the Carse of Gowrie and the southern ends of Strathmore, Strath Tay and beyond. Moreover, Dunsinane was evidently fortified in antiquity. Its summit and slopes are enclosed by rubble banks, which mark the course of collapsed stone walls or ramparts.[75] The summit of the hill is crowned by a heavily fortified multivallate (multiple-ramparted) 'citadel', sub-circular in plan and defended by three closely spaced, dry-stone-revetted ramparts. The citadel is approached by a winding trackway on the north-east, which penetrates the ramparts obliquely, probably leading to a single narrow entrance passage.

To the north and south of the citadel, two lower terraces are enclosed by a single rampart to form a pair of outer annexes. The larger, southern, annexe encloses an area of 2.16 ha and contains several crescentic and circular scooped and raised platforms. These are probably house sites, although it is unclear if they are contemporary with the hillfort. In contrast, the wall of the southern annexe is overlain by the remains of a later stone-walled hut circle or shieling. The nature of the hillfort's occupation is unknown, but may have been permanent, seasonal or, if used as a refuge in times of danger, occasional. Furthermore, the strongly fortified citadel may have been used in a different manner from the more lightly defended outer annexes.

An aerial view of the hillfort citadel, Dunsinane Hill, Perthshire. The multiple ramparts and ground disturbed by early excavations, particularly at the eastern end of the interior, are clearly visible. (Crown copyright: Royal Commission on the Ancient and Historical Monuments of Scotland)

The hillfort's importance is indicated by its location and defences. It occupies the summit of a prominent hill and its citadel's defences are on a massive scale; the inner wall alone is up to 9 m thick. The ramparts also occupy an area that is out of proportion to the space enclosed; approximately 3.7 times that of the interior, which is only 0.1 ha in area. The Royal Commission justifiably describes Dunsinane as 'the most spectacular of the fortifications in south-east Perth[shire] . . . unparalleled in the rest of the area'.[76] The labour required for the fort's construction must have been considerable, and yet only a relatively small group could have lived within the citadel's tiny interior at any one time. The fort's strength and location therefore reflect the power and status of its occupants. Who were they and when did they live?

Dating

Dunsinane Hill was a focus of activity at various times during prehistory. Two cup-marked stones on the summit indicate Neolithic or early Bronze Age (*c.* 3200–1400 BC) activity there. The intriguing discovery, somewhere on Dunsinane, of two bronze swords, since lost, also attests a late Bronze Age (*c.* 900–500 BC) presence.[77] But in both cases the nature of the activity, whether occupation or something more transient, and its duration are unknown.

It is unlikely that a single group built and occupied the hillfort. Rather than being of unitary construction, the fortifications belong to more than one phase. For example, the citadel's outer rampart overlies an earlier trackway that approaches the summit through what appears to be the original entrance into the northern annexe. The wall enclosing the northern annexe is poorly preserved, suggesting that it has been extensively robbed to provide building material for the citadel. The southern annexe wall, which is further away from the citadel, is better preserved. This implies that the citadel is later than at least the northern annexe and possibly its southern counterpart. The citadel, therefore, was probably constructed within the interior of an earlier hillfort. While two phases of construction are apparent from the fort's surface appearance alone, excavation may reveal more. The citadel may overlie an earlier fortification on the summit, while its massive defences may not be contemporary; the ramparts could have been strengthened or extra ramparts added subsequently. Dunsinane's ramparts may attest a complex sequence of fortification and refortification, perhaps over an extended period.

The construction technique employed in Dunsinane's ramparts may help to date the hillfort. Traces of outer and inner revetments, façades of large stones retaining a rubble core, survive on the southern annexe wall. But fragments of vitrified rock, scattered around the citadel's ramparts and another three in the southern enclosure wall, attest a more complex construction in at least one phase. Vitrification occurs when rocks are subjected to extreme temperatures, about 1,200°C, causing them to melt or soften. As the molten rock cools it solidifies into a glassy, slag-like mass, often distorted and fused with fragments of unvitrified rock.[78] The temperatures required are generated by the intense burning of reinforcing timber beams within the ramparts, a process which has been reproduced experimentally.[79]

Vitrification is found widely in Scottish hillforts, particularly in central and eastern Scotland and around the Moray Firth, and is often the only indication that their ramparts were timber-laced. Beam-slots, voids within the rampart left when the timbers decay naturally, survive only rarely. Radiocarbon dates from vitrified ramparts range from around the seventh century BC to the second century AD, indicating that this is a late Bronze Age and Iron Age phenomenon. Consistent with this, Iron Age activity at Dunsinane may be indicated by a bronze spiral finger-ring, found in nineteenth century excavations but since lost.[80] However, radiocarbon dating also demonstrates that timber-lacing was

Castle Law, Abernethy, Perthshire. The outer face of the hillfort's inner rampart, exposed in excavations by David Christison in 1896–8. The beam slots, left when the timber lacing has rotted away, are clearly visible as regularly spaced voids in the stonework. (Crown copyright: Royal Commission on the Ancient and Historical Monuments of Scotland)

employed in Pictish fortifications at Burghead (Moray), Portknockie (Banff) and Dundurn (Perthshire),[81] while the vitrified ramparts at the Mote of Mark, Kirkcudbrightshire, probably date to the seventh century.[82]

Even if its vitrified ramparts are Iron Age in date, Dunsinane may still have been (re)fortified or (re)occupied during the early medieval period. In multi-phase hillforts with evidence of vitrification, the timber-laced ramparts usually belong to an early phase. This may also be the case at Dunsinane, where no vitrified material is detectable *in situ*, as a fused mass of rampart core material, although this may be revealed by excavation. This suggests that material from a vitrified rampart, presumably belonging to an earlier hillfort on Dunsinane, was reused in later fortifications.

The date of these later ramparts is unknown, but some Iron Age hillforts were reoccupied during the early medieval period, as at Craig Phadraig. Alternatively, the fort's construction may date to the early Middle Ages. Radiocarbon dating demonstrates that Clatchard Craig, Fife, which was initially interpreted as a reoccupied Iron Age hillfort, actually belongs to the early medieval period.[83] Hillforts in Scotland belong to a wider chronological range than was once suspected and may be identified as a integral element of the Pictish settlement pattern. But Pictish hillforts vary considerably in plan and construction and cannot be distinguished from Iron Age hillforts by surface appearance alone. Although excavation is required to establish whether Dunsinane was (re)occupied and/or (re)fortified by the Picts, this is clearly a possibility.

One thing is certain. Despite its traditional name and description, Dunsinane is not a castle. The earliest Scottish castles date from the twelfth century and the structure on Dunsinane Hill pre-dates this, belonging instead to a class of later prehistoric and/or early medieval hillforts.

Historical Evidence

Even if Dunsinane was a Pictish hillfort in at least its later phase(s), this still leaves a considerable gap between the eclipse of the Pictish kingdom in the mid-ninth century and Macbeth's reign in the mid-eleventh. Fortunately, the only documentary source recording early medieval activity at Dunsinane falls within this gap.

The regnal lists record the killing of Kenneth II (971–95) at Fettercairn through the treachery of Finuele, daughter of the *comes* (literally 'earl', probably mormaer) of Angus, after Kenneth had slain her only son at a place which is spelled in different manuscript versions as *Dunfinoen*, *Dunsinoen*, *Dunismoen* or *Dunsion*.[84] Fordun identified this as Dunsinane: 'The king had ordered her [Finuele's] only son to be put to death at Dunsinane, whether by the severity of the law or because of some crime or for any other cause I do not know'.[85] Local tradition also maintains that Dunsinane was 'a secure place of residence' of Kenneth III (?997–1005) and other, unspecified, kings, although the evidence for this – if any – is unclear.[86]

Doubts have been expressed about the identification of the place concerned with Dunsinane. Alcock suggested that the length of time between the compilation of the regnal lists and the events they record may have resulted in a spurious tradition concerning Kenneth's killing of Finuele's son being attached to this prominent landmark.[87] But the Scottish regnal lists originated in the eleventh century, not much later than the event concerned. Although they survive only as later copies, this is characteristic of early medieval texts and is insufficient grounds for dismissing this evidence. Alcock also points to Dunsinane's altitude, which is considerably higher than other known early medieval fortifications in Scotland. Yet the significance of altitude is unclear. In Dunsinane's case, accessibility may have been sacrificed for a more defensive location which also enabled the defences of a pre-existing hillfort to be reused. Moreover, Dunsinane's ostensibly anomalous altitude masks the fact that the hill rises from a valley floor which is already around 125 m above sea-level. The final weakness in Alcock's argument is that he does not identify an alternative candidate for *Dunsinoen*.

A strong case can be made that Dunsinane was the place mentioned in the regnal lists and an early medieval fortified royal centre. David Christison, who pioneered the study of Scottish hillforts, remarked that 'Dunsinnan . . . seems to be one of the very few primitive Scottish fortresses mentioned by the early annalists; at least there is no other existing claimant for the honour of being *Dunsinoen*'.[88] Alcock has demonstrated the importance of hillforts as historically recorded centres of royal power in early medieval Scotland. Although many may have been abandoned by the eleventh century in favour of lower-lying palace complexes such as Scone and Forteviot, others survived into the medieval period as important royal castles. Although not in the same league as Edinburgh or Stirling, Dunsinane appears to have been a fortified royal centre that was either still in use or was reoccupied by the late tenth century. A key factor here was location; Dunsinane is only 12 km north-east of the royal inauguration centre of Scone. Alternatively, Dunsinane may not have been occupied continuously, but may have been reused during times of political instability, such as the end of Macbeth's reign.

Antiquarian Interest

Dunsinane's traditional status as 'Macbeth's Castle' stimulated extensive antiquarian interest. In 1772, Sir John Sinclair, founder of the *Statistical Account of Scotland*, 'collected all the traditions respecting the history of Macbeth that were current in the neighbourhood', including how Macbeth built his 'castle' on Dunsinane on the advice of witches who lived nearby.[89] Sinclair also (mis)translated Dunsinane as 'the hill of ants', attributing its name to 'the great labour and industry so essentially requisite for collecting the materials of so vast a building'.[90] In contrast, reflecting his perceived superhuman status and qualities, Macbeth was known locally as 'The Giant' and Dunsinane as 'the Giant's House'.[91] Despite being misled by local folklore, Sinclair's description and sketch plan reveal that, unlike other visitors, he appreciated the layout of the hillfort, identifying its central citadel, outer annexes and associated trackways.

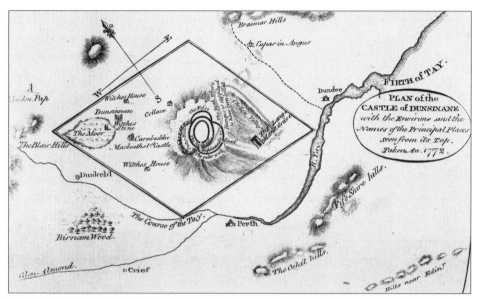

Sir James Sinclair's plan of the castle of Dunsinane. Although dated 1772, when Sinclair conducted his fieldwork at Dunsinane, the plan was not published until 1796. (Crown copyright: Royal Commission on the Ancient and Historical Monuments of Scotland)

Inspired by its traditional association with Macbeth, Dunsinane drew antiquarians and travellers alike, becoming an established attraction on the Enlightenment tour of Scotland. Pennant visited Dunsinane on his second tour, in 1772, but was less impressed with the hillfort than its setting: 'No place could be better adapted for the seat of a jealous tyrant; the sides are steep, and of the most difficult ascent; the summit commanding a view to a great distance in front and rear. At present there are not any remains of this celebrated fortress: its place is now a verdant area . . . surrounded by two deep ditches.[92] In contrast, John Williams, who visited Dunsinane before 1777, described it as 'well fortified, being defended by a strong rampart which went quite round the upper part of the hill'.[93] The first to describe the phenomenon of vitrified forts, Williams assessed that Dunsinane belonged to a larger group of 'fortified hills'.

Dunsinane's fame spread rapidly: 'the traveller will consider Dunsinnan as holy ground', declared one antiquarian in 1827 and by 1831 its attraction was so great that the feet of its many visitors had worn tracks to the summit of 'the spell-bound height'.[94] Early antiquarians approached Dunsinane with preconceived ideas. Heavily influenced by the hill's mythological associations, the hillfort was accepted as Macbeth's castle without question.

Early Excavations

From the outset, antiquarians were interested in what lay beneath the surface at Dunsinane. The earliest recorded excavations there occurred in or before 1772, when Pennant noted that 'The hill has been dug into; but nothing was discovered, excepting some very black corn'.[95] Possibly referring to this, a 1797 account states that 'Several years ago, some gentlemen, in digging a pit near the middle of the area [the citadel], discovered pieces of the bones of animals, brick, and burnt corn'.[96] Dr James Playfair, then minister of Meigle and later principal of St Andrews University, excavated at Dunsinane shortly before 1799, when he claimed to have 'discovered a part of it [the hillfort] as entire as when it was originally constructed'.[97]

Dunsinane continued to attract the attentions of antiquarians and was the scene of further excavations during the mid-nineteenth century.[98] These were undertaken in 1854 by William Nairne, who owned the hill, by T.M. Nairne in 1857 and by Alexander Laing in 1867.[99] Dunsinane was disturbed on other occasions. According to local tradition, Macbeth 'deposited his most valuable effects in times of emergency . . . This encouraged them [local people] to excavate the top of the hill, as they were satisfied a proper degree of perseverance was only required to find the treasure'.[100] The extent of these various excavations is apparent from the disturbed ground within and around the citadel.

These excavations were poorly conducted and recorded, even by the standards of the day, and it is difficult to interpret their results. But some details may be gleaned from the limited accounts available. From its external face, Playfair cut a trench 6.4 m through the innermost rampart, revealing it to be 'nicely built of large stone, bedded in clay or mortar' and surviving to a height of 1.5–1.8 m.[101] Although he claimed that the wall was 'cemented with red mortar', this was probably a clay binding. In contrast, William Nairne's

Dunsinane Hill, Perthshire. Dr A. Wise's section of the citadel, showing the rampart resting on boulder foundations and the twin subterranean chambers of the probable souterrain. (Crown copyright: Royal Commission on the Ancient and Historical Monuments of Scotland)

excavations reportedly revealed an 'earthen wall' resting on a foundation of 'layers of large packed boulders' where the underlying surface was uneven.[102] Andrew Stewart's unpublished account of the same excavations described the wall more accurately as 'strongly built of large stones, both inside and out, while the filling in is a mass of loose stones, entirely without manipulation of mortar'.[103] These discrepancies emphasise the poor standard of excavation and recording employed.

Playfair's excavations revealed that the citadel's inner wall was equally well preserved around its entire circuit, having been protected by collapsed rampart material. Although the rampart's original height could not be determined, the 'immense mass' of rubble on the summit indicated that it must have been considerable. James Robertson remarked that if this debris was removed, 'Macbeth's fortress on Dunsinnan hill would be one of the most remarkable monuments of antiquity in Britain'.[104]

Early accounts of Dunsinane do not refer to, or even deny, the presence of vitrification.[105] However, large quantities of vitrified rocks were discovered within the citadel in 1854. These included a fused lump within the rampart which Christison thought was reused from an earlier vitrified rampart, although it may belong to *in situ* vitrified rampart core material.[106] Possibly supporting the latter interpretation, Laing extracted several sizeable vitrified rocks from the rampart's foundations in 1867.[107]

Playfair's excavations through the rampart also extended across the centre of the citadel's interior. This exposed occupation deposits, a paved area and, behind the rampart, a pit containing cattle, sheep and hare bones. Despite excavating to a depth of 0.9 m, no traces of buildings were detected. William Nairne excavated at both ends of the interior and, in contrast, exposed foundation walls 0.3 m high 'within one-half of a large circular opening towards the west of the area, which seems to have been an open court', while a mass of rubble in the south-east was interpreted as the remains of a tower.[108] These structures are not mentioned in Wise's account of the 1854 excavations.

There are also conflicting descriptions of two subterranean chambers discovered within the east of the interior in 1854.[109] Both had been disturbed by earlier excavations. The chambers were either straight sided, with vertical, mortared walls, or figure-of-eight-shaped in plan, unmortared and corbelled, that is, with each successive course of stonework projecting inwards until the gap could be roofed with a lintel. Two sloping entrances provided access to one chamber, which was linked to the other by two narrow passages. The chambers and passages contained a (probably rotary) quernstone, for grinding

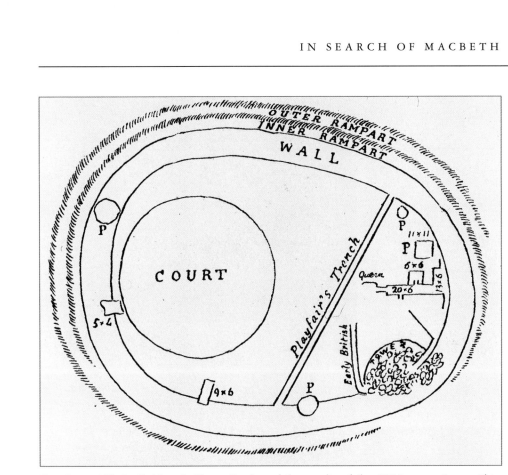

Dunsinane Hill, Perthshire. A. Stewart's plan of the results of the 1854 excavations within the citadel. (Crown copyright: Royal Commission on the Ancient and Historical Monuments of Scotland)

grain; cattle, deer and horse bones; and human skeletal remains, including the skulls of two adults and one child, perhaps belonging to crouched inhumations. Wise believed that the 'child had been destroyed and buried with its parents; a barbarous custom by no means uncommon among rude savage races'.[110]

Although recently interpreted as a hilltop burial chamber predating the fort,[111] Wise's interpretation that the hillfort's inhabitants stored foodstuffs and valuables there appears more likely.[112] Subterranean structures known as souterrains are common in Angus and Perthshire, where their heaviest concentration is in the Carse of Gowrie, immediately south of Dunsinane.[113] Usually elongated or crescentic in form, but occasionally bi-lobed as at Dunsinane, these were the storage structures of associated surface settlements and occasionally occur within hillforts. Although dating evidence is meagre, souterrains probably belong to the period between the first century BC and second century AD, suggesting that Dunsinane was occupied at about that time.

The souterrain at Newmill, Bankfoot, Perthshire. A composite view of the souterrain and, beyond it, the post-holes of the associated timber round house. The gap in the stone lining towards the bulbous terminal of the souterrain was caused by a mechanical excavator before the site was identified. (Crown copyright: Royal Commission on the Ancient and Historical Monuments of Scotland)

The mid-nineteenth century antiquarians saw beyond Dunsinane's traditional association with Macbeth. Despite their poor standards of excavation and publication, they based their conclusions on empirical observation and comparison with other excavated hillforts. The souterrain, vitrified ramparts and spiral ring pointed to the hillfort's construction in 'a period of great antiquity' and Dunsinane's status as 'a strong British fortification . . . prepared by an ancient people, who had advanced so far in refinement as to have felt the importance of uniting in considerable bodies to defend themselves against their powerful enemies'.[114] If Macbeth had a fortification on Dunsinane, it probably occupied the site of a pre-existing Iron Age hillfort.

Conclusions

Dunsinane is a complex monument with probably multiple phases of fortification and occupation, perhaps extending over 1,500 years or more. It probably originated as an Iron Age hillfort with timber-laced ramparts. The hilltop was refortified, possibly by the Picts, using vitrified material from those ramparts. Dunsinane may have been a fortified royal centre of the province of Gowrie, perhaps complementing the ritual centre at Scone. After the eclipse of Pictish power in the mid-ninth century, Dunsinane, like other royal centres, may have retained its role under the early Scottish kings. Dunsinane's link with the historical Macbeth, and even its fortification and occupation during the early medieval period, are unconfirmed. But the regnal lists and Fordun imply Dunsinane's position as a royal centre of Kenneth II, only about thirty-five years before Macbeth's reign began, when it may have performed a similar function. The medieval tradition that Dunsinane was fortified by Macbeth and was the site of his battle against Malcolm and Siward is plausible. Macbeth's fortress is unlikely to have been the earliest on the hilltop, but he may have reused earlier fortifications, perhaps strengthening them in times of instability or as a vainglorious symbol of his own status and power. Macbeth's interest in fortifications is perhaps indicated by the fact that he welcomed the Norman castellans who fled from the Welsh Marches in 1052 and were still there two years later, when they died fighting for Macbeth in the Battle of the Seven Sleepers.

Only excavations conducted to modern standards and accompanied by scientific dating techniques will unravel the complexity of Dunsinane's prehistory and determine if it was also an early medieval hillfort. Whether any early medieval activity could be dated with sufficient accuracy for it to be associated with Macbeth's reign is another matter. The antiquarian excavations, although poorly conducted and recorded, give an intriguing insight into Dunsinane's archaeological potential. At least a third of the citadel's interior shows no signs of disturbance, while the areas investigated previously may merit re-excavation. Dunsinane may yet yield its secrets and with them, perhaps, evidence of its status as Macbeth's fortified royal centre.

THE DUNSINANE AREA

Dunsinane's prominence within the Macbeth myth is reflected in the rich topographical mythology of south-east Perthshire. Attracted by Macbeth's traditional association with Dunsinane, visiting antiquarians sought to locate key episodes from the myth within the surrounding landscape, recording the

Macbeth's Law, Lawton House, Perthshire. According to local tradition, Macbeth dispensed justice from this impressive mound, which is probably a prehistoric funerary monument or a medieval motte. (The Author)

traditions associated with nearby monuments. These traditions interpreted traces of earlier, often prehistoric, human activity with reference to Macbeth. The monuments concerned form two groups, one surrounding Dunsinane itself and the other near Meigle, 14 km north-east of Dunsinane.

According to local tradition, Dunsinane was not Macbeth's original castle: 'Macbeth, after his elevation to the throne . . . resided for 10 years at Cairnbeddie . . . which the country people call Carn-beth, or Macbeth's Castle, and where the vestiges of his castle are still to be seen'.[115] This comprises a roughly rectangular enclosure, measuring 70 m by 60 m, within a wide ditch, 6.5 km west of Dunsinane (NO 150308).[116] Now damaged by ploughing, only traces of a circular, flat-topped mound are visible in the southern corner of the enclosure. Although resembling a motte and bailey superficially, the site's poor defensive location, in a hollow, casts doubt on this interpretation. When disturbed in the early nineteenth century the mound reportedly yielded 'horse shoes . . . in great abundance' and 'handles of swords and dirks'.[117] The date and function of this monument are unclear but there is no evidence to suggest a link with the historical Macbeth. This is equally true of other locations.

The King's Seat (NO 231330), 2 km north-east of Dunsinane, is, at 377 m, the highest of the Sidlaw Hills. According to tradition this is where 'Macbeth sat, as on a watch-tower, for it commands a more comprehensive view than Dunsinane. Here his scout might be placed who brought him the fatal news of the march of Birnam wood'.[118] On its summit, 'the ruin of a circular inclosure, similar to Macbeth's castle, but much smaller', was interpreted as Macbeth's 'watch-tower or out-post', from which the hill gained its name.[119] However, the ruins actually belong to a prehistoric burial cairn.

At the feet of Dunsinane and the King's Seat were 'several tumuli composed of earth and stones of a pyramidical form, called here Lawes. One of a considerable size . . . called Law-town, is supposed to have been that from which Macbeth administered justice to his people', hence its name.[120] Now known as Macbeth's Law (NO 201345), this circular, flat-topped mound, 5 m high and with a low terrace around part of its base, stands in the grounds of Lawton House, near Kinrossie, 3 km north-north-west of Dunsinane. It may be a prehistoric funerary monument, a medieval motte, or both.[121] This tradition may indicate that Macbeth's Law is an early medieval court hill, several of which reused ancient barrows or cairns.[122] But there is no evidence to suggest that the monument's association with Macbeth is anything other than mythological.

The Lang Man's Grave and Bandirran stone circle, Perthshire, with Dunsinane Hill in the background, as sketched by J. Skene in 1832. The Lang Man's Grave marks Macbeth's burial place, according to eighteenth century tradition. (Crown copyright: Royal Commission on the Ancient and Historical Monuments of Scotland; NMRS PTD 320/1)

Revealing the influence of Shakespeare's *Macbeth*, the locations of Macbeth's death and burial feature prominently in local tradition: 'when Malcolm prepared to attack the castle [Dunsinane] . . . he [Macbeth] immediately deserted it, and flying, ran up the opposite hill [the King's Seat], pursued by MacDuff; but finding it impossible to escape, he threw himself from the top of the hill, was killed upon the rocks, and buried at the Lang Man's Grave.'[123] The Lang Man's Grave was 'a great stone lying on the ground, ten feet long' at the eastern foot of Dunsinane Hill, while two similar stones nearby were said 'to mark the graves of the leaders who fell in the storm of Macbeth's Castle'.[124] These may be the twin monoliths at Bandirran (NO 210310) or the two massive fallen boulders belonging to the small stone circle nearby.[125]

The second group of monuments are at Belliduff (NO 289442), on the estate of Belmont Castle, and were believed to mark the site of Macbeth's last battle. A map of the Belmont estate (1758) records that Macbeth was buried under a mound known as 'Belle-duff'.[126] Local tradition painted a vivid picture of the events supposedly associated with it:

> on its [Belmont's] environs lay the last scene of the tragedy of Macbeth. In one place is shewn his Tumulus, called Belly Duff, or . . . the memorial of his fall; for to tyrants no such respect was paid; and their remains were treated with the utmost indignity among the northern nations . . . By the final syllable, I should choose to style it a monument to perpetuate the memory of the gallant Mac-duff. It is a verdant mount, surrounded by two terraces, with a cop at the top. . . . The battle, which began beneath the castle of Dunsinane, might have spread as far as this place. Here the great stand might have been made; here Mac-duff might have summoned the usurper to yield; and here I imagine him uttering his last defiance.[127]

Excavations in 1855 revealed an 'ancient stone coffin', probably a Bronze Age short cist, 0.6 m beneath the centre of the mound, suggesting that Belliduff was another prehistoric funerary monument.[128]

Nearby monuments were reputed to mark the burial places of the battle's distinguished dead, although their interpretation evidently varied over time:

> In a field on the other side of the house is another monument to a hero of that day, to the memory of the brave young Seward, who fell, slain on the spot by Macbeth. A stupendous stone marks the place; twelve feet [3.6 m] high above ground, and eighteen feet and a half [5.6 m] in girth in the thickest place. The

quantity below the surface of the earth is only two feet eight inches [0.8 m]; the weight, on accurate computation, amounts to twenty tons; yet I have been assured that no stone of this species is to be found within twenty miles. . . . Near the great stone is a small tumulus, called Duff's-know; where some other commander is supposed to have fallen.[129]

But by the late eighteenth century, this monolith was reputed 'to commemorate the death of one of his [Macbeth's] generals' and, reflecting a further transformation, was known as Macbeth's Stone by the mid-nineteenth century.[130] By this time a smaller monolith was referred to as Seward's Stone. Macbeth's Stone (NO 280435) is a superb example of its type, decorated with many cupmarks.[131] There appear to be no other recorded traditions concerning the cairn at Duff's Knowe (NO 278433).

Macbeth's Stone, Belmont, Perthshire. This impressive monument was erected to comemorate the young Siward, one of Macbeth's generals, or Macbeth himself, according to eighteenth- and nineteenth-century traditions. But it is more likely to date from the Neolithic or early Bronze Age, some three or four millennia earlier. (Crown copyright: Royal Commission on the Ancient and Historical Monuments of Scotland)

Despite this rich topographical tradition, these monuments are most unlikely to have been associated with the historical Macbeth. Although none have been excavated to modern standards, these standing stones and burial mounds are almost certainly prehistoric monuments, most probably belonging to the Neolithic or early Bronze Age. In contrast, 'Macbeth's Castle' at Cairnbeddie, if a motte and bailey castle, probably post-dates Macbeth, belonging to the twelfth or thirteenth centuries AD. Another Macbeth was sheriff of Scone in the late twelfth century and it is possible that he, and not Macbeth, King of Scots, is commemorated in the name; Scone lies only 5 km south-west of Cairnbeddie. The increased frequency of the name during the twelfth century probably also accounts for the two 'Macbeth's Castles' in Peebles-shire.[132]

The traditions associated with Dunsinane and neighbouring monuments represent an important but neglected dimension of the Macbeth myth. Although originating in the Macbeth of the medieval chroniclers and

Shakespeare, these traditions subsequently diverged to form a rich and unique body of topographical mythology. While some myths may have been stimulated by the enquiries of antiquarians and travellers, it is clear that several monuments were already linked with Macbeth in local tradition by the 1770s. This inspired antiquarians to trace the myth within the landscape, 'reading' monuments as the physical testimony of specific episodes in Macbeth's reign.

This mapping of the myth is most evident in Sinclair's account, which reports that Macbeth was advised to build his castle on Dunsinane Hill by 'two of the most famous witches in the kingdom [who] lived on each hand of Macbeth, one at Collace, the other not far from Dunsinnan-house, at a place called the Cape . . . The moor where the witches met . . . is yet pointed out by the country people, and there is a stone still preserved, which is called the witches stone'.[133] The stone concerned is probably one of the pair at Loanhead (NO 148329).[134] Sinclair, obviously believing these to be historical events, carried this approach to its logical conclusion in his plan of Dunsinane and its environs. This shows the locations not only of Dunsinane, Carnbeddie, the Lang Man's Grave, Birnam Wood and the Moor, but also the witches' houses and stone and 'the road where Banquo is supposed to have been killed'.

MACBETH'S BURIAL PLACE

The locations of Macbeth's death and burial are the subject of several conflicting traditions. The regnal lists[135] and later chroniclers consistently record that Macbeth was killed at Lumphanan and there is no reason to doubt this. In contrast, Shakespeare's Macbeth is killed in battle at Dunsinane for dramatic effect, while local tradition relates how Macbeth threw himself from the summit of the nearby King's Seat.

These locations all feature in the various traditions concerning Macbeth's burial place. The regnal lists record that Macbeth was 'buried in the island of Iona', as does an elegy preserved in Bower's *Scotichronicon*:

The island of Iona possesses these men [Macbeth and Lulach] buried in peace
In the tomb of the kings until Judgement Day.[136]

But Macbeth was buried at the Lang Man's Grave, according to Perthshire tradition. In contrast, Aberdeenshire folklore maintained that Macbeth was fatally wounded on the Brae of Strettum at Carnbady.[137] Macbeth was then buried in Macbeth's Cairn (NJ 578053) where a monolith, Macbeth's Stone, supposedly marked the spot:

> Macbeth's Cairn lies about a measured mile [1.6 km] north from the kirk [of Lumphanan], on the brow of a low hill, is 40 yards [36.6 m] in circumference, and rises pretty high in the middle. Farther up the hill are several smaller cairns. It is said . . . that Macbeth, flying from the south, had but few men with him when he reached Lumphanan; that he endeavoured to hide himself at a town called Cairn Baddy, but flying from hence went about a mile north, till M'Duff, out-riding his company, came up with him at that place where the cairn now lies, killed him in single combat, and brought back his head.[138]

Once again, prehistoric monuments feature prominently in the topographical mythology of Macbeth. Although any of these monuments may have been used as later burial places, their association with Macbeth is more likely to represent a later tradition, influenced by the knowledge that Macbeth was killed nearby. Instead, the role of these myths is to rationalise the presence of impressive prehistoric monuments within the contemporary landscape. But the best-known monument in this area, a massive motte and bailey fortification known as the Peel of Lumphanan (NJ 576037), is probably of thirteenth-century date and is therefore unconnected with Macbeth.

The identification of Lulach's burial place faces an identical problem. Local tradition presents a very different account from the regnal lists and chronicles, claiming that Lulach was buried near the 'bleedy faulds', near Alford Moss in the parish of Tough, Aberdeenshire: 'on the brow of a hill, there is a large stone standing perpendicular, about 9½ feet [2.9 m] round, and 12½ [3.8 m] high . . . Beneath it, tradition says that one of Macbeth's sons is interred'.[139] This is Luath's Stone (NJ 641149), on Green Hill overlooking the Howe of Alford. According to local folklore, 'Luath' was buried near where he fell.[140] But the reference to Macbeth's sons, rather than his step-son, casts doubt on the reliability of this tradition, while the identification of Luath with Lulach is questionable. Luath (Gaelic, 'swift, noble') was one of Cuthullin's hunting dogs in James Macpherson's 'Works of Ossian' and Luath's Stone may have acquired its name from this or other mythological associations. Moreover, Luath's Stone is neither near Essie, nor even in Strathbogie, but 25 km to the south-west. Luath's Stone is unlikely to mark Lulach's burial but is, once again, probably a Neolithic or early Bronze Age monolith.

Macbeth's final resting place? The Reilig Odhráin and St Oran's Chapel, Iona, and the tombs of the Scottish kings, c. 1880. The then unrestored Benedictine abbey stands in the background. (Crown copyright: Royal Commission on the Ancient and Historical Monuments of Scotland)

Returning to Macbeth, which of the traditions concerning his burial place are correct? Where is Macbeth's final resting place? This is no minor detail. As John Marsden claims, 'his burial among the tombs of the kings on Iona serves as confirmation of the legitimacy of Macbeth's right to that high-kingship [sic, the kingship of the Scots]'.[141] The same assertion is made about Lulach: 'burial on Iona is firm evidence that he was regarded as a legitimate successor to an ancient line of Scottish kings'.[142] Where his body was buried reveals much about the perception of Macbeth's royal status and concepts and practices of early Scottish kingship in general.

Iona, a tiny island off the west coast of Scotland, is the cradle of Christianity in Scotland north of the Forth–Clyde isthmus. St Columba (or Columcille), who may have been granted the island by a King of Dál Riata, founded a monastery there in or shortly after 563.[143] Iona had an enduring symbolic significance to the early Scottish kingship and its special status is apparent from its recorded role as a royal burial place. Sixteen early Scottish kings, from Kenneth mac Alpin in 858 until Donald II (whose bones were translated to Iona from Dunkeld) sometime after about 1099, were buried on Iona, according to the regnal lists, after which Dunfermline became the burial place of the medieval Scottish kings. Iona is portrayed as the burial ground of the Scottish kings in successive chronicles, and also in Shakespeare's *Macbeth*:

ROSS	Where is Duncan's body?
	Carried to Colmkill,
MACDUFF	The sacred storehouse of his predecessors
	And guardian of their bones.[144]

The royal burial ground on Iona is traditionally identified as Reilig Odhráin (St Oran's Cemetery).[145] The surviving memorial stones, many of which are now in the abbey museum, date from the eighth century until the present day and include about 150 medieval graveslabs. St Oran's Chapel, which stands inside the cemetery, belongs to the twelfth century. Yet the appearance of Reilig Odhráin dates only from the nineteenth century. The gravestones were excavated in about 1834[146] and arranged in two parallel rows and enclosed with iron railings in about 1859, while Reilig Odhráin was enclosed in 1875. The rows of stones, the 'ridge of the kings' and the 'ridge of the chiefs', are traditionally believed to include the graveslabs of the early Scottish kings and the medieval Lords of the Isles respectively.

The inclusion of Macbeth in the long list of early Scottish kings buried on Iona seems suspect. After killing Macbeth at Lumphanan, would Malcolm have had Macbeth's body transported to a remote island on the other side of Scotland? More crucially, would Malcolm have permitted Macbeth's burial alongside the Scottish kings, including Malcolm's own father, Duncan, whom Macbeth had killed and seized the kingship from? Or

St Oran's Chapel, Iona, possibly built as a family burial chapel by Somerled, Lord of the Isles, who died in 1164. The decorative doorway, with its characteristically Romanesque dog-tooth moulding, indicates a twelfth-century date. The chapel was restored and reroofed in 1957. (Crown copyright: Royal Commission on the Ancient and Historical Monuments of Scotland)

were Macbeth's remaining followers responsible for his burial on Iona and Malcolm simply powerless to prevent it? But perhaps Macbeth's kingship, regardless of the circumstances under which he obtained it, entitled him to be buried with his royal predecessors on Iona? All these interpretations strain credulity. More probably, a scribe was simply adhering to established convention in placing Macbeth's burial on Iona, regardless of the historical reality.

Macbeth's final resting place cannot be identified with certainty, but seems more likely to have been at or near Lumphanan than on Iona. But in many ways the identification of Macbeth's burial place and even the fact of his death seem irrelevant. Macbeth, more than any other Scottish monarch, lives on, his name, deeds and reputation immortalised in mythology and drama.

Notes

ASC   *Anglo-Saxon Chronicle*
AT   *Annals of Tigernach*
AU   *Annals of Ulster*
CS   *Chronicum Scotorum*
ESSH   *Early Sources of Scottish History*, ed. A.O. Anderson (1990)
NSA   *New Statistical Account of Scotland* (1845)
OSA   *[Old] Statistical Account of Scotland* (1791–9)
RCAHMS   Royal Commission on the Ancient and Historical Monuments of Scotland
RCHM(E)   Royal Commission on Historical Monuments (England)
s.a.   *sub anno* ('under the year', refering to annalistic entries)
SAEC   *Scottish Annals from English Chroniclers*, ed. A.O. Anderson 1991)

Introduction

1. Donaldson, G. 1990: 56.

1. Scotland in the Age of Macbeth

1. Most Scottish entries are conveniently collected, in translation, in ESSH and SAEC.
2. Smyth 1972; Bannerman 1974: 9–26.
3. Cowan, E.J. 1980.
4. Anderson, M.O. 1980: 43–76, 261–91.
5. Watson 1926; Nicolaisen 1976.
6. There is no overall survey of the archaeology of early medieval Scotland, although Laing 1975: 20–88, 177–207; Ritchie and Ritchie 1981: 142–82; Laing and Laing 1993; Foster 1996 are all useful. However, the eleventh century, which bridges the early medieval and medieval periods, is particularly poorly covered in the literature.
7. The excavations most relevant to this study are reported in Alcock, Alcock and Driscoll 1989; Alcock and Alcock 1992. Alcock 1981 provides an overview.
8. These peoples have received very uneven coverage in the archaeological and historical literature. On the Picts see Wainwright (ed.) 1955; Henderson 1967; Friell and Watson (eds) 1984; Small (ed.) 1987; Sutherland 1994; Cummins 1995; Nicoll (ed.) 1995; Henry (ed.) 1997; on the Scots see Bannerman 1974; Anderson, M.O. 1982; on the Picts and Scots see Laing and Laing 1993; Foster 1996; on the Angles see Jackson 1959; on the Britons see Kirby 1962; Macquarrie 1993; on the Angles and Britons see Jackson 1963; Nicolaisen 1964; on the Vikings see Crawford 1987; Morris and Rackham 1992; Batey, Jesch and Morris (eds) 1993; Ritchie, A. 1993; Crawford (ed.) 1995; Graham-Campbell and Batey 1998.
9. Cowan, E.J. 1982; Crawford 1995.
10. Anderson, M.O. 1960; Anderson, A.O. 1963; Barrow 1973: 139–61; Kirby 1975a; 1975b; Duncan 1976.
11. Nicolaisen 1976: 123–36.
12. On which see Byrne 1973.
13. AT s.a. 1040, 1058; AU s.a. 1058, 1093.

14. Aitchison 1994a.
15. Adomnán, *Vita S. Columbae*: 188–9. On which see Enright 1985a; 1985b: 5–78; Meckler 1990.
16. Stevenson 1927. On the Irish system see Ó Corráin 1971.
17. Aitchison 1998: 116–17.
18. Fordun 2: 289; not in Bower.
19. For a comprehensive account see Aitchison forthcoming.
20. Bannerman 1989.
21. Alcock 1982; Alcock and Alcock 1992: 218–41. See also Foster 1998.
22. Fordun, Bower 2: 421. Bower's *Scotichronicon*, a continuation of Fordun's *Chronicle*, is available in a recent translation and is therefore cited in preference throughout.
23. Skene 1890, Vol. 3: 49–60; Jackson 1972: 102–10; Duncan 1978: 108–11; Smyth 1989: 219–20.
24. On the Pictish provinces see Skene 1890, Vol. 3: 42–8; Henderson 1975a; Broun forthcoming.
25. AU s.a. 917, 1014; AT s.a. 976. All entries in AU before 1014 are ante-dated by one year.
26. Bannerman 1993.
27. AU s.a. 738; *Scottish Chronicle*, ed. Anderson, M.O. 1980: 252; ESSH 1: 236, 473.
28. AT s.a. 1029; AU s.a. 1020, 1085, 1130; *Book of Leinster* 1: 98.
29. Regnal lists, ed. Anderson, M.O. 1980: 267, 275, 283–4; ESSH 1: 513.
30. Duncan 1978: 164–5.
31. Boece 2: 164–5; Holinshed 2: 252; Shakespeare, *Macbeth* Act 5, Scene 9.
32. Barrow 1973: 7–68; Grant, A. 1993. For an archaeological perspective see Driscoll 1991.
33. Loyn 1955; 1992.
34. Symeon, *De Obsessione Dunelmi*: 98.
35. Bower 2: 417.
36. Jackson 1972: 110–14; Grant, A. 1993: 42.
37. Jackson 1972: 30, 33, 112–14; Bannerman 1993: 26–7.
38. *Acts of the Parliaments of Scotland*, Vol. 1: 663–5; Duncan 1978: 107.
39. Barrow 1973: 47; Grant, A. 1993: 48–9, 73, 76.
40. Driscoll 1991; 1998a.
41. Driscoll 1998b. On the Irish evidence see Aitchison 1994b; Herity 1995.
42. Barrow 1992: 217–46.
43. Jones, G.R.J. 1984.
44. Boece 2: 164–5.
45. Donaldson, G. 1953; Cowan, I.B. 1973; 1975; Barrow 1981: 61–83; Macquarrie 1992.
46. Watson 1926: 244–338; Macdonald, A. 1973; 1979; Nicolaisen 1976: 128–30; Taylor, S. 1996; Barrow 1989: 76–8; Clancy forthcoming.
47. Jackson 1972: 32, 35, 78, 123.
48. AU s.a. 864.
49. AU s.a. 1093.
50. AU s.a. 964; *Scottish Chronicle*, ed. Anderson, M.O. 1980: 252; ESSH 1: 471–3.
51. O'Dwyer 1981; Clancy 1996.
52. Trans. Macquarrie 1992: 131. See also ESSH 2: 76. For the edited text see Hinde 1868, Vol. 1: 247.
53. Hudson, B.T. 1994a.
54. Jackson 1972: 30, 34, 50.
55. Ibid.: 32.
56. Donaldson, G. 1973; Fernie 1987.
57. RCAHMS 1982: 41–2, 137–8; Ritchie, A. 1997: 98–100.
58. Cruden 1986: 6–13; Fernie 1987: 393–4.
59. Cruden 1986: 14–20; Fernie 1987: 403–7; Cameron 1994.
60. Trans. after Colgrave and Mynors 1969: 223.
61. AU s.a. 781.
62. Jones, Keiller and Maude 1993.
63. Ed. Anderson, M.O. 1980: 252; ESSH 1: 395–7.
64. Ed. Anderson, M.O. 1980: 252; ESSH 1: 452.
65. Ed. Anderson, M.O. 1980: 252, 267, 275, 283; ESSH 1: 453.
66. ESSH 1: 453.
67. Ed. Anderson, M.O. 1980: 267, 275, 283; ESSH 1: 473.
68. Trans. Jackson 1957: 133.
69. Sellar 1993.
70. ASC s.a. 1078, D text.
71. AU s.a. 1085.
72. AU s.a. 1116.
73. AU s.a. 1130.

74. ASC s.a. 1080 (for 1130), D text.
75. According to one's interpretation of the *Holyrood Chronicle*: 142, 142–3, n. 2.

2. The Path to the Throne

1. AT s.a. 1058; AU s.a. 1058; CS s.a. 1056.
2. Ed. Jackson 1957: 132.
3. *Liber Cartarum*: 114.
4. Apocrypha, 1 and 2 Maccabees.
5. Pinkerton 1789, Vol. 2: 164–5.
6. AU s.a. 1014, 1041, 1086; AFM s.a. 1106.
7. Ellis 1980: 13; Bannerman 1986: 1; Hudson, B.T. 1992: 352–3.
8. Ó Corráin and Maguire 1981: 127.
9. ESSH 2: 232; MacBeth 1921: 36.
10. Ed. Heist 1965: 211; Bitel 1990: 35.
11. Chadwick 1951: 8, n. 2, 12; Cowan, E.J. 1993: 129.
12. MacBeth 1921: x, 111. Erskine 1930; Ellis 1980; Tranter 1987: 21–5; Cowan, E.J. 1993 all give the name as MacBeth.
13. E.g. Hudson, B.T. 1994b; *Prophecy of Berchán*: 224–7; Foster 1996: 113; Marsden 1997: 191.
14. Ed. O'Brien 1962: 329–30. On medieval royal genealogies in general see Dumville 1977.
15. Trans Pálsson and Edwards 1981: 36–7.
16. *Chronicle of Huntingdon*: 210; Wyntoun 4: 258–9; ESSH 1: 593, n. 3; but see Anderson, A.O. 1928; ESSH 1: 579, n. 8.
17. Boece 2: 143.
18. Fordun 2: 173; not in Bower.
19. Wyntoun 4: 273.
20. *Orkneyinga Saga*, trans Pálsson and Edwards 1981: 38.
21. Wyntoun 4: 275.
22. Bartlett and Mackay 1989; Goodman and Tuck 1992; Neville 1998.
23. AT s.a. 1020; AU s.a. 1020.
24. Trans Pálsson and Edwards 1981: 27–8.
25. ASC, E text.
26. ASC, A text.
27. Ed. Whitelock 1955, Vol. 1: 311.
28. ASC s.a. 1054; ESSH 1: 591.
29. Hudson, B.T. 1992: 351–3.
30. *Life of Edward the Confessor*: 42–3.
31. ESSH 1: 591–2; Hudson, B.T. 1992: 356; Lawson 1993: 104.
32. Trans. Jackson 1972: 34.
33. AT s.a. 1029; AU s.a. 1029.
34. AU s.a. 1032.
35. On the *comitatus* in general, see Evans 1997.
36. Lucas 1967.
37. Trans Pálsson and Edwards 1981: 35–6.
38. Trans. Hudson, B.T. 1996: 91.
39. *Prophecy of Berchán*: 84, 87; *Duan Albanach*: 129, 133.
40. Marstrander 1913: 116.
41. Trans. Hudson, B.T. 1996: 88; Jackson 1957: 133; ESSH 1: 602.
42. *Liber Cartarum*: 114; Lawrie (ed.) 1905: 5.
43. AU s.a. 1033.
44. Wyntoun 4: 275.
45. AU s.a. 1033.
46. Fordun, Bower 2: 383, 385, 411.
47. Regnal list E, ed. Anderson, M.O. 1980: 254; ESSH 1: 603.
48. Regnal lists, ed. Anderson, M.O. 1980: 284; ESSH 1: 573.
49. ESSH 1: 576.
50. Trans. Hudson, B.T. 1996: 90.
51. Fordun, Bower 2: 411.
52. ESSH 1: 576.
53. Ed. and trans. France 1989: 55, 57; ESSH 1: 546.
54. Fordun 2: 173–4; not in Bower. On 'abthane' see Fordun 2: 412–13; ESSH 1: 576–7, n. 7.
55. SAEC: 85, n. 4.
56. Bower 2: 409, 411.
57. Fordun, Bower 2: 419; see also *Chronicle of Carlisle*, ESSH 1: 593, n. 3. On Cumbria's status see Kapelle 1979: 27–49.
58. Donaldson, G. 1995: 106–7.
59. Trans. Hudson, B.T. 1996: 90.
60. ESSH 1: 572, 579.
61. Bower 2: 419.
62. Trans Pálsson and Edwards 1981: 50–5.
63. Taylor, A.B. 1937; *Orkneyinga Saga*, trans. Taylor, A.B. 1938: 361.
64. Trans Pálsson and Edwards 1981: 50.
65. Trans. Hudson, B.T. 1996: 91.
66. Boece 2: 144, 146–9.
67. Trans. Taylor, A.B. 1938: 173.
68. Trans Pálsson and Edwards 1981: 60.
69. Regnal list I; ed. Anderson, M.O. 1980: 284; Fordun, Bower 2: 419.
70. Symeon, *Historia Regum*: 99.
71. Symeon, *Historia Dunelmensis Ecclesiae*: 64.

3. Macbeth, King of Scots

1. Bower 2: 419, 421.
2. ESSH 1: 579.
3. Ed. Anderson, M.O. 1980: 268, 276, 284.
4. Bower 2: 421; see also *Verse Chronicle*, ESSH 1: 576.
5. Fordun 2: 420.
6. *Moray Register*: 30, no. 36; ESSH 1: 581.
7. Marianus Scotus, ESSH 1: 579.
8. Symeon, *Historia Dunelmensis Ecclesiae*: 64.
9. AT s.a. 1040; CS s.a. 1038.
10. Fordun, Bower 2: 419.
11. Wyntoun 4: 273–5.
12. Fordun, Bower 2: 427.
13. Ibid. 2: 427.
14. Trans Pálsson and Edwards 1981: 75.
15. Ibid.: 58–71.
16. Fordun, Bower 2: 419.
17. Ibid. 2: 427.
18. Ibid. 2: 427.
19. AT s.a. 1045; see also AU s.a. 1045.
20. ESSH 1: 583–4, n. 6 and 7.
21. *Annals of Durham*, SAEC: 84.
22. Bower 2: 427, 429, 437, 439.
23. *Lebor Bretnach*: 10–14. On which see Mac Eoin 1964: 139; Dumville 1976: 259.
24. ESSH 1: 274, n. 5; Cowan, E.J. 1984: 125. On the myth in general see Hudson, B.T. 1991.
25. Anderson, M.O. 1974; Smyth 1989: 186–7; Macquarrie 1992: 118–21.
26. *Liber Cartarum*: 114; Lawrie (ed.) 1905: 5–6, no. 5.
27. Taylor, S. 1995: 146–7.
28. *Dunfermline Register*: 3, no. 1.
29. *Liber Cartarum*: 115–16; Lawrie (ed.) 1905: 7, no. 8; 11–12, no. 14; 19, no. 23.
30. On the medieval pilgrimage to Rome see Birch 1998.
31. See e.g. Dalrymple 1776, Vol. 1: 3, n.; Macintosh, J. 1892, Vol. 1: 140, n. 48.
32. Marianus is not to be confused with his namesake and contemporary, Marianus Scotus of Ratisbon, who founded the first of the *Schottenklöster*, Irish monasteries in Austria and southern Germany.
33. Kenney 1929: 615, n. 316.
34. After ESSH 1: 588. Several later chronicles also record this episode, but their accounts are derivative and provide neither independent corroboration nor additional information; Symeon, *Historia Regum*: 120; Florence of Worcester, 1: 204; Wyntoun 4: 276–7; *Chronicle of Melrose*: 111.
35. Wilmart 1929.
36. Lawson 1993: 102–4.
37. Symeon, *Historia Regum*: 114.
38. *Chronicle of Huntingdon*: 198.
39. AT s.a. 1028, 1029; AU s.a. 1028, 1030, 1031.
40. ASC s.a. 1031, D text.
41. Notably Freeman 1867, Vol. 2: 54–5, 118.
42. CS s.a. 854; AT s.a. 1034; AU s.a. 1034.
43. *Encomium Emmae Reginae*: 37.
44. Kenney 1929: 601.
45. Symeon, *Historia Regum*: 120.
46. AU s.a. 1051.
47. William of Malmesbury, *Vita Wulfstani*: 16–17; see also ASC s.a. 1061.
48. Symeon, *Historia Regum*: 114.
49. *Orkneyinga Saga*: 74–5.
50. Mann 1925, Vol. 6: 19–182; Barraclough 1968: 73–4; Maxwell-Stuart 1997: 81.
51. Stenton 1971: 566–8; Barlow 1997: 118–26.
52. ASC s.a. 1052, E text.
53. Trans. after SAEC 84. See also Symeon, *Historia Regum*: 123.
54. On the identification: Round 1964: 251–2; Stenton 1971: 562, n.; Barlow 1997: 94; on the site: RCHM(E) 1931: 64; Higham and Barker 1992: 43–5; Shoesmith 1996: 104–6.
55. Fordun, Bower 2: 439, 427.
56. Gaimar, ed. Bell 1960: 160; trans Hardy and Martin 1889: 160.
57. Fordun 2: 184–91; not in Bower.
58. Fordun, Bower 3: 17.
59. Bower 3: 19.
60. ESSH 1: 593.
61. ESSH 1: 593.
62. Trans. Wright 1866, Vol. 1: 389–91.
63. ASC s.a. 1054, D text.
64. Symeon, *Historia Regum*: 124.
65. Wyntoun 4: 297, 299.
66. ASC s.a. 1054, C and D texts.
67. Florence of Worcester, 1: 212.
68. AU s.a. 1054.
69. Florence of Worcester, 1: 212.

70. ESSH 1: 593, n. 2; 2: 37; SAEC, 96.
71. *Chronicle of Huntingdon*: 204; Shakespeare, *Macbeth*, Act 5, Scene 9.
72. Wyntoun 4: 299.
73. There is no evidence to support Stephens' (1876) claim that the battle was fought at Dundee.
74. Bower 3: 17.
75. Ibid. 3: 19.
76. *Chronicle of Melrose*: 112; see also ESSH 1: 593, n. 3.
77. ESSH 1: 602.
78. Bower 3: 23.
79. Regnal lists; ESSH 1: 600.
80. AU s.a. 1058; *Verse Chronicle*, ESSH 1: 601.
81. Bower 3: 19.
82. Marianus, *Chronicle*; ESSH 1: 579, 602.
83. As Marsden (1997: 200) describes it.
84. Regnal list E, ESSH 1: 603.
85. AT s.a. 1058.
86. ESSH 1: 602.
87. Bower 3: 21, 23.
88. Lynch 1991: 74.
89. ESSH 1: 602.
90. Trans. Jackson 1957: 133.
91. Ed. Anderson, M.O. 1980: 284; ESSH 1: 603.
92. *Verse Chronicle*, ESSH 1: 604.
93. AU s.a. 1058.
94. Bower 3: 23.
95. AT s.a. 1058.

4. The Making of the Myth

1. Bergin 1970: 4; see also Flower 1947: 67–106; Carney 1973; Williams, J.E.C. 1971.
2. Bannerman 1989.
3. Thomson 1969.
4. *Prophecy of Berchán*: 193–5; trans. Hudson, B.T. 1996: 91.
5. Broun forthcoming.
6. Aitchison 1994a: 62–3.
7. Trans. after Kelly 1976: 7.
8. Trans. Hudson, B.T. 1996: 90.
9. Ibid.: 92.
10. Trans. Jackson 1957: 133.
11. Hudson, B.T. 1990.
12. s.a. 1039 (for 1040), s.a. 1056 (for 1057); ESSH 1: 600–1; trans. Stevenson 1856: 110, 112.
13. Fordun 2: xiv.
14. Bower 2: xv; on Fordun's methods and sources see Fordun 2: xlix–li; Bower 1: xiv–xxxii; 2: xv–xxi.
15. Scott 1971: 200.
16. Bower 2: 421.
17. Ibid. 3: 21.
18. Ibid. 2: 427.
19. Ibid. 2: 429.
20. Ibid. 2: 437.
21. Ibid. 2: 439.
22. Ibid. 2: 399.
23. Donaldson and Morpeth 1996: 35.
24. Marsden 1997: 203.
25. Wyntoun 4: 277.
26. Ibid. 4: 277, 276.
27. Ibid. 4: 259.
28. Ibid. 4: 287, 301.
29. Ibid. 4: 279.
30. Ibid. 4: 273.
31. Ibid. 4: 279.
32. Ibid. 4: 299.
33. Ibid. 4: 301.
34. Ibid. 4: 301.
35. Chadwick 1951; Cowan, E.J. 1993: 132.
36. On which see Rees and Rees 1961: 207–341.
37. On which see Aitchison 1998.
38. Byrne 1973: 99.
39. Wyntoun 4: 294.
40. Kieckhefer 1976: 18–23.
41. Bower 3: 25.
42. Ibid. 3: 23.
43. Trans. Constable 1892: 120–3.
44. Ibid.: 120–1.
45. Nicholson 1974: 586.
46. Boece 2: 143. All quotations here are given in modern English from Bellenden's Scots translation.
47. Ibid. 2: 144.
48. Ibid. 2: 151.
49. Ibid. 2: 151, 152.
50. Ibid. 2: 153.
51. Ed. Cody 1888, Vol. 1: 306–8. On Leslie see Donaldson and Morpeth 1996: 77–8.
52. McFarlane 1981; Donaldson and Morpeth 1996: 89–91.
53. Trans. Aikman 1855, Vol. 1: 335.
54. Ibid., Vol. 1: 343.
55. Holinshed: 239; ed. Boswell-Stone 1968: 18.

56. The New Cambridge Shakespeare edition (ed. Braunmuller 1997) provides a wide-ranging introduction. The New Penguin Shakespeare (ed. Hunter, G.K. 1995) and Arden Shakespeare (ed. Muir 1971) editions are also useful.

57. Paul 1950; Clark, A.M. 1981.

58. Jack 1955.

59. Larner 1973; Clark, S. 1977; Cowan, E.J. 1983.

60. On which see Arbuckle 1957.

61. Stallybrass 1982; *Shakespearean Criticism* 29 (1996), 39 (1998).

62. Law 1952; Bullough 1973: 423–527; Muir 1977: 208–17; Wells and Taylor 1987: 543–8.

63. Holinshed: 206–9; ed. Boswell-Stone 1968: 22–3, 26–31.

64. Shakespeare, *Macbeth*, Act 2, Scene 4.

65. Holinshed: 208–9, 210; ed. Boswell-Stone 1968: 31–2.

66. Shakespeare, *Macbeth*, Act 3, Scene 4.

67. Holinshed: 218.

68. Ibid.: 246–8.

69. Shakespeare, *Macbeth*, Act 4, Scene 1.

70. Ibid., Act 1, Scene 1.

71. Sinclair 1797: 244.

72. The quotations are from the 1708 edition, 13–14.

73. Ibid.: 95–7.

74. Cowan, E.J. 1993: 117. On Archibald, see Donaldson and Morpeth 1996: 149–50.

75. Keltie 1875, Vol. 1: 54.

76. Barrow 1975: 112–13.

77. MacIntosh 1822: 35.

78. Erskine 1930: 7. See also Adam 1957; Dunnett 1988; Stewart 1988: 5–8; Fleming 1997: 7–10.

79. Ellis 1980: x; MacMillan 1959: 3; MacBeth 1921: 1.

80. Cowan, E.J. 1993: 118.

81. Ellis 1980: x.

82. MacBeth 1921: 1.

83. Bain 1928: 53; Stopes 1916: 112.

84. Braunmuller 1997: 70, 78.

85. Stewart, A. 1826: 31.

86. Pinkerton 1789, Vol. 2: 197.

87. Innes 1860: 118; Tranter 1987: 25; Grant, I.F. 1930: 11.

88. Stopes 1916: 86.

89. Ritchie, R.L.G. 1954: 7.

90. Skene 1886, Vol. 1: 404.

91. Stopes 1916: 83; Donaldson, G. 1990: 56.

92. Aitchison forthcoming, Chapt. 4.

93. Chambers 1827, Vol. 2: 376.

94. McKerracher 1984; Gerber 1992: 105–11.

95. Vickers 1974–81; *Shakespearean Criticism* 3 (1986): 165–355; 20 (1993): 1–424 provide a comprehensive coverage. Muir (ed.) 1966; Wain (ed.) 1968; Muir and Edwards (eds) 1977; Brown, J.R. (ed.) 1982 are useful anthologies of the most important criticism; Foakes (1990) and Wheeler (1990: 897–939) are helpful guides to the literature.

96. Pepys, Vol. 8: 7; entry dated 7 January 1667.

97. Stone 1941.

98. Billington 1995.

99. Huggett 1981; Opie and Tatem 1989: 396.

100. Sinfield 1992.

101. Moody 1958; Downer 1966: 290–310.

102. Davies 1780, Vol. 2: 136.

103. Steer and Bannerman 1977: 103.

104. Sellar 1981: 106.

105. Lincoln 1905, Vol. 9: 85; letter dated 17 August 1863.

106. White 1999.

107. Rosen and Porter 1984.

108. Thurber 1942: 33.

109. Ball 1968; Jorgens 1977: 148–74; Rothwell and Melzer 1990: 147–71; Buchan 1991: 27–30.

110. Shakespeare, *Macbeth*, Act 5, Scene 8.

111. Mullin 1976.

112. Hutton 1960; Davies 1988: 83–99.

113. Osborne 1997.

114. Carruthers (ed.) 1996: introduction.

115. Davies 1988: 152–66; Donaldson, G. 1990: 69–91; Goodwin 1994: 169–91.

116. Mulryne 1992.

117. Wain 1968: 30.

118. Schlegel 1815, Vol. 2: 198.

119. Freud 1957, Vol. 14: 324.

5. *In Search of Macbeth*

1. E.g. Dundurn and Dumbarton Rock, on which see Alcock *et al.* 1989; Alcock and Alcock 1990.

2. Boece 2: 149.

3. Shakespeare, *Macbeth*, Act 1, Scene 2.

4. RCAHMS 1933: 21–2, no. 23; Lang 1975: 209, 211, 227. See also Lang 1984; 1994. On Inchcolm Abbey itself see Fawcett and McRoberts 1989.

5. Holinshed, Vol. 2: 243; ed. Boswell-Stone 1968: 23.

6. Shakespeare, *Macbeth*, Act 1, Scene 3.

7. Shaw 1882, Vol. 2: 173; see also Grant and Leslie 1798: 179.

8. Johnson 1775: 36.

9. Boswell 1785: 122–3.

10. Johnson 1775: 37.

11. Douglas 1934.

12. Bain 1928: 463.

13. MacGibbon and Ross 1887, Vol. 2: 315.

14. Trans. from *Cawdor Book*: 20.

15. MacGibbon and Ross 1887, Vol. 2: 113–25.

16. MacGibbon and Ross 1887, Vol. 2: 314–23.

17. MacGibbon and Ross 1887, Vol. 2: 113.

18. Dunbar 1899: 15.

19. Shaw 1882, Vol. 2: 270.

20. Small and Cottam 1972; Small 1975: 85.

21. Henderson 1975b; on other possible sites see Alcock 1981: 159–61.

22. Boswell 1785: 139.

23. Johnson 1775: 39.

24. OSA 9 (1791): 632–3; NSA 14 (1845): 12. The latter account is dated January 1835.

25. Shaw 1882, Vol. 3: 90; MacDonald 1975: 125.

26. OSA 9 (1791): 633.

27. For a more detailed account of Scone see Aitchison forthcoming, Chapt. 5.

28. Bower 2: 319, 327.

29. Bower 3: 107.

30. Fordun 1: 227; 2: 218; not in Bower.

31. *Chronicle of Melrose*, ESSH 2: 159–60.

32. Bower 2: 415, 417.

33. Cowan and Easson 1976: 50.

34. *Liber Cartarum*: 113; Lawrie (ed.) 1905: 4; see also the commentary in *Vita Sancti Servani*: 126.

35. *Vita Sancti Servani*: 140, 149.

36. AU s.a. 703.

37. Macquarrie 1992: 113.

38. *Liber Cartarum*: 113; Lawrie (ed.) 1905: 4.

39. *Liber Cartarum*: 114–17; Reeves 1864: 51–3; Lawrie (ed.) 1905: 5–7, 9, 11, 19.

40. *Liber Cartarum*: 188–9; Lawrie (ed.) 1905: 187.

41. *Vitae S. Columbae*: lx.

42. *Liber Cartarum*: 113; Hadden and Stubbs 1964, Vol. 2: 227–8; see also Anderson, M.O. 1980: 57–8.

43. NSA 9 (1845): 2–3, 74; Kerr 1882: 163.

44. In a letter from Michael Bruce, quoted in Kerr 1882: 163.

45. RCAHMS 1933: 305–6, no. 581; Fawcett 1994: 23–4.

46. Annan 1862; Kerr 1882.

47. Boece 2: 158.

48. Wyntoun 4: 284–7.

49. RCAHMS 1933: 209, no. 421.

50. Book 10, fol. ccv.

51. OSA 12 (1792): 552, n.

52. OSA 16 (1791): 529.

53. MacGibbon and Ross 1892, Vol. 4: 260–4; RCAHMS 1933: 280–3, no. 535.

54. OSA 10 (1793): 136–7.

55. Bower 2: 437.

56. Wyntoun 4: 299.

57. Hudson, H.N. (ed.) 1908: xxiii–xxiv; Furness (ed.) 1915: 398–400; Porter and Clarke 1901: 126–32; Cowan, E.J. 1993: 132.

58. Breeze 1997.

59. Camden 1590, Vol. 2: 40.

60. OSA 6 (1792): 359–60; Dingwall 1997: 163.

61. Gilbert 1979: 45, 178–9.

62. Hunter, T. 1883: 9, 73.

63. Pennant 1774: 80; the engraving is from the 1790 edition.

64. The Bodleian Library, MS M.D. Mendelssohn d. 2, fol. 13r. Unfortunately this sketch is too faint to reproduce here.

65. NSA 10 (1845): 1006.

66. M'Lean 1865: 70.

67. Hunter, T. 1883: 80.

68. NSA 10 (1845): 1007; account dated January 1843.

69. Hunter, T. 1883: 73.

70. Pakenham 1996: 106.

71. Wyntoun 4: 281, 283.

72. Boece 1: 156.

73. Ibid. 2: 156.

74. Shakespeare, *Macbeth*, Act 5, Scene 5.
75. RCAHMS 1994: 55–7.
76. Ibid.: 55.
77. Coles 1962: 125.
78. MacKie 1969; 1976; Small 1975.
79. Ralston 1987a. On hillfort fortifications in general see Ralston 1995.
80. Brown, T. 1873: 378–9.
81. Small 1969; Edwards and Ralston 1978; Ralston 1987b; Alcock 1981; 1984: 21–2; Alcock *et al.* 1989.
82. Laing 1975: 36.
83. Close-Brooks 1987a; 1987b.
84. Ed. Anderson, M.O. 1980: 275, 284.
85. Bower 2: 377.
86. OSA 9 (1792): 154.
87. Alcock 1981: 174, 178; see also ESSH 1: 513, n. 4.
88. Christison 1900: 85.
89. Sinclair 1797: 242.
90. Ibid.: 243.
91. OSA 9 (1792): 154; Sinclair 1797: 243.
92. Pennant 1776, Vol. 2: 178–9.
93. Williams 1777: 52.
94. Chambers 1827, Vol. 2: 375; Knox 1831: 196.
95. Pennant 1776, Vol. 2: 179.
96. OSA 20 (1797): 241.
97. Playfair 1819, Vol. 1: 488.
98. Chalmers 1887, Vol. 1: 406–14; Chambers 1827, Vol. 2: 374–5; Knox 1831: 192–8.
99. Wise 1859; Brown, T. 1873.
100. Wise 1859: 93, 95.
101. Playfair 1819, Vol. 1: 488.
102. Wise 1859: 95.
103. Quoted in Christison 1900: 89.
104. Robertson 1799: 570.
105. Williams, J. 1777: 52; Knox 1831: 196.
106. Christison 1900: 89–91.
107. Brown, T. 1873: 379.
108. Stewart, quoted in Christison 1900: 90.
109. Stewart, quoted in Christison 1900: 90; Wise 1859: 96–7.
110. Wise 1859: 99.
111. RCAHMS 1994: 57.
112. Wise 1859: 99.
113. Wainwright 1963; RCAHMS 1994: 63–8, 70–5, 159–60.

114. Brown, T. 1873: 380; Wise 1859: 99.
115. Sinclair 1797: 242.
116. Christison 1900: 46; RCAHMS 1994: 106.
117. NSA 10 (1845): 874.
118. Pennant 1776, Vol. 2: 179.
119. OSA 9 (1793): 154.
120. Pennant 1776, Vol. 2: 179–80; see also OSA 13 (1793): 537, n; Robertson 1799: 380, n.
121. RCAHMS 1994: 16, 106.
122. Driscoll 1998b: 153–4.
123. Sinclair 1797: 244.
124. Pennant 1776, Vol. 2: 179; Chambers 1827, Vol. 2: 376.
125. RCAHMS 1994: 33, 34, 151, 152.
126. Wise 1859: 94, n. 3. Enquiries at the Scottish Records Office, National Library of Scotland's Map Library, Perth and Kinross Council Archive and the RCAHMS have failed to locate a copy of this map.
127. Pennant 1776, Vol. 2: 175, 176; see also OSA 1 (1791): 505–6.
128. Jervise 1859: 246; Wise 1859: 94, n. 3.
129. Pennant 1776, Vol. 2: 177.
130. OSA 1 (1791): 505–6; NSA 10 (1845): 234; Jervise 1859: 246.
131. RCAHMS 1994: 34.
132. On which see Chalmers 1889, Vol. 4: 917–18.
133. Sinclair 1797: 243 and n.
134. RCAHMS 1994: 152.
135. Ed. Anderson, M.O. 1980: 268, 276, 284; ESSH 1: 600.
136. Bower 3: 23.
137. OSA 6 (1791–2): 269; NSA 12 (1845): 1083, 1092.
138. OSA 6 (1791–2): 388, n.
139. OSA 8 (1791–2): 269.
140. NSA 12: 613.
141. Marsden 1994: 90; echoing Stewart, A. 1826: 32.
142. Marsden 1994: 95.
143. Ritchie, A. 1997: 31–46.
144. Shakespeare, *Macbeth*, Act 2, Scene 4.
145. RCAHMS 1982: 250; Ritchie, A. 1997: 100–1.
146. Laing, D. 1859.

Bibliography

PRIMARY SOURCES

The Acts of the Parliaments of Scotland, eds T. Thomson and C. Innes, 12 vols, Edinburgh, A. & C. Black, 1814–75

Anglo-Saxon Chronicle, trans. M. Swanton, *The Anglo-Saxon Chronicle*, London, J.M. Dent, 1996

Annals of the Four Masters, ed. and trans. J. O'Donovan, *Annala Rioghachta Eireann: Annals of the Kingdom of Ireland by the Four Masters, from the Earliest Period to the Year 1616*, 7 vols, Dublin, Hodges and Smith, 1848, 1851

Annals of Tigernach, ed. and trans. W. Stokes, *The Annals of Tigernach*, 2 vols, Felinfach, Dyfed, Llanerch, 1993; first published in *Revue Celtique* 16 (1895): 374–419; 17 (1896): 6–33, 119–263, 337–420; 18 (1897): 9–59, 150–97, 268–303, 313–449

Annals of Ulster, eds and trans S. MacAirt and G. MacNiocaill, *The Annals of Ulster (to AD 1131)*, Dublin, Dublin Institute for Advanced Studies, 1983

Audacht Morainn, ed. and trans. F. Kelly, Dublin, Dublin Institute for Advanced Studies, 1976

Bede. *Historia Ecclesiastica Gentis Anglorum*, eds and trans B. Colgrave and R.A.B. Mynors, *Bede's Ecclesiastical History of the English People*, Oxford, Clarendon Press, 1969

Bellenden, John. *Croniklis of the Scots*, eds R.W. Chambers and W.W. Seton, *Bellenden's Translation of the History of Hector Boece*, Glasgow, Maclehose, Jackson & Co., 1919

Boece, Hector. *Scotorum Historiae*, eds E.C. Batho and H.W. Husbands, *The Chronicles of Scotland, Compiled by Hector Boece, Translated into Scots by John Bellenden, 1531*, 2 vols, Edinburgh, Scottish Text Society, 1938, 1941

Book of Leinster, eds R.I. Best, O. Bergin and M.A. O'Brien, *The Book of Leinster, formerly Lebar na Núachongbála*, Vol. 1, Dublin, Dublin Institute for Advanced Studies, 1954

Bower, Walter. *Scotichronicon*, gen. ed. D.E.R. Watt, *Scotichronicon, by Walter Bower in Latin and English*, 9 vols, Aberdeen and Edinburgh, Aberdeen University Press, 1989–98

Buchanan, George. *Rerum Scoticarum Historia*, 1582, trans. J. Aikman, *The History of Scotland, from the Earliest Period to the Present Time*, 6 vols, Glasgow, Blackie & Son, 1855

Cawdor Book, ed. C. Innes, *The Book of the Thanes of Cawdor: a Series of Papers Selected from the Charter Room at Cawdor, 1236–1742*, Edinburgh, Spalding Club, 1859

Chronicle of Holyrood, ed. M.O. Anderson, *A Scottish Chronicle known as the Chronicle of Holyrood*, Edinburgh, Scottish History Society, 1938

Chronicle of Huntingdon, ed. and trans. T. Forester, *The Chronicle of Henry of Huntingdon*, London, H.G. Bohn, 1853

Chronicle of Melrose, trans. J. Stevenson, *Chronicle of Melrose*, in *The Church Historians of England*, Pre-Reformation Series 4.1, London, Seeleys, 1856: pp. 79–242

Chronicum Scotorum, ed. and trans. W.M. Hennessy, *Chronicum Scotorum: a Chronicle of Irish Affairs, from the Earliest Times to AD 1135*, London, Public Record Office, 1866

Corpus Genealogiarum Hiberniae, ed. M.A. O'Brien, Dublin, Dublin Institute for Advanced Studies, 1962

Duan Albanach, ed. and trans. K. Jackson, 'The Duan Albanach', *Scottish Historical Review* 36 (1957): 125–37

Dunfermline Register: Registrum de Dunfermelyn, Edinburgh, Bannatyne Club, 1842

Encomium Emmae Reginae, ed. and trans. A. Campbell, *Encomium Emmae Reginae*, London, Camden Society, 1949; reprinted, with a supplementary introduction by S. Keynes, Cambridge, Cambridge University Press, 1998

Florence of Worcester. *Chronicon ex Chronicis*, ed. B. Thorpe, *Florentii Wigorniensis Monachi Chronicon ex Chronicis*, 2 vols, London, English Historical Society, 1848–9

Fordun, John of. *Chronica Gentis Scotorum*, ed. W.F. Skene, *Johannis de Fordun Chronica Gentis Scotorum*, Edinburgh, 1871; trans. F.J.H. Skene, *John of Fordun's Chronicle of the Scottish Nation*, Edinburgh, Historians of Scotland, 1872; reprinted 2 vols, Felinfach, Dyfed, Llanerch, 1993

Gaimar, Geffrei. *L'estoire des Engleis*, trans. T.D. Hardy and C.T. Martin, *Lestorie des Engles solum la Translacion Maistre Geffrei Gaimar*, Vol. 2, London, Public Record Office, 1889; ed. A. Bell, *L'estoire des Engleis*, Oxford, Basil Blackwell for the Anglo-Norman Society, 1960

Glaber, Rudulfus. *Historiarum Libri Quinque*, ed. and trans. J. France, *Historiarum Libri Quinque: Five Books of the Histories*, Oxford, Clarendon Press, 1989

Holinshed, Raphael. *The Historie of Scotland*, Vol. 2 of *Chronicles of England, Scotland and Ireland*, 3 vols in 2, London, 1577; ed. W.G. Boswell-Stone, *Shakespeare's Holinshed: the Chronicle and the Plays Compared*, New York, Dover, 1968; first published 1896

Langtoft, Pierre de. *Chronicle*, ed. and trans. T. Wright, *The Chronicle of Pierre de Langtoft*, 2 vols, London, Public Record Office, 1866, 1868

Leslie, John. *De Origine, Moribus et Rebus Gestis Scotorum libri decem*, 1578, trans. J. Dalrymple, ed. E.G. Cody, *The Historie of Scotland*, 2 vols, Edinburgh, Scottish Text Society, 1888, 1895

Lebor Bretnach, ed. A.G. van Hamel, *Lebor Bretnach: the Irish Version of the Historia Brittonum of Nennius*, Dublin, 1932

Liber Cartarum, ed. T. Thomson, *Liber Cartarum Prioratus Sancti Andree in Scotia*, Edinburgh, Bannatyne Club, 1841

Life of King Edward the Confessor, ed. and trans. F. Barlow, *The Life of King Edward who Rests at Westminster*, London, Thomas Nelson & Sons, 1962

Mair (or Major), John. *Historia Maioris Britanniae (1521)*, trans. A. Constable, *A History of Greater Britain, as well England as Scotland*, Edinburgh, Æ.J.G. Mackay, 1892

Marianus Scotus. *Mariani Scotti Chronicon*, ed. G. Waitz, *Monumenta Germaniae Historica, Scriptores*, 5, Berlin, Deutsches Institut für Erforschung des Mittelalters, 1844: pp. 481–562

Moray Register, ed. C. Innes, *Registrum Episcopatus Moraviensis*, Edinburgh, Bannatyne Club, 1837

Orkneyinga Saga, trans. A.B. Taylor, *The Orkneyinga Saga*, Edinburgh, Oliver & Boyd, 1938; trans H. Pálsson and P. Edwards, *Orkneyinga Saga: the History of the Earls of Orkney*, Harmondsworth, Penguin, 1981

Prophecy of Berchán, ed. and trans. B.T. Hudson, *Prophecy of Berchán: Irish and Scottish High-Kings of the Early Middle Ages*, Westport, Conn., Greenwood, 1996

Scottish Chronicle, ed. M.O. Anderson 1980: pp. 249–53; ed. B.T. Hudson, *Scottish Historical Review* 77 (1998)

Stewart, William. *The Buik of the Croniclis of Scotland*, ed. W.B. Turnbull, *The Buik of the Croniclis of Scotland; or a Metrical Version of the History of Hector Boece*, 3 vols, London, Public Record Office, 1858

Symeon of Durham. *Historia Dunelmensis Ecclesiae*, trans. J. Stevenson, *Simeon's History of the Church of Durham*, London, Seeleys, 1855; reprinted Felinfach, Dyfed, Llanerch, 1988

——. *Historia Regum*, trans. J. Stevenson, *Simeon of Durham's History of the Kings*, London, Seeleys, 1857; reprinted Felinfach, Dyfed, Llanerch, 1987

——. *De Obsessione Dunelmi*, trans. J. Stevenson, *Simeon's Account of the Siege of Durham*, in J. Stevenson (trans.), *Simeon's History of the Church of Durham*, Felinfach, Dyfed, Llanerch, 1988: pp. 97–100

Turgot. *Vita S. Margaretae Scotorum Reginae*, ed. I.H. Hinde, in *Symeonis Dunelmensis Opera et Collectanea*, Vol. 1, Durham, Surtees Society, 1868: pp. 234–54; trans. A.O. Anderson 1990, Vol. 2: pp. 59–88

Verse Chronicle, ed. J. Stevenson, *Chronica de Mailros*, Edinburgh, Bannatyne Club, 1835: pp. 223–9; eds A.O. Anderson, M.O. Anderson and W.C. Dickinson, *Chronicle of Melrose*, xxiv–xxvi (facsimile edition); ed. and trans. D. Brown and A.B. Scott, 'Liber Extravagans', in *Scotichronicon*, Vol. 9

Vita Sancti Colmani de land Elo, ed. W.W. Heist, *Vitae Sanctorum Hiberniae: Ex Codice Olim Salmanticensi nunc Bruxellensi*, Bruxelles, Société des Bollandistes, 1965: pp. 209–24

Vita S. Columbae, eds and trans A.O. Anderson and M.O. Anderson, *Adomnán's Life of Columba*, Oxford, Clarendon Press, 1991

Vita Sancti Servani, ed. and trans. A. Macquarrie, '*Vita Sancti Servani*: the Life of St Serf', *Innes Review* 44 (2) (1993): 122–52

William of Malmesbury. *De Gestis Regum Anglorum*, ed. W. Stubbs, 2 vols, London, Public Record Office, 1887, 1889

——. *Vita Wulfstani*, ed. R.R. Darlington, *The Vita Wulfstani of William of Malmesbury*, London, Camden Society, 1928

Wyntoun, Andrew of. *Orygynale Cronykil of Scotland*, ed. F.J. Amours, *The Original Chronicle of Andrew of Wyntoun*, 6 vols, Edinburgh, Scottish Text Society, 1903–14

SECONDARY SOURCES

Adam, R.J. 1957. 'The Real Macbeth: King of Scots, 1040–1054', *History Today* 7.6: 381–7

Aitchison, N.B. 1994a. 'Kingship, Society and Sacrality: Rank, Power, and Ideology in Early Medieval Ireland', *Traditio* 49: 45–75

——. 1994b. *Armagh and the Royal Centres in Early Medieval Ireland: Monuments, Cosmology and the Past*, Woodbridge, Cruithne/Boydell & Brewer

——. 1998. 'Regicide in Early Medieval Ireland', in G. Halsall (ed.), *Violence and Society in the Early Medieval West*, Woodbridge, Boydell Press: pp. 108–25

——. Forthcoming. *Scotland's Stone of Destiny: Myth, History and Nationhood*, Stroud, Tempus

Alcock, L. 1981. 'Early Historic Fortifications in Scotland', in G. Guilbert (ed.), *Hill-Fort Studies: Essays for A.H.A. Hogg*, Leicester, Leicester University Press: pp. 150–80

——. 1982. 'Forteviot: a Pictish and Scottish Royal Church and Palace', in S.M. Pearce (ed.), *The Early Church in Western Britain and Ireland: Studies Presented to C.A. Ralegh Radford*, BAR British Series 102, Oxford, British Archaeological Reports: pp. 211–39

——. 1984. *A Survey of Pictish Settlement Archaeology*, in Friell and Watson (eds) 1984: pp. 7–41

Alcock, L. and Alcock, E.A. 1990. 'Reconnaissance Excavations on Early Historic Fortifications and Other Royal Sites in Scotland, 1974–1984: 4, Excavations at Alt Clut, Clyde Rock, Strathclyde, 1974–75', *Proceedings of the Society of Antiquaries of Scotland* 120: 95–149

——. 1992. 'Reconnaissance Excavations on Early Historic Fortifications and Other Royal Sites in Scotland, 1974–1984: 5, A. Excavations & Other Fieldwork at Forteviot, Perthshire, 1981; B. Excavations at Urquhart Castle, Inverness-shire, 1983; C. Excavations at Dunnottar, Kincardineshire, 1984', *Proceedings of the Society of Antiquaries of Scotland* 122: 215–87

Alcock, L., Alcock, E.A. and Driscoll, S.T. 1989. 'Reconnaissance Excavations on Early Historic Fortifications and Other Royal Sites in Scotland, 1974–1984: 3: Excavations at Dundurn, Strathearn, Perthshire, 1976–77', *Proceedings of the Society of Antiquaries of Scotland* 119: 189–226

Anderson, A.O. 1928. 'Macbeth's Relationship to Malcolm II', *Scottish Historical Review* 25: 377

——. 1963. 'Anglo-Scottish Relations from Constantine II to William', *Scottish Historical Review* 42: 1–20

——. (ed.). 1990. *Early Sources of Scottish History, AD 500 to 1286*, 2 vols, Stamford, Paul Watkins; first published 2 vols, Edinburgh, Oliver & Boyd, 1922

——. (ed.). 1991. *Scottish Annals from English Chroniclers, AD 500 to 1286*, 2 vols, Stamford, Paul Watkins; first published London, David Nutt, 1908

Anderson, M.O. 1960. 'Lothian and the Early Scottish Kings', *Scottish Historical Review* 39: 98–112

——. 1974. 'St Andrews Before Alexander I', in G.W.S. Barrow (ed.), *The Scottish Tradition: Essays in Honour of Ronald Gordon Cant*, Edinburgh, Scottish Academic Press: pp. 1–13

——. 1980. *Kings and Kingship in Early Scotland*, second edn; first published Edinburgh, Scottish Academic Press, 1973

——. 1982. 'Dalriada and the Creation of the Kingdom of the Scots', in D. Whitelock, R. McKitterick and D. Dumville (eds), *Ireland in Early Medieval Europe: Studies in Memory of Kathleen Hughes*, Cambridge, Cambridge University Press: pp. 106–32

Annan, R. 1862. 'Notes on the Antiquities of Kinross-shire: 2, On the Culdees, and the Inch or Island of St Serf's, Lochleven', *Proceedings of the Society of Antiquaries of Scotland* 3 (1857–60): 382–8

Anon. 1708. *A Key to the Drama . . . Containing the Life, Character, and Secret History of Mackbeth*, London, J. Woodward

Anon. 1828. *The Secret History of Mac-beth, King of Scotland*, Peterhead, Peter Buchan

Anon. 1841. *Memoirs of the Court of Scotland . . . Containing the Secret History of Macbeth*, Edinburgh

Arbuckle, W.F. 1957. 'The "Gowrie Conspiracy"', *Scottish Historical Review* 36: 1–24, 89–110

Bain, G. 1928. *History of Nairnshire*, second edn; first published Nairn, 'Telegraph', 1893

Ball, R.H. 1968. *Shakespeare on Silent Film: a Strange Eventful History*, London, George Allen & Unwin

Bannerman, J. 1974. *Studies in the History of Dalriada*, Edinburgh, Scottish Academic Press

——. 1986. *The Beatons: a Medical Kindred in the Classical Gaelic Tradition*, Edinburgh, John Donald

——. 1989. 'The King's Poet and the Inauguration of Alexander III', *Scottish Historical Review* 68: 120–49

——. 1993. 'MacDuff of Fife', in Grant and Stringer (eds), 1993: pp. 20–38

Barlow, F. 1997. *Edward the Confessor*, new edn, London, Yale University Press; first published Eyre & Spottiswoode, 1970

Barraclough, G. 1968. *The Medieval Papacy*, London, Thames & Hudson

Barrow, G.W.S. 1973. 'Pre-feudal Scotland: Shires and Thanes', in G.W.S. Barrow, *The Kingdom of the Scots: Government, Church, and Society From the Eleventh to the Fourteenth Century*, London, Edward Arnold

——. 1975. 'Macbeth and Other Mormaers of Moray', in Maclean (ed.), 1975: pp. 109–22

——. 1981. *Kingship and Unity: Scotland 1000–1306*, London, Edward Arnold

——. 1989. 'The Lost Gàidhealtachd of Medieval Scotland', in W. Gillies (ed.), *Gaelic and Scotland: Alba agus a' Ghàidhlig*, Edinburgh, Edinburgh University Press: pp. 67–88

——. 1992. 'Popular Courts', in G.W.S. Barrow, *Scotland and its Neighbours in the Middle Ages*, London, Hambledon: pp. 217–46; first published as 'Popular Courts in Early Medieval Scotland, Some Suggested Place-name Evidence', *Scottish Studies* 25 (1981): 1–24

Bartlett, R. and MacKay, A. (eds). 1989. *Medieval Frontier Societies*, Oxford, Clarendon Press

Batey, C.E., Jesch, J. and Morris, C.D. (eds). 1993. *The Viking Age in Caithness, Orkney and the North Atlantic*, Edinburgh, Edinburgh University Press

Bergin, O. 1970. *Irish Bardic Poetry: Texts and Translations, together with an Introductory Lecture*, comps and eds D. Greene and F. Kelly, Dublin, Dublin University Press

Billington, M. 1995. 'Is this Macbeth I See Before Me?', the *Guardian*, 27 September 1995: p. 12

Birch, D.J. 1998. *Pilgrimage to Rome in the Middle Ages: Continuity and Change*, Woodbridge, Boydell Press

Bitel, L.M. 1990. *Isle of the Saints: Monastic Settlement and Christian Community in Early Ireland*, Ithaca, Cornell University Press

Boswell, J. 1785. *The Journal of a Tour to the Hebrides, with Samuel Johnson*, London, Charles Dilly; ed. I. McGowan, *Journey to the Hebrides*, Edinburgh, Canongate, 1996

Braunmuller, A.R. (ed.). 1997. *Macbeth*, The New Cambridge Shakespeare, Cambridge, Cambridge University Press

Breeze, D.J. 1997. 'The Great Myth of Caledon', in Smout (ed.), 1997: pp. 47–51; first published in *Scottish Forestry* 46 (1992): 331–5

Broun, D. Forthcoming. 'Recreating Ancient Alba: the Seven Pictish Kingdoms in *De situ Albanie*', in E.J. Cowan and R.A. McDonald (eds), *Alba* (provisional title only), Edinburgh

Brown, J.R. (ed.). 1982. *Focus on Macbeth*, London, Routledge & Kegan Paul

Brown, T. 1873. 'Notes Relating to Dunsinnane Hill', *Proceedings of the Society of Antiquaries of Scotland* 9 (1870–2): 378–80

Buchan, L.M. 1991. *Still in Movement: Shakespeare on Screen*, Oxford, Oxford University Press

Bullough, G. 1973. *Narrative and Dramatic Sources of Shakespeare*, Vol. 7, London, Routledge & Kegan Paul

Byrne, F.J. 1973. *Irish Kings and High-Kings*, London, B.T. Batsford

Camden, W. 1590. *Britannia, or a Chorographicall Description of the Most Flourishing Kingdomes, England, Scotland, and Ireland*, trans. P. Holland, 2 vols, revised and enlarged edition Londini, Georgii Bishop & Ioannis Norton; first published London, Radulphum Newbery, 1586

Cameron, N. 1994. 'St Rule's Church, St Andrews, and Early Stone-Built Churches in Scotland', *Proceedings of the Society of Antiquaries of Scotland* 124: 367–78

Carney, J. 1973. 'Society and the Bardic Poet', *Studies: an Irish Quarterly Review* 62: 233–50

Carruthers, B. (ed.). 1996. *Macbeth by William Shakespeare: The Screenplay*, Stratford-upon-Avon, Cromwell Productions

Chadwick, N.K. 1949–51. 'The Story of Macbeth: a Study in Gaelic and Norse Tradition', *Scottish Gaelic Studies* 6 (1949): 189–211; 7 (1951): 1–25

Chalmers, G. 1887–94. *Caledonia: or, a Historical and Topographical Account of North Britain from the Most Ancient to the Present Times*, 9 vols; new edn, Paisley, Alexander Gardner; first published 3 vols, London, T. Cadell, 1807–24

Chambers, R. 1827. *The Picture of Scotland*, 2 vols, Edinburgh, William Tait

——. 1849. *The History of Scotland*, 2 vols, rev. edn, London, Richard Bentley

Christison, D. 1900. 'The Forts, "Camps", and Other Field-Works of Perth, Forfar and Kincardine', *Proceedings of the Society of Antiquaries of Scotland* 34 (1899–1900): 43–120

Clancy, T.O. 1996. 'Iona, Scotland, and the Célí Dé', in Crawford, 1996: pp. 111–30

——. Forthcoming. 'Annat in Scotland and the Origins of the Parish', *Innes Review*

Clark, A.M. 1981. *Murder Under Trust, or the Topical Macbeth, and Other Jacobean Matters*, Edinburgh, Scottish Academic Press

Clark, S. 1977. 'King James's *Daemonologie*: Witchcraft and Kingship', in S. Anglo (ed.), *The Damned Art: Essays in the Literature of Witchcraft*, London, Routledge & Kegan Paul: pp. 156–81

Close-Brooks, J. 1987a. 'Excavations at Clatchard Craig, Fife 1953–4 and 1959–60', *Proceedings of the Society of Antiquaries of Scotland* 116 (1986): 117–84

——. 1987b. 'Clatchard Craig, a Pictish Hillfort in Fife', in Small (ed.), 1987: pp. 27–30

Coles, J. 1962. 'Scottish Late Bronze Age Metalwork: Typology, Distributions and Chronology'. *Proceedings of the Society of Antiquaries of Scotland* 93 (1959–60): 16–134

Cowan, E.J. 1980. 'The Scottish Chronicle in the Poppleton Manuscript', *Innes Review* 32: 3–21

——. 1982. 'Caithness in the Sagas', in J.R. Baldwin (ed.), *Caithness: a Cultural Crossroads*, Edinburgh, Scottish Society for Northern Studies: pp. 25–44

——. 1983. 'The Darker Vision of the Scottish Renaissance: the Devil and Francis Stewart', in I.B. Cowan and D. Shaw (eds), *The Renaissance and Reformation in Scotland*, Edinburgh, Scottish Academic Press: pp. 125–40

——. 1984. 'Myth and Identity in Early Medieval Scotland', *Scottish Historical Review* 63: 111–35

——. 1993. 'The Historical MacBeth', in Sellar (ed.), 1993: pp. 117–41

Cowan, I.B. 1973. 'The Post-Columban Church', *Records of the Scottish Church History Society* 18: 245–60

——. 1975. 'Early Ecclesiastical Foundations', in McNeill and Nicholson, 1975: pp. 17–19, 119–22

Cowan, I.B. and Easson, D.E. 1976. *Medieval Religious Houses: Scotland*, second edn, London, Longman; first published Longmans, Green, 1957

Crawford, B.E. 1987. *Scandinavian Scotland*, Leicester, Leicester University Press

——. 1995. *Earl and Mormaer: Norse-Pictish Relationships in Northern Scotland*, Rosemarkie, Groam House Museum

——. (ed.). 1995. *Scandinavian Settlement in Northern Britain*, Leicester, Leicester University Press

——. (ed.). 1996. *Scotland in Dark Age Britain*, St Andrews, Scottish Cultural Press

Cruden, S. 1986. *Scottish Medieval Churches*, Edinburgh, John Donald

Cummins, W.A. 1995. *The Age of the Picts*, Stroud, Sutton Publishing

Dalrymple, D. (Lord Hailes). 1776. *Annals of Scotland; from the Accession of Malcolm III, Surnamed Canmore, to the Accession of Robert I*, 2 vols, Edinburgh, J. Murray

Davies, A. 1988. *Filming Shakespeare's Plays: the Adaptations of Laurence Olivier, Orson Welles, Peter Brook and Akira Kurosawa*, Cambridge, Cambridge University Press

Davies, T. 1780. *Memoirs of the Life of David Garrick*, 2 vols, London, the author

Dingwall, C. 1997. 'Coppice Management in Highland Perthshire', in Smout (ed.), 1997: pp. 162–75

Donaldson, G. 1953. 'Scottish Bishops' Sees Before the Reign of David I', *Proceedings of the Society of Antiquaries of Scotland* 87 (1952–3): 106–17; a revised version appears in Donaldson, G. 1985: pp. 11–24

——. 1973. 'Scotland's Earliest Church Buildings', *Records of the Scottish Church History Society* 18: 1–9; a revised version appears in Donaldson, G. 1985: pp. 1–10

——. 1985. *Scottish Church History*, Edinburgh, Scottish Academic Press

——. 1990. *A Northern Commonwealth: Scotland and Norway*, Edinburgh, Saltire

——. 1995. 'Reflections on the Royal Succession', in G. Donaldson (ed. J. Kirk), *Scotland's History: Approaches and Reflections*, Edinburgh, Scottish Academic Press: pp. 103–17

Donaldson, G. and Morpeth, R.S. 1996. *Who's Who in Scottish History*, n.p. (Cardiff), Welsh Academic Press; first published Oxford, Blackwell, 1973

Donaldson, P.S. 1990. 'Surface and Depth: Throne of Blood as Cinematic Allegory', in P.S. Donaldson, *Shakespearean Films/Shakespearean Directors*, London, Unwin Hyman: pp. 69–91

Douglas, R. 1934. *Annals of the Royal Burgh of Forres*, Elgin

Downer, A.S. 1966. *The Eminent Tragedian: William Charles Macready*, London, Oxford University Press

Driscoll, S.T. 1991. 'The Archaeology of State Formation in Scotland', in W.S. Hanson and E.A. Slater (eds), *Scottish Archaeology: New Perceptions*, Aberdeen, Aberdeen University Press: pp. 81–111

——. 1998a. 'Formalising the Mechanisms of State Power: Early Scottish Lordship from the Ninth to the Thirteenth Centuries', in Foster *et al.* (eds), 1998: pp. 32–58

——. 1998b. 'Picts and Prehistory: Cultural Resource Management in Early Medieval Scotland', *World Archaeology* 30: 142–58

Dumville, D.N. 1976. 'The Textual History of "Lebor Bretnach": a Preliminary Study', *Éigse* 16 (1975–6): 255–73

——. 1977. 'Kingship, Genealogies and Regnal Lists', in P.H. Sawyer and I. Wood (eds), 1977, *Early Medieval Kingship*, Leeds, School of History, University of Leeds: pp. 72–104

Dunbar, A.H. 1899. *Scottish Kings: a Revised Chronology of Scottish History, 1005–1625*, second edn, Edinburgh, D. Douglas, 1906

Duncan, A.M.M. 1976. 'The Battle of Carham', *Scottish Historical Review* 55: 20–8

——. 1978. *Scotland: the Making of the Kingdom*, rev. edn; first published Edinburgh, Oliver & Boyd, 1975

Dunnett, D. 1988. 'The Real Macbeth', *The Story of Scotland* 4: 88–93

Edwards, K.J. and Ralston, I. 1978. 'New Dating and Environmental Evidence from Burghead, Moray', *Proceedings of the Society of Antiquaries of Scotland* 109 (1977–8): 202–10

Ellis, P.B. 1980. *MacBeth, High King of Scotland 1040–57 AD*, London, Frederick Muller; reprinted Belfast, Blackstaff, 1990

Enright, M.J. 1985a. 'Royal Succession and Abbatial Prerogative in Adomnán's *Vitae Columbae*', *Peritia* 4: 83–103

——. 1985b. *Iona, Tara and Soissons: the Origin of the Royal Anointing Ritual*, Berlin, de Gruyter

Erskine, R. 1930. *Mac Beth: Being a Sketch of the Historical Figure as Opposed to That of Some Tradition and the Drama*, Inverness, Robert Carruthers & Sons

Evans, S.S. 1997. *The Lords of Battle: Image and Reality of the Comitatus in Dark-Age Britain*, Woodbridge, Boydell Press

Fawcett, R. 1994. *Scottish Abbeys and Priories*, London, B.T. Batsford/Historic Scotland

Fawcett, R. and McRoberts, D. 1989. *Inchcolm Abbey and Island*, Edinburgh, HMSO

Feachem, R. 1977. *Guide to Prehistoric Scotland*, second edn; first published London, B.T. Batsford, 1963

Fernie, E. 1987. 'Early Church Architecture in Scotland', *Proceedings of the Society of Antiquaries of Scotland* 116 (1986): 393–411

Fleming, M. 1997. *The Real Macbeth and Other Stories from Scottish History*, Edinburgh, Mercat Press

Flower, R. 1947. *The Irish Tradition*, Oxford, Clarendon Press

Foakes, R.A. 1990. 'Macbeth', in S. Wells (ed.), *Shakespeare: a Bibliographical Guide*, rev. edn; first published Oxford, Clarendon Press, 1973: pp. 259–74

Forsyth, R. 1805–8. *The Beauties of Scotland*, 5 vols, Edinburgh, T. Bonar & J. Brown; first published 1772

Foster, S.M. 1996. *Picts, Gaels and Scots: Early Historic Scotland*, London, B.T. Batsford/Historic Scotland

——. 1998. 'Before *Alba*: Pictish and Dál Riata Power Centres from the Fifth to Late Ninth Centuries AD', in Foster *et al.* (eds), 1998: pp. 1–31

Foster, S.M., Macinnes, A. and MacInnes, R. (eds). 1998. *Scottish Power Centres: from the Early Middle Ages to the Twentieth Century*, Glasgow, Cruithne Press

Freeman, E.A. 1867–79. *The History of the Norman Conquest of England, its Causes and Results*, 6 vols, Oxford, Clarendon Press

Freud, S. 1957. *The Standard Edition of the Complete Psychological Works*, ed. J. Strachey, Vol. 14, London, Hogarth Press/Institute of Psycho-Analysis

Friell, J.G.P. and Watson, W.G. (eds). 1984. *Pictish Studies: Settlement, Burial and Art in Dark Age Northern Britain*, BAR British Series 125, Oxford, British Archaeological Reports

Furness, H.H. (ed.). 1915. *Macbeth*, New Variorum edn, rev. edn, Philadelphia, J.B. Lippincott & Co.; first published 1873

Garrick, D. 1744. *An Essay on Acting . . . the Mimical Behaviour of a Certain Fashionable Faulty Actor . . . {with} a Short Criticism on his Acting of Macbeth*, London, W. Bickerton

Gerber, P. 1992. *The Search for the Stone of Destiny*, Edinburgh, Canongate; new edn published 1997 as *Stone of Destiny*

Gilbert, J.M. 1979. *Hunting and Hunting Reserves in Medieval Scotland*, Edinburgh, John Donald

Goodman, A. and Tuck, A. 1992. *War and Border Societies in the Middle Ages*, London, Routledge

Goodwin, J. 1994. *Akira Kurosawa and Intertextual Cinema*, Baltimore, John Hopkins University Press

Graham-Campbell, J. and Batey, C.E. 1998. *Vikings in Scotland: an Archaeological Survey*, Edinburgh, Edinburgh University Press

Grant, A. 1993. 'Thanes and Thanages, from the Eleventh to the Fourteenth Centuries', in Grant and Stringer (eds), 1993: pp. 39–81

Grant, A. and Stringer, K. (eds). 1993. *Medieval Scotland: Crown, Lordship and Community. Essays Presented to G.W.S. Barrow*, Edinburgh, Edinburgh University Press

Grant, I.F. 1930. *The Social and Economic Development of Scotland before 1603*, Edinburgh, Oliver & Boyd

Grant, J. and Leslie, W. 1798. *A Survey of the Province of Moray: Historical, Geographical and Political*, Aberdeen, Isaac Forsyth

Hadden, A. and Stubbs, W. 1964. *Councils and Ecclesiastical Documents Relating to Great Britain and Ireland*, 2 vols, Oxford, Clarendon Press; first published 1869–78

Henderson, I. 1967. *The Picts*, London, Thames & Hudson

——. 1975a. 'Pictish Territorial Divisions', in McNeill and Nicholson, 1975: pp. 8–9, 114

——. 1975b. 'Inverness, a Pictish Capital', in Maclean (ed.), 1975: pp. 9–108

Henry, D. (ed.). 1997. *The Worm, the Germ and the Thorn: Pictish and Related Studies Presented to Isabel Henderson*, Balgavies, Angus, Pinkfoot Press

Herity, M. 1995. 'Motes and Mounds at Royal Sites in Ireland', *Journal of the Royal Society of Antiquaries of Ireland* 123 (1993): 127–51

Higham, R. and Barker, P. 1992. *Timber Castles*, London, B.T. Batsford

Honeyman, B. 1977. *Macbeth, King of Scots*, London, Hale

Hudson, B.T. 1990. 'From *Senchus* to *Histoire*: Traditions of King Duncan I', *Studies in Scottish Literature* 25: 100–20

——. 1991. 'The Conquest of the Picts in Early Scottish Literature', *Scotia: Interdisciplinary Journal of Scottish Studies* 15: 13–25

——. 1992. 'Cnut and the Scottish Kings', *English Historical Review* 107: 350–60

——. 1994a. 'Kings and Church in Early Scotland', *Scottish Historical Review* 73: 145–70

——. 1994b. *Kings of Celtic Scotland*, Westport, Conn., Greenwood

Hudson, H.N. (ed.). 1908. *The Tragedy of Macbeth*, New Hudson Shakespeare, ed. and rev. E.C. Black, Boston, Ginn & Co.

Huggett, R. 1981. *The Curse of Macbeth and other Theatrical Superstitions, an Investigation*, Chippenham, Picton

Hunter, G.K. (ed.). 1995. *Macbeth*, The New Penguin Shakespeare, rev. edn; first published Harmondsworth, Penguin, 1967

Hunter, T. 1883. *Woods, Forests, and Estates of Perthshire*, Perth, Henderson, Robertson & Co.

Hutton, C. 1960. *Macbeth: the Making of the Film*, London, Max Parrish

Innes, C. 1860. *Scotland in the Middle Ages: Sketches of Early Scotch History and Social Progress*, Edinburgh, Edmonston & Douglas

Jack, J.H. 1955. 'Macbeth, King James and the Bible', *ELH: a Journal of English Literary History* 22: 173–93

Jackson, K.H. 1959. 'Edinburgh and the Anglian Occupation of Lothian', in P. Clemoes (ed.), *The Anglo-Saxons: Studies in some Aspects of their History and Culture*, London, Bowes & Bowes: pp. 35–42

——. 1963. 'Angles and Britons in Northumbria and Cumbria', in K.H. Jackson, *Angles and Britons*, O'Donnell Lectures, Cardiff, University of Wales Press, 1963: pp. 60–84

——. 1972. *The Gaelic Notes in the Book of Deer*, Cambridge, Cambridge University Press

Jervise, A. 1859. 'Notices Descriptive of the Localities of Certain Sculptured Stone Monuments in Forfarshire, &c. – Meigle, Essie, Glamis, Thornton, and Cossins', *Proceedings of the Society of Antiquaries of Scotland* 2 (1854–7): 187–99, 242–51

Johnson, S. 1775. *A Journey to the Western Islands of Scotland*, London, J. Pope; ed. I. McGowan, *Journey to the Hebrides*, Edinburgh, Canongate, 1996

Jones, B., Keillar, I. and Maude, K. 1993. 'The Moray Aerial Survey: Discovering the Prehistoric and Proto-Historic Landscape', in Sellar (ed.), 1993: pp. 47–74

Jones, G.R.J. 1984. 'The Multiple Estate: a Model for Tracing the Inter-Relationships of Society, Economy and Habitat', in K. Biddick (ed.), *Archaeological Approaches to Medieval Europe*, Kalamazoo, Mich., Medieval Institute Publications, Western Michigan University: pp. 9–42

Jorgens, J.J. 1977. *Shakespeare on Film*, Bloomington, Indiana University Press

Kapelle, W.E. 1979. *The Norman Conquest of the North: the Region and its Transformation, 1000–1135*, London, Croom Helm

Keltie, J.S. 1875. *A History of the Scottish Highland, Highland Clans and Highland Regiments*, 2 vols, Edinburgh, A. Fullerton & Co.

Kenney, J.F. 1929. *The Sources for the Early History of Ireland: Ecclesiastical*, New York, Columbia University Press; second edn Dublin, 1993

Kerr, A. 1882. 'Description of the Ecclesiastical Remains Existing upon St Serf's Island, Lochleven', *Proceedings of the Society of Antiquaries of Scotland* 16 (1881–2): 159–68

Kieckhefer, R. 1976. *European Witch Trials: their Foundations in Popular and Learned Culture, 1300–1500*, London, Routledge & Kegan Paul

Kirby, D.P. 1962. 'Strathclyde and Cumbria: a Survey of Historical Development to 1092', *Transactions of the Cumberland and Westmorland Antiquarian and Archaeological Society* 62: 77–94

——. 1975a. 'The Evolution of the Frontier, *c.* 400–1018', in McNeill and Nicholson, 1975: pp. 24–6, 124–5

——. 1975b. 'The Evolution of the Frontier 1018–1237', in McNeill and Nicholson, 1975: pp. 52–4

Knox, J. 1831. *The Topography of the Basin of the Tay*, Edinburgh, J. Anderson & W. Hunter

Laing, D. 1859. 'On the Present State of the Ruins of Iona, and their Preservation', *Proceedings of the Society of Antiquaries of Scotland* 2 (1854–7): 7–12

Laing, L. 1975. *The Archaeology of Late Celtic Britain and Ireland c. 400–1220 AD*, London, Methuen & Co.

Laing, L. and J. 1993. *The Picts and the Scots*, Stroud, Sutton Publishing

Lang, J. 1975. 'Hogback Monuments in Scotland', *Proceedings of the Society of Antiquaries of Scotland* 105 (1972–4): 206–35

——. 1984. 'The Hogback. A Viking Colonial Monument', *Anglo-Saxon Studies in Archaeology and History* 3: 83–176

——. 1994. 'The Govan Hogbacks: a Reappraisal', in A. Ritchie (ed.), *Govan and its Early Medieval Sculpture*, Stroud, Sutton Publishing: pp. 123–31

Larner, C. 1973. 'James VI and I and Witchcraft', in A.G.R. Smith (ed.), *The Reign of James VI and I*, London, Macmillan: pp. 74–90

Law, R.A. 1952. 'The Composition of Macbeth with Reference to Holinshed', *Texas Studies in English* 31: 35–41

Lawrie, A.C. (ed.). 1905. *Early Scottish Charters Prior to AD 1153*, Glasgow, James Maclehose & Sons

Lawson, M.K. 1993. *Cnut: the Danes in England in the Early Eleventh Century*, London, Longman

Lincoln, A. 1905. *Complete Works of Abraham Lincoln*, eds J.G. Nicolay and J. Hay, new edn; first published New York, Frances D. Tandy Co., 1984

Loyn, H. 1955. 'Gesiths and Thegns in England from the Seventh to the Tenth Century', *English Historical Review* 70: 529–40

——. 1992. 'Kings, Gesiths and Thegns', in M. Carver (ed.), *The Age of Sutton Hoo: the Seventh Century in North-Western Europe*, Woodbridge, Boydell Press: pp. 75–9

Lucas, A.T. 1967. 'The Plundering and Burning of Churches in Ireland, 7th to 16th Century', in E. Rynne (ed.), *North Munster Studies: Essays in Commemoration of Monsignor Michael Moloney*, Limerick, Limerick Field Club: pp. 172–229

Lynch, M. 1992. *Scotland: a New History*, London, Pimlico; first published London, Century, 1991

MacBeth, J. 1921. *MacBeth: King, Queen and Clan*, Edinburgh, W.J. Hay

Macdonald, A. 1973. '*"Annat"* in Scotland: a Provisional Review', *Scottish Studies* 17: 135–46

——. 1979. 'Gaelic *cill (Kil(l)-)* in Scottish Place-names', *Bulletin of the Ulster Place-Name Society* 2: 9–19

MacDonald, D.J. 1975. 'Life in Early Inverness', in Maclean (ed.), 1975: pp. 124–40

Mac Eoin, G.S. 1964. 'On the Irish Legend of the Origin of the Picts', *Studia Hibernica* 4: 138–54

MacFarlane, I.D. 1981. *Buchanan*, London, Duckworth

MacGibbon, D. and Ross, T. 1887–92. *The Castellated and Domestic Architecture of Scotland from the Twelfth to the Eighteenth Century*, 5 vols, Edinburgh, D. Douglas

MacIntosh, D. 1822. *The History of Scotland: from the Invasion of the Romans till the Union with England*, second edn, London; first published Edinburgh, 1821

McKerracher, A.C. 1984. 'Where is the Real Stone?', *The Scots Magazine* 122 (December 1984): 271–9

MacKie, E.W. 1969. 'Timber-Laced and Vitrified Walls in Iron Age Forts: Causes of Vitrifaction', *Glasgow Archaeological Journal* 1: 69–71

——. 1976. 'The Vitrified Forts of Scotland', in D.W. Harding (ed.), *Hillforts: Later Prehistoric Earthworks in Britain and Ireland*, London, Academic Press: pp. 205–35

Maclean, L. (ed.). 1975. *The Hub of the Highlands: the Book of Inverness and District*, Inverness, Inverness Field Club

M'Lean, C. 1865. *Historical and Descriptive Dunkeld: its Straths and Glens*, Dunkeld, A. M'Lean; first published 1857

MacMillan, S. 1959. *A Vindication of MacBeth and His Claims,* Ipswich, Mass.

McNeill, P. and Nicholson, R. (eds). 1975. *An Historical Atlas of Scotland, c. 400–c. 1600*, St Andrews Atlas Committee of the Conference of Scottish Medievalists; rev. and enlarged edn, eds P.G.B. McNeill and H.L. MacQueen, *An Atlas of Scottish History to 1707*, Edinburgh, 1996

Macquarrie, A. 1992. 'Early Christian Religious Houses in Scotland: Foundation and Function', in J. Blair and R. Sharpe (eds), *Pastoral Care before the Parish*, Leicester, Leicester University Press: pp. 110–33

——. 1993. 'The Kings of Strathclyde, *c.* 400–1018', in Grant and Stringer (eds), 1993: pp. 1–19

Mann, H.K. 1925. *The Lives of the Popes in the Middle Ages: The Popes of the Gregorian Renaissance, St Leo IX to Honorius II, 1049–1130*, Vol. 6 (*1049–73*); first published London, Kegan Paul, Trench, Trubner & Co., 1910

Marsden, J. 1994. *The Tombs of the Kings: an Iona Book of the Dead*, Felinfach, Dyfed, Llanerch

——. 1997. *Alba of the Ravens: in Search of the Celtic Kingdom of the Scots*, London, Constable

Marshall, W. 1880. *Historic Scenes in Perthshire*, Edinburgh, W. Oliphant

Marstrander, C.J.S. (ed.). 1913. *Dictionary of the Irish Language: D-degóir*, Dublin, Royal Irish Academy

Maxwell-Stuart, P.G. 1997. *Chronicle of the Popes: the Reign-by-Reign Record of the Papacy from St Peter to the Present*, London, Thames & Hudson

Meckler, M. 1990. 'Colum Cille's Ordination of Aedan mac Gabrain', *Innes Review* 41: 139–50

Moody, R. 1958. *The Astor Place Riot,* Bloomington, Ind., Indiana University Press

Morris, C.D. and Rackham, D.J. (eds). 1992. *Norse and Later Settlement and Subsistence in the North Atlantic*, Glasgow, Department of Archaeology, University of Glasgow

Muir, K. (ed.). 1966. *Shakespeare Survey*, Cambridge, Cambridge University Press

——. (ed.). 1971. *Macbeth,* The Arden Shakespeare, tenth edn; first published London, Methuen, 1951

——. 1977. *The Sources of Shakespeare's Plays*, London, Methuen

Muir, K. and Edwards, P. (eds). 1977. *Aspects of 'Macbeth'*, Cambridge, Cambridge University Press

Mullin, M. 1976. 'Strange Images of Death: Sir Herbert Beerbohm Tree's Macbeth, 1911', *Theatre Survey* 17: 125–42

Mulryne, R. 1992. 'From Text to Foreign Stage: Yukio Ninagawa's Cultural Translation of Macbeth', in P. Kennan and M. Tempera (eds), *Shakespeare from Text to Stage*, Bologna, CLUEB: pp. 131–43

Neville, C.J. 1998. *Violence, Custom and Law: the Anglo-Scottish Border Lands in the Later Middle Ages*, Edinburgh, Edinburgh University Press

Nicholson, R. 1974. *Scotland: the Later Middle Ages*, Edinburgh, Oliver & Boyd

Nicolaisen, W.F.H. 1964. 'Celts and Anglo-Saxons in the Scottish Border Counties', *Scottish Studies* 8: 141–71

——. 1976. *Scottish Place-Names*, London, B.T. Batsford

Nicoll, E.H. (ed.). 1995. *A Pictish Panorama*, Balgavies, Angus, Pinkfoot Press

Ó Corráin, D. 1971. 'Irish Regnal Succession: a Reappraisal', *Studia Hibernica* 11: 7–39

Ó Corráin, D. and Maguire, F. 1981. *Gaelic Personal Names*, Dublin, Academy Press

O'Dwyer, P. 1981. *Céli Dé: Spiritual Reform in Ireland, 750–900*, Dublin, Editions Tailliura

Opie, I. and Tatem, M. (eds). 1989. *A Dictionary of Superstitions*, Oxford, Oxford University Press

Osborne, L.E. 1997. 'Poetry in Motion: Animating Shakespeare', in L.E. Boose and R. Burt (eds), *Shakespeare, the Movie: Popularizing the Plays on Film, TV, and Video*, London, Routledge, 1997: pp. 103–20

Pakenham, T. 1996. *Meetings with Remarkable Trees*, London, Weidenfeld & Nicolson

Paul, H.N. 1950. *The Royal Play of Macbeth*, New York, Macmillan Co.

Pennant, T. 1774. *A Tour in Scotland; MDCCLXIX*, third edn, London, Benjamin White; reprinted Perth, Melven Press, 1979

——. 1776. *A Tour in Scotland and Voyage to the Hebrides, MDCCLXXII*, 3 vols, second edn, London, Benjamin White

Pepys, S. 1974. *The Diary of Samuel Pepys. Volume VIII, 1667*, eds R. Latham and W. Matthews, London, G. Bell & Sons

Pinkerton, J. 1787–9. *An Enquiry into the History of Scotland Preceding the Reign of Malcolm III, or the Year 1056: a Dissertation on the Origin and Progress of the Scythians*, 2 vols, London

Playfair, J. 1819. *A Geographical and Statistical Description of Scotland*, 2 vols, Edinburgh, Archibald Constable & Co.

Porter, C. and Clarke, H.A. 1901. *Shakespeare Studies: Macbeth*, New York, American Book Co.

Radford, C.A.R. 1942. 'The Early Christian Monuments of Scotland', *Antiquity* 16: 1–18

Ralston, I. 1987a. 'The Yorkshire Television Vitrified Wall Experiment at East Tullos, City of Aberdeen District', *Proceedings of the Society of Antiquaries of Scotland* 116 (1986): 17–40

——. 1987b. 'Portknockie: Promontory Forts and Pictish Settlement in the North-East', in Small (ed.), 1987: pp. 15–26

——. 1995. 'Fortifications and Defence', in M.J. Green (ed.), *The Celtic World*, London, Routledge: pp. 59–81

RCAHMS. 1933. *Eleventh Report with Inventory of Monuments and Constructions in the Counties of Fife, Kinross, and Clackmannan*, Edinburgh, HMSO

——. 1982. *Argyll: an Inventory of the Monuments*, Vol. 4: *Iona*, n.p. (Edinburgh), RCAHMS

——. 1994. *South-East Perth: an Archaeological Landscape*, n.p. (Edinburgh), RCAHMS

RCHM(E). 1931. *An Inventory of the Historical Monuments of South-West Herefordshire*, London, HMSO

Rees, A. and Rees, B. 1961. *Celtic Heritage: Ancient Tradition in Ireland and Wales*, London, Thames & Hudson

Reeves, W. 1864. *The Culdees of the British Islands*, Dublin, privately published; reprinted, Felinfach, Dyfed, Llanerch, 1994

Ritchie, A. 1993. *Viking Scotland*, London, B.T. Batsford/Historic Scotland

——. 1997. *Iona*, London, B.T. Batsford/Historic Scotland

Ritchie, G. and Ritchie, A. 1981. *Scotland: Archaeology and Early History*, London, Thames & Hudson; reprinted Edinburgh, Edinburgh University Press, 1991

Ritchie, R.L.G. 1954. *The Normans in Scotland*, Edinburgh, Edinburgh University Press

Robertson, J. 1799. *General View of the Agriculture in the County of Perth: with Observations on the Means of its Improvement*, Perth, Board of Agriculture

Rosen, D. and Porter, A. (eds). 1984. *Verdi's 'Macbeth': a Sourcebook*, Cambridge, Cambridge University Press

Rothwell, K.S. and Melzer, A.H. 1990. *Shakespeare on Screen: an International Filmography and Videography*, London, Mansell

Round, J.H. 1964. *Feudal England: Historical Studies on the Eleventh and Twelfth Centuries*, London, George Allen & Unwin; first published Swan, Sonnenscheon & Co., 1895

Rumble, A. (ed.). 1994. *The Reign of Cnut: King of England, Denmark and Norway*, Leicester, Leicester University Press

Schlegel, A.W. 1815. *A Course of Lectures on Dramatic Art and Literature*, trans. J. Black, 2 vols, London, Baldwin, Craddock & Joy

Scott, W.W. 1971. 'Fordun's Description of the Inauguration of Alexander II', *Scottish Historical Review* 50: 198–200

Sellar, D. 1981. 'Highland Family Origins – Pedigree Making and Pedigree Faking', in L. Maclean (ed.), *The Middle Ages in the Highlands*, Inverness, Inverness Field Club: pp. 103–16

——. 'Sueno's Stone and its Interpreters', in Sellar (ed.), 1993: pp. 97–116

—— (ed.). 1993. *Moray: Province and People*, Edinburgh, Scottish Society for Northern Studies

Shaw, L. 1882. *The History of the Province of Moray*, ed. and enlarged by J.F.S. Gordon, 3 vols, Glasgow, T.D. Morison; first published Edinburgh, W. Auld, 1775

Shoesmith, R. 1996. *A Guide to Castles & Moated Sites in Herefordshire*, Wooton Almeley, Herefordshire, Logaston

Sinclair, Sir John. 1797. 'Additional Information Respecting the Castle of Dunsinnan, or Dunsinane', *The Statistical Account of Scotland* 20: 242–6; reprinted in D.J. Withrington and I.R. Grant (gen eds), *The Statistical Account of Scotland, Vol. 11: South and East Perthshire, Kinross-shire*, Wakefield, E.P. Publishing, 1976: pp. 80–5

Sinfield, A. 1992. '*Macbeth*: History, Ideology, and Intellectuals', in A. Sinfield, *Faultlines, Cultural Materialism and the Politics of Dissident Reading*, Oxford, Clarendon Press: pp. 95–108

Skene, W.F. (ed.). 1867. *Chronicles of the Picts, Chronicles of the Scots, and Other Early Memorials of Scottish History*, Edinburgh

——. 1886–90. *Celtic Scotland: a History of Ancient Alban*, second edn, 3 vols, Edinburgh, D. Douglas; first published 1876–80

Small, A. 1969. 'Burghead', *Scottish Archaeological Forum* 1: 61–8

——. 1975. 'The Hill-Forts of the Inverness Area', in Maclean (ed.), 1975: pp. 78–90

—— (ed.). 1987. *The Picts: a New Look at Old Problems*, Dundee, n.p.

Small, A. and Cottam, M.B. 1972. *Craig Phadrig: Interim Report on 1971 Excavation*, Dundee, Department of Geography, University of Dundee

Smout, T.C. (ed.). 1997. *Scottish Woodland History*, Edinburgh, Scottish Cultural Press

Smyth, A.P. 1972. 'The Earliest Irish Annals: Their First Contemporary Entries, and the Earliest Centres of Recording', *Proceedings of the Royal Irish Academy* 72C: 1–48

——. 1989. *Warlords and Holy Men: Scotland AD 80–1000*, Edinburgh, Edinburgh University Press; first published London, Edward Arnold, 1984

Stallybrass, P. 1982. 'Macbeth and Witchcraft', in Brown, J.R. (ed.), 1982: pp. 189–209

Steer, K. and Bannerman, J. 1977. *Late Medieval Monumental Sculpture in the West Highlands*, Edinburgh, RCAHMS

Stenton, F.M. 1989. *Anglo-Saxon England*, third edn, Oxford, Oxford University Press; first published Oxford, Clarendon Press, 1943

Stephens, G. 1876. *Macbeth, Earl Siward and Dundee: a Contribution to Scottish History from the Rune-Finds of Scandinavia*, Edinburgh, Oliver & Boyd

Stevenson, J.H. 1927. 'The Law of the Throne – Tanistry and the Introduction of the Law of Primogeniture: a Note on the Succession of the Kings of Scotland from Kenneth MacAlpin to Robert Bruce', *Scottish Historical Review* 25: 1–12

Stewart, A. 1826. *The History of Scotland, from the Roman Invasion till the Suppression of the Rebellion in 1745*, Edinburgh, Oliver & Boyd

Stewart, B. *Macbeth, Scotland's Warrior King*, Poole, Firebird; also published as J. Matthews and B. Stewart, *Celtic Battle Heroes: Cuchulainn, Boadicea, Fionn MacCumhail, Macbeth*, Poole, Firebird, 1988: pp. 143–87

Stone, G.W., Jr. 1941. 'Garrick's Handling of *Macbeth*', *Studies in Philology* 38: 609–28; reprinted in Wain (ed.), 1968: pp. 33–48

Stopes, C.C. 1916. *Shakespeare's Industry*, London, G. Bell & Sons

Sutherland, E. 1994. *In Search of the Picts: a Celtic Dark Age Nation*, London, Constable

Taylor, A.B. 1937. 'Karl Hundason, "King of Scots"', *Proceedings of the Society of Antiquaries of Scotland* 71 (1936–7): 334–42

Taylor, S. 1995. 'The Scandinavians in Fife and Kinross: the Onomastic Evidence', in Crawford (ed.), 1995: pp. 141–67

——. 1996. 'Place-names and the Early Church in Eastern Scotland', in Crawford (ed.), 1996: pp. 93–110

Thomson, D.S. 1969. 'Gaelic Learned Orders and Literati in Medieval Scotland', *Scottish Studies* 12: 57–78

Thurber, J. 1942. *My World – and Welcome to It*, London, Hamish Hamilton

Tranter, N. 1987. *The Story of Scotland*, London, Routledge & Kegan Paul; reprinted n.d., Glasgow, Neil Wilson

Vickers, B. 1974–81. *Shakespeare: the Critical Heritage*, 6 vols, London, Routledge & Kegan Paul

Wain, J. 1968a. 'Introduction', in Wain (ed.), 1968: pp. 11–30

—— (ed.). 1968b. *Shakespeare: Macbeth*, Basingstoke, Macmillan

Wainwright, F.T. (ed.). 1955. *The Problem of the Picts*, Edinburgh, Thomas Nelson; reprinted Perth, Melven Press, 1980

——. 1963. *The Souterrains of Southern Pictland*, London, Routledge & Kegan Paul

Watson, W.J. 1926. *The History of the Celtic Place-Names of Scotland*, Edinburgh, William Blackwood & Sons

Wells, S. and Taylor, G. 1987. *William Shakespeare: a Textual Companion*, Oxford, Clarendon Press

Wheeler, T. 1990. '*Macbeth*': an Annotated Bibliography*, New York, Garland

White, D. 1999. 'Once More into the Office . . .', the *Guardian*, 12 June 1999

Whitelock, D. (ed.). 1955. *English Historical Documents, c. 500–1042*, London, Eyre & Spottiswoode; reprinted London, Eyre & Methuen, 1979

Williams, J. 1777. *An Account of Some Remarkable Ancient Ruins Lately Discovered in the Highlands and Northern Parts of Scotland*, Edinburgh, W. Creech

Williams, J.E.C. 1971. 'The Court Poet in Medieval Ireland', *Proceedings of the British Academy* 57: 85–136

Wilmart, A. 1929. 'La Trinité des Scots à Rome et les Notes du *Vat. Lat.* 378', *Revue Bénédictine* 41: 218–30

Wise, T.A. 1859. 'Notice of Recent Excavations in the Hill Fort of Dunsinane, Perthshire', *Proceedings of the Society of Antiquaries of Scotland* 2 (1854–7): 93–9

Index

Numbers in *italic* refer to illustrations.